THE DAILY STUDY BIBLE SERIES
REVISED EDITION

THE LETTERS TO
TIMOTHY, TITUS,
AND
PHILEMON

THE LETTERS TO
TIMOTHY, TITUS,
AND
PHILEMON

REVISED EDITION

Translated
with an Introduction and Interpretation
by
WILLIAM BARCLAY

THE WESTMINSTER PRESS
PHILADELPHIA

Revised Edition
Copyright © 1975 William Barclay

First published by The Saint Andrew Press
Edinburgh, Scotland

Timothy and Titus, First Edition, 1956; Second Edition, 1960

Philemon, First Edition, 1957; Second Edition, 1960

Published by The Westminster Press ®
Philadelphia, Pennsylvania

PRINTED IN THE UNITED STATES OF AMERICA

4   5   6   7   8   9

Library of Congress Cataloging in Publication Data

Bible. N.T. Pastoral epistles. English. Barclay.
    1975.
    The letters to Timothy, Titus, and Philemon.

    (The Daily study Bible series. — Rev. ed.)
    1. Bible. N.T. Pastoral epistles — Commentaries.
2. Bible. N.T. Philemon — Commentaries.
I. Bible. N.T. Philemon. English. Barclay.
1975. II. Barclay, William, lecturer in the Univer-
sity of Glasgow. III. Title. IV. Series.
BS2733.B28   1975   227'.8'077   75-26553
ISBN 0-664-21311-1
ISBN 0-664-24111-5 pbk.

GENERAL INTRODUCTION

The Daily Study Bible series has always had one aim—to convey the results of scholarship to the ordinary reader. A. S. Peake delighted in the saying that he was a "theological middleman", and I would be happy if the same could be said of me in regard to these volumes. And yet the primary aim of the series has never been academic. It could be summed up in the famous words of Richard of Chichester's prayer—to enable men and women "to know Jesus Christ more clearly, to love him more dearly, and to follow him more nearly".

It is all of twenty years since the first volume of *The Daily Study Bible* was published. The series was the brain-child of the late Rev. Andrew McCosh, M.A., S.T.M., the then Secretary and Manager of the Committee on Publications of the Church of Scotland, and of the late Rev. R. G. Macdonald, O.B.E., M.A., D.D., its Convener.

It is a great joy to me to know that all through the years *The Daily Study Bible* has been used at home and abroad, by minister, by missionary, by student and by layman, and that it has been translated into many different languages. Now, after so many printings, it has become necessary to renew the printer's type and the opportunity has been taken to restyle the books, to correct some errors in the text and to remove some references which have become outdated. At the same time, the Biblical quotations within the text have been changed to use the Revised Standard Version, but my own original translation of the New Testament passages has been retained at the beginning of each daily section.

There is one debt which I would be sadly lacking in courtesy if I did not acknowledge. The work of revision and correction has been done entirely by the Rev. James Martin, M.A., B.D., minister of High Carntyne Church, Glasgow. Had it not been for him this task would never have been undertaken, and it is impossible for me to thank him enough for the selfless toil he has put into the revision of these books.

It is my prayer that God may continue to use *The Daily Study Bible* to enable men better to understand His word.

Glasgow   WILLIAM BARCLAY

CONTENTS

viii

2 TIMOTHY

CONTENTS

A GENERAL INTRODUCTION
TO THE LETTERS OF PAUL

THE LETTERS OF PAUL

There is no more interesting body of documents in the New Testament than the letters of Paul. That is because of all forms of literature a letter is most personal. Demetrius, one of the old Greek literary critics, once wrote, "Every one reveals his own soul in his letters. In every other form of composition it is possible to discern the writer's character, but in none so clearly as the epistolary." (Demetrius, *On Style,* 227). It is just because he left us so many letters that we feel we know Paul so well. In them he opened his mind and heart to the folk he loved so much; and in them, to this day, we can see that great mind grappling with the problems of the early church, and feel that great heart throbbing with love for men, even when they were misguided and mistaken.

THE DIFFICULTY OF LETTERS

At the same time, there is often nothing so difficult to understand as a letter. Demetrius (*On Style,* 223) quotes a saying of Artemon, who edited the letters of Aristotle. Artemon said that a letter ought to be written in the same manner as a dialogue, because it was one of the two sides of a dialogue. In other words, to read a letter is like listening to one side of a telephone conversation. So when we read the letters of Paul we are often in a difficulty. We do not possess the letter which he was answering; we do not fully know the circumstances with which he was dealing; it is only from the letter itself that we can deduce the situation which prompted it. Before we can hope to understand fully any letter Paul wrote, we must try to reconstruct the situation which produced it.

THE ANCIENT LETTERS

It is a great pity that Paul's letters were ever called *epistles.* They are in the most literal sense *letters.* One of the great lights shed on the interpretation of the New Testament has been the discovery and the publication of the *papyri*. In the ancient world, *papyrus* was the substance on which most documents were written. It was composed of strips of the pith of a certain bulrush that grew on the banks of the Nile. These strips were laid one on top of the other to form a substance very like brown paper. The sands of the Egyptian desert were ideal for preservation, for papyrus, although very brittle, will last forever so long as moisture does not get at it. As a result, from the Egyptian rubbish heaps, archaeologists have rescued hundreds of documents, marriage contracts, legal agreements, government forms, and, most interesting of all, private letters. When we read these private letters we find that there was a pattern to which nearly all conformed; and we find that Paul's letters reproduce exactly that pattern. Here is one of these ancient letters. It is from a soldier, called Apion, to his father Epimachus. He is writing from Misenum to tell his father that he has arrived safely after a stormy passage.

"Apion sends heartiest greetings to his father and lord Epimachus. I pray above all that you are well and fit; and that things are going well with you and my sister and her daughter and my brother. I thank my Lord Serapis [his god] that he kept me safe when I was in peril on the sea. As soon as I got to Misenum I got my journey money from Caesar—three gold pieces. And things are going fine with me. So I beg you, my dear father, send me a line, first to let me know how you are, and then about my brothers, and thirdly, that I may kiss your hand, because you brought me up well, and because of that I hope, God willing, soon to be promoted. Give Capito my heartiest greetings, and my brothers and Serenilla and my friends. I sent you a little picture of myself painted by Euctemon. My military name is Antonius Maximus. I pray for your good health. Serenus sends good wishes, Agathos Daimon's boy, and Turbo, Gallonius's son." (G. Milligan, *Selections from the Greek Papyri*, 36).

Little did Apion think that we would be reading his letter to his father 1800 years after he had written it. It shows how little human nature changes. The lad is hoping for promotion quickly. Who will Serenilla be but the girl he left behind him? He sends the ancient equivalent of a photograph to the folk at home. Now that letter falls into certain sections. (i) There is a greeting. (ii) There is a prayer for the health of the recipients. (iii) There is a thanksgiving to the gods. (iv) There are the special contents. (v) Finally, there are the special salutations and the personal greetings. Practically every one of Paul's letters shows exactly the same sections, as we now demonstrate.

(i) *The Greeting: Romans* 1: 1; 1 *Corinthians* 1: 1; 2 *Corinthians* 1: 1; *Galatians* 1: 1; *Ephesians* 1: 1; *Philippians* 1: 1; *Colossians* 1: 1, 2; 1 *Thessalonians* 1: 1; 2 *Thessalonians* 1: 1.

(ii) *The Prayer:* in every case Paul prays for the grace of God on the people to whom he writes: *Romans* 1: 7; 1 *Corinthians* 1: 3; 2 *Corinthians* 1: 2; *Galatians* 1: 3; *Ephesians* 1: 2; *Philippians* 1: 3; *Colossians* 1: 2; 1 *Thessalonians* 1: 1; 2 *Thessalonians* 1: 2.

(iii) *The Thanksgiving: Romans* 1: 8; 1 *Corinthians* 1: 4; 2 *Corinthians* 1: 3; *Ephesians* 1: 3; *Philippians* 1: 3; 1 *Thessalonians* 1: 3; 2 *Thessalonians* 1: 3.

(iv) *The Special Contents:* the main body of the letters.

(v) *Special Salutations and Personal Greetings: Romans* 16; 1 *Corinthians* 16: 19; 2 *Corinthians* 13: 13; *Philippians* 4: 21, 22; *Colossians* 4: 12–15; 1 *Thessalonians* 5: 26.

When Paul wrote letters, he wrote them on the pattern which everyone used. Deissmann says of them, "They differ from the messages of the homely papyrus leaves of Egypt, not as letters but only as the letters of Paul." When we read Paul's letters we are not reading things which were meant to be academic exercises and theological treatises, but human documents written by a friend to his friends.

THE IMMEDIATE SITUATION

With a very few exceptions, all Paul's letters were written to meet an immediate situation and not treatises which he sat down to write in the peace and silence of his study. There

THE LETTERS OF PAUL

was some threatening situation in Corinth, or Galatia, or Philippi, or Thessalonica, and he wrote a letter to meet it. He was not in the least thinking of us when he wrote, but solely of the people to whom he was writing. Deissmann writes, "Paul had no thought of adding a few fresh compositions to the already extant Jewish epistles; still less of enriching the sacred literature of his nation. . . . He had no presentiment of the place his words would occupy in universal history; not so much that they would be in existence in the next generation, far less that one day people would look at them as Holy Scripture." We must always remember that a thing need not be transient because it was written to meet an immediate situation. All the great love songs of the world were written for one person, but they live on for the whole of mankind. It is just because Paul's letters were written to meet a threatening danger or a clamant need that they still throb with life. And it is because human need and the human situation do not change that God speaks to us through them today.

THE SPOKEN WORD

One other thing we must note about these letters. Paul did what most people did in his day. He did not normally pen his own letters but dictated them to a secretary, and then added his own authenticating signature. (We actually know the name of one of the people who did the writing for him. In *Romans* 16: 22 Tertius, the secretary, slips in his own greeting before the letter draws to an end). In 1 *Corinthians* 16: 21 Paul says, "This is my own signature, my autograph, so that you can be sure this letter comes from me." (cp. *Colossians* 4: 18; 2 *Thessalonians* 3: 17.)

This explains a great deal. Sometimes Paul is hard to understand, because his sentences begin and never finish; his grammar breaks down and the construction becomes involved. We must not think of him sitting quietly at a desk, carefully polishing each sentence as he writes. We must think of him striding up and down some little room, pouring out a torrent

Paul composed his letters, he had in his mind's eye a vision of words, while his secretary races to get them down. When of the folk to whom he was writing, and he was pouring out his heart to them in words that fell over each other in his eagerness to help.

INTRODUCTION TO THE LETTERS TO
TIMOTHY AND TITUS

PERSONAL LETTERS

1 and 2 *Timothy* and *Titus* have always been regarded as forming a separate group of letters, different from the other letters of Paul. The most obvious difference is that they, along with the little letter to *Philemon,* are written to *persons,* whereas all other Pauline letters are written to *Churches.* The Muratorian Canon, which was the earliest official list of New Testament books, says that they were written "from personal feeling and affection." They are private rather than public letters.

ECCLESIASTICAL LETTERS

But it very soon began to be seen that, though these are personal and private letters, they have a significance and a relevance far beyond the immediate. In 1 *Timothy* 3: 15 their aim is set down. They are written to Timothy "that you may know how one ought to behave in the household of God, which is the Church of the living God." So, then, it came to be seen that these letters have not only a personal significance, but also what one might call an *ecclesiastical* significance. The Muratorian Canon says of them that, though they are personal letters written out of personal affection, "they are still hallowed in the respect of the Catholic Church, and *in the arrangement of ecclesiastical discipline."* Tertullian said that Paul wrote "two letters to Timothy and one to Titus, which were composed *concerning the state of the Church (de ecclesiastico statu)."* It is not then surprising that the first name given to them was *Pontifical Letters,* that is, written by the *pontifex,* the priest, the controller of the Church.

PASTORAL LETTERS

Bit by bit they came to acquire the name by which they

are still known—The Pastoral Epistles. In writing of 1 *Timothy*
Thomas Aquinas, as long ago as 1274, said, "This letter is as
it were *a pastoral rule* which the Apostle delivered to
Timothy." In his introduction to the second letter, he writes,
"In the first letter he gives Timothy instructions concerning
ecclesiastical order; in this second letter he deals with a *pastoral
care* which should be so great that it will even accept
martyrdom for the sake of the care of the flock." But this
title, The Pastoral Epistles, really became affixed to these
letters in 1726 when a great scholar, Paul Anton by name,
gave a series of famous lectures on them under that title.

These letters then deal with the care and organization of
the flock of God; they tell men how to behave within the
household of God; they give instructions as to how God's
house should be administered, as to what kind of people
the leaders and pastors of the Church should be, and as to
how the threats which endanger the purity of Christian faith
and life should be dealt with.

THE GROWING CHURCH

The supreme interest of these letters is that we get in them
a picture of the infant Church. In those early days it was an
island in a sea of paganism. The people in it were only one
remove from their heathen origin. It would have been so
easy for them to relapse into the pagan standards from
which they had come; the tarnishing atmosphere was all
around. It is most significant that missionaries tell us that of
all letters the Pastoral Epistles speak most directly to the
situation of the younger Churches. The situation with which
they deal is being re-enacted in India, in Africa, in China
every day. They can never lose their interest because in them
we see, as nowhere else, the problems which continually beset
the growing Church.

THE ECCLESIASTICAL BACKGROUND OF THE PASTORALS

From the beginning these letters have presented problems
to New Testament scholars. There are many who have felt

that, as they stand, they cannot have come directly from the hand and pen of Paul. That this is no new feeling may be seen from the fact that Marcion, who, although he was a heretic, was the first man to draw up a list of New Testament books, did not include them among Paul's letters. Let us then see what makes people doubt their direct Pauline authorship.

In them we are confronted with the picture of a Church with a fairly highly developed ecclesiastical organization. There are *elders* (1 *Timothy* 5: 17–19; *Titus* 1: 5–6); there are *bishops,* superintendents or overseers (1 *Timothy* 3: 1–7; *Titus* 1: 7–16); there are *deacons* (1 *Timothy* 3: 8–13). From 1 *Timothy* 5: 17, 18 we learn that by that time elders were even salaried officials. The elders that rule well are to be counted worthy of a double pay and the Church is urged to remember that the labourer is worthy of his hire. There is at least the beginning of the order of widows who became so prominent later on in the early Church (1 *Timothy* 5: 3–16). There is clearly here a quite elaborate structure within the Church, too elaborate some would claim for the early days in which Paul lived and worked.

THE DAYS OF CREEDS

It is even claimed that in these letters we can see the days of creeds emerging. The word *faith* changed its meaning. In the earliest days it is always *faith in a person*; it is the most intimate possible personal connection of love and trust and obedience with Jesus Christ. In later days it became *faith in a creed*; it became the acceptance of certain doctrines. It is said that in the Pastoral Epistles we can see this change emerging.

In the later days men will come who will depart from the *faith* and give heed to doctrines of devils (1 *Timothy* 4: 1). A good servant of Jesus Christ must be nourished in the words of *faith and good doctrine* (1 *Timothy* 4: 6). The heretics are men of corrupt minds, reprobate concerning the *faith* (2 *Timothy* 3: 8). The duty of Titus is to rebuke men that they may be sound in the *faith* (*Titus* 1: 13).

This comes out very particularly in an expression peculiar to the Pastorals. Timothy is urged to keep hold of "the truth that has been entrusted to you" (2 *Timothy* 1: 14). The word for *that has been entrusted* is *parathēkē*. *Parathēkē* means a *deposit* which has been entrusted to a banker or someone else for safe-keeping. It is essentially something which must be handed back or handed on absolutely unchanged. That is to say the stress is on *orthodoxy*. Instead of being a close, personal relationship to Jesus Christ, as it was in the thrilling and throbbing days of the early Church, faith has become the acceptance of a creed. It is even held that in the Pastorals we have echoes of the earliest creeds.

> "God was manifested in the flesh;
> Vindicated in the Spirit;
> Seen by angels;
> Preached among the nations;
> Believed on in the world;
> Taken up in glory" (1 *Timothy* 3: 16).

That indeed sounds like the fragment of a creed to be recited.

"Remember Jesus Christ, risen from the dead, descended from David, as preached in my gospel" (2 *Timothy* 2: 8).

That sounds like a reminder of a sentence from an accepted creed.

Within the Pastorals there undoubtedly are indications that the day of insistence on acceptance of a creed has begun, and that the days of the first thrilling personal discovery of Christ are beginning to fade.

A DANGEROUS HERESY

It is clear that in the forefront of the situation against which the Pastoral Epistles were written there was a dangerous heresy which was threatening the welfare of the Christian Church. If we can distinguish the various characteristic features of that heresy, we may be able to go on to identify it.

It was characterized by *speculative intellectualism*. It

produced questions (1 *Timothy* 1: 4); those involved in it doted about questions (1 *Timothy* 6: 4); it dealt in foolish and unlearned questions (2 *Timothy* 2: 23); its foolish questions are to be avoided (*Titus* 3: 9). The word used in each case for *questions* is *ekzētēsis,* which means *speculative discussion.* This heresy was obviously one which was a playground of the intellectuals, or rather the pseudo-intellectuals of the Church.

It was characterized by *pride.* The heretic is proud, although in reality he knows nothing (1 *Timothy* 6: 4). There are indications that these intellectuals set themselves on a plane above the ordinary Christian; in fact they may well have said that complete salvation was outside the grasp of the ordinary man and open only to them. At times the Pastoral Epistles stress the word *all* in a most significant way. The grace of God, which brings salvation, has appeared to *all* men (*Titus* 2: 11). It is God's will that *all* men should be saved and come to a knowledge of the truth (1 *Timothy* 2: 4). The intellectuals tried to make the greatest blessings of Christianity the exclusive possession of a chosen few; and in contradistinction the true faith stresses the all-embracing love of God.

There were within that heresy two opposite tendencies. There was a tendency to *asceticism.* The heretics tried to lay down special food laws, forgetting that everything God has made is good (1 *Timothy* 4: 4, 5). They listed many things as impure, forgetting that to the pure all things are pure (*Titus* 1: 15). It is not impossible that they regarded sex as something unclean and belittled marriage, and even tried to persuade those who were married to renounce it, for in *Titus* 2: 4 the simple duties of the married life are stressed as being binding on the Christian.

But this heresy also issued in *immorality.* The heretics even invaded private houses and led away weak and foolish women in evil desires (2 *Timothy* 3: 6). They professed to know God, but denied him by their deeds (*Titus* 1: 16). They were out to impose upon people and to make money out of their false teaching. To them gain was godliness (1 *Timothy* 6: 5); they taught and deceived for base gain (*Titus* 1: 11).

On the one hand this heresy issued in an unchristian asceticism, and on the other it produced an equally unchristian immorality.

It was characterized, too, by *words* and *tales* and *genealogies*. It was full of godless chatter and useless controversies (1 *Timothy* 6: 20). It produced endless genealogies (1 *Timothy* 1: 4; *Titus* 3: 9). It produced myths and fables (1 *Timothy* 1: 4; *Titus* 1: 14).

It was at least in some way and to some extent tied up with *Jewish legalism*. Amongst its devotees were those of the circumcision (*Titus* 1: 10). The aim of the heretics was to be teachers of the law (1 *Timothy* 1: 7). It pressed on men Jewish fables and the commandments of men (*Titus* 1: 14).

Finally, these heretics denied *the resurrection of the body*. They said that any resurrection that a man was going to experience had been experienced already (2 *Timothy* 2: 18). This is probably a reference to those who held that the only resurrection the Christian experienced was a spiritual one when he died with Christ and rose again with him in the experience of baptism (*Romans* 6: 4).

THE BEGINNINGS OF GNOSTICISM

Is there any heresy which fits all this material? There is, and its name is *Gnosticism*. The basic thought of Gnosticism was that all matter is essentially evil and spirit alone is good. That basic belief had certain consequences.

The Gnostic believed that matter is as eternal as God; and that when God created the world he had to use this essentially evil matter. That meant that to them God could not be the direct creator of the world. In order to touch this flawed matter he had to send out a series of emanations—they called them aeons—each one more and more distant from himself until at last there came an emanation or aeon so distant that it could deal with matter and create the world.

Between man and God there stretched a series of these emanations, each with his name and genealogy. So Gnosticism literally had endless fables and endless genealogies. If a man was ever to get to God, he must, as it were, ascend this ladder of emanations; and to do that he needed a very special kind of knowledge including all kinds of passwords to get him past each stage. Only a person of the highest intellectual calibre could hope to acquire this knowledge and know these passwords and so get to God.

Further, if matter was altogether evil, the body was altogether evil. From that, two opposite possible consequences sprang. Either the body must be held down so that a rigorous asceticism resulted, in which the needs of the body were as far as possible eliminated and its instincts, especially the sex instinct, as far as possible destroyed; or it could be held that, since it was evil, it did not matter what was done with the body and its instincts and desires could be given full rein. The Gnostic therefore became either an ascetic or a man to whom morality had ceased to have any relevance at all.

Still further, if the body was evil, clearly there could be no such thing as its resurrection. It was not the resurrection of the body but its destruction to which the Gnostic looked forward.

All this fits accurately the situation of the Pastoral Epistles. In Gnosticism we see the intellectualism, the intellectual arrogance, the fables and the genealogies, the asceticism and the immorality, the refusal to contemplate the possibility of a bodily resurrection, which were part and parcel of the heresy against which the Pastoral Epistles were written.

One element in the heresy has not yet been fitted into place— the Judaism and the legalism of which the Pastoral Epistles speak. That too finds its place. Sometimes Gnosticism and Judaism joined hands. We have already said that the Gnostics insisted that to climb the ladder to God a very special knowledge was necessary; and that some of them insisted that for the good life a strict asceticism was essential. It was the claim of certain of the Jews that it was precisely the Jewish law and the Jewish food regulations which provided that special knowledge and necessary asceticism; and so there were times when Judaism and Gnosticism went hand in hand.

It is quite clear that the heresy at the back of the Pastoral Epistles was Gnosticism. Some have used that fact to try to prove that Paul could have had nothing to do with the writing of them, because, they say, Gnosticism did not emerge until much later than Paul. It is quite true that the great formal systems of Gnosticism, connected with such names as Valentinus and Basilides, did not arise until the second century; but these great figures only systematized what was already there. The basic ideas of Gnosticism were there in the atmosphere which surrounded the early Church, even in the days of Paul. It is easy to see their attraction, and also to see that, if they had been allowed to flourish unchecked, they could have turned Christianity into a speculative philosophy and wrecked it. In facing Gnosticism, the Church was facing one of the gravest dangers which ever threatened the Christian faith.

THE LANGUAGE OF THE PASTORALS

The most impressive argument against the direct Pauline origin of the Pastorals is a fact which is quite clear in the Greek but not so clear in any English translation. The total number of words in the Pastoral Epistles is 902, of which 54 are proper names; and of these 902 words, no fewer than 306 never occur in any other of Paul's letters. That is to say more than a third of the words in the Pastoral Epistles are totally absent from Paul's other letters. In fact 175 words in the Pastoral Epistles occur nowhere else in the New Testament at all; although it is only fair to say that there are 50 words in the Pastoral Epistles which occur in Paul's other letters and nowhere else in the New Testament.

Further, when the other letters of Paul and the Pastorals say the same thing they say it in different ways, using different words and different turns of speech to express the same idea.

Again, many of Paul's favourite words are absent entirely from the Pastoral Epistles. The words for the *cross* (stauros) and *to crucify* (stauroun) occur 27 times in Paul's other letters, and never in the Pastorals. *Eleutheria* and the kindred words which have to do with *freedom* occur 29 times in Paul's other letters, and never in the Pastorals. *Huios, son* and *huiothesia, adoption,* occur 46 times in Paul's other letters, and never in the Pastorals.

Moreover, Greek has many more of those little words called *particles* and *enclitics* than English has. Sometimes they indicate little more than a tone of voice; every Greek sentence is joined to its predecessor by one of them; and they are often virtually untranslatable. Of these particles and enclitics there are 112 which Paul uses altogether 932 times in his other letters that never occur in the Pastorals.

There is clearly something which has to be explained here. The vocabulary and the style make it hard to believe that Paul wrote the Pastoral Epistles in the same sense as he wrote his other letters.

PAUL'S ACTIVITIES IN THE PASTORALS

But perhaps the most obvious difficulty of the Pastorals is that they show Paul engaged in activities for which there is no room in his life as we know it from the book of Acts. He has clearly conducted a mission in Crete (*Titus* 1: 5). And he proposes to spend a winter in Nicopolis, which is in Epirus (*Titus* 3: 12). In Paul's life as we know it that particular mission and that particular winter just cannot be fitted in. But it may well be that just here we have stumbled on the solution to the problem.

WAS PAUL RELEASED FROM HIS ROMAN IMPRISONMENT?

Let us sum up. We have seen that the Church organization of the Pastorals is more elaborate than in any other Pauline letter. We have seen that the stress on orthodoxy sounds like second or third generation Christianity, when the thrill of the new discovery is wearing off and the Church is on the way to becoming an institution. We have seen that Paul is depicted as carrying out a mission or missions which cannot be fitted into the scheme of his life as we have it in *Acts*. But *Acts* leaves it quite uncertain what happened to Paul in Rome. It ends by telling us that he lived for two whole years in a kind of semi-captivity, preaching the gospel without hindrance (*Acts* 28: 30, 31). But it does not tell us how that captivity ended, whether in Paul's release or his execution. It is true that the general assumption is that it ended in his condemnation and death; but there is a by no means negligible stream of tradition which tells that it ended in his release, his liberty for two or three further years, his re-imprisonment and his final execution about the year A.D. 67.

Let us look at this question, for it is of the greatest interest.

First, it is clear that when Paul was in prison in Rome, he did not regard release as impossible; in fact, it looks as if he expected it. When he wrote to the Philippians, he said that he was sending Timothy to them, and goes on, "And I trust in the Lord that shortly I myself shall come also" (*Philippians* 2: 24). When he wrote to Philemon, sending back the runaway Onesimus, he says, "At the same time prepare a guest room for me, for I am hoping through your prayers to be granted to you" (*Philemon* 22). Clearly he was prepared for release, whether or not it ever came.

Second, let us remember a plan that was very dear to Paul's heart. Before he went to Jerusalem on that journey on which he was arrested, he wrote to the Church at Rome, and in that letter he is planning a visit to Spain. "I hope to see you in passing," he writes, "as I go to Spain." "I shall go on by way of you," he writes, "to Spain" (*Romans* 15: 24, 28). Was that visit ever paid?

Clement of Rome, when he wrote to the Church at Corinth about A.D. 90, said of Paul that he preached the gospel in the East and in the West; that he instructed the whole world (that is, the Roman Empire) in righteousness; and that he went to the extremity (*terma*, the terminus) of the West, before his martyrdom. What did Clement mean by *the extremity of the West?* There are many who argue that he meant nothing more than Rome. Now it is true that someone writing away in the East in Asia Minor would probably think of Rome as *the extremity of the West.* But Clement *was writing from Rome;* and it is difficult to see that for any-one in Rome *the extremity of the West* could be anything else but Spain. It certainly seems that Clement believed that Paul reached Spain.

The greatest of all the early Church historians was Eusebius. In his account of Paul's life he writes: "Luke who wrote the Acts of the Apostles, brought his history to a close at this point, after stating that Paul had spent two whole years at Rome as a prisoner at large, and preached the word of God without constraint. Thus, after he had made his defence, it is said that the Apostle was sent again on the ministry of preaching, and that on coming to the same city a second time he suffered martyrdom" (Eusebius: *Ecclesiastical History*, 2.22.2). Eusebius has nothing to say about Spain, but he did know the story that Paul had been released from his first Roman imprisonment.

The Muratorian Canon, that first list of New Testament books, describes Luke's scheme in writing Acts: "Luke related to Theophilus events of which he was an eye-witness, as also, in a separate place, he evidently declares the martyrdom of Peter (he probably refers to *Luke* 22: 31, 32); but omits the journey of Paul from Rome to Spain."

In the fifth century, two of the great Christian fathers are definite about this journey. Chrysostom in his sermon on 2 *Timothy* 4: 20 says: "Saint Paul after his residence in Rome departed to Spain." Jerome in his *Catalogue of Writers* says that Paul "was dismissed by Nero that he might preach Christ's gospel in the West."

Beyond doubt a stream of tradition held that Paul journeyed to Spain.

This is a matter on which we will have to come to our own decision. The one thing which makes us doubt the historicity of that tradition is that in Spain itself there is not and never was any tradition that Paul had worked and preached there, no stories about him, no places connected with his name. It would be indeed strange if the memory of such a visit had become totally obliterated. It could well be that the whole story of Paul's release and journey to the west arose simply as a deduction from his expressed intention to visit Spain (*Romans* 15). Most New Testament scholars do not think that Paul was released from his imprisonment; the general consensus of opinion is that his only release was by death.

PAUL AND THE PASTORAL EPISTLES

What then shall we say of Paul's connection with these letters? If we can accept the tradition of his release, and of his return to preaching and teaching, and of his death as late as A.D. 67, we might well believe that as they stand they came from his hand. But, if we cannot believe that—and the evidence is on the whole against it—are we to say that they have no connection with Paul at all?

We must remember that the ancient world did not think of these things as we do. It would see nothing wrong in issuing a letter under the name of a great teacher, if it was sure that the letter said the things which that teacher would say under the same circumstances. To the ancient world it was natural and seemly that a disciple should write in his master's name. No one would have seen anything wrong in one of Paul's disciples meeting a new and threatening situation with a letter under Paul's name. To regard that as forgery is to misunderstand the mind of the ancient world. Are we then to swing completely to the other extreme and say that some disciple of his issued these letters in Paul's name years after he was dead, and at a time when the Church was much more highly organized than ever it was during his lifetime?

As we see it, the answer is no. It is incredible that any

disciple would put into Paul's mouth a claim to be the chief
of sinners (1 *Timothy* 1: 15); his tendency would be to stress
Paul's holiness, not to talk about his sin. It is incredible that
anyone writing in the name of Paul would give Timothy the
homely advice to drink a little wine for the sake of his health
(1 *Timothy* 5: 23). The whole of 2 *Timothy* 4 is so personal and
so full of intimate, loving details that no one but Paul could
have written it.

Wherein lies the solution? It may well be that something
like this happened. It is quite obvious that many letters of
Paul went lost. Apart from his great public letters, he must
have had a continuous private correspondence; and of that we
possess only the little letter to Philemon. It may well be that
in the later days there were some fragments of Paul's
correspondence in the possession of some Christian teacher.
This teacher saw the Church of his day and his locality in
Ephesus threatened on every side. It was threatened with
heresy from without and from within. It was threatened with
a fall away from its own high standards of purity and truth.
The quality of its members and the standard of its office-
bearers were degenerating. He had in his possession little
letters of Paul which said exactly the things that should be
said, but, as they stood, they were too short and too
fragmentary to publish. So he amplified them and made them
supremely relevant to the contemporary situation and sent
them out to the Church.

In the Pastoral Epistles we are still hearing the voice of
Paul, and often hearing it speak with a unique personal
intimacy; but we think that the form of the letters is due to a
Christian teacher who summoned the help of Paul when the
Church of the day needed the guidance which only he could
give.

THE LETTERS TO TIMOTHY

1 TIMOTHY

THE ROYAL COMMAND

1 *Timothy* 1 : 1, 2

> Paul, an apostle of Christ Jesus, by the royal command of God,
> our Saviour, and of Jesus Christ, our Hope, writes this letter to
> Timothy, his true child in the faith. Grace, mercy and peace be to
> you from our Lord Jesus Christ.

NEVER a man magnified his office as Paul did. He did not
magnify it in pride; he magnified it in wonder that God had
chosen him for a task like that. Twice in the opening words
of this letter he lays down the greatness of his privilege.

(i) First, he calls himself *an apostle of Christ Jesus. Apostle*
is the Greek word *apostolos*, from the verb *apostellein* which
means *to send out;* an *apostolos* was *one who was sent
out.* As far back as Herodotus it means an *envoy*, an
ambassador, one who is sent out to represent his country and
his king. Paul always regarded himself as the envoy and
ambassador of Christ. And, in truth, that is the office of every
Christian. It is the first duty of every ambassador to form a
liaison between the country to which he is sent and the
country from which he has come. He is the connecting link.
And the first duty of every Christian is to be a connecting
link between his fellow-men and Jesus Christ.

(ii) Secondly, he says that he is an apostle *by the royal
command of God.* The word he uses is *epitagē.* This is the
word Greek uses for the injunctions which some inviolable law
lays on a man; for the royal command which comes to a man
from the king; and above all for the instructions which come
to a man either directly or by some oracle from God. For
instance, a man in an inscription dedicates an altar to the
goddess Cybele *kat'epitagēn,* in accordance with the command
of the goddess, which, he tells us, had come to him in a
dream. Paul thought of himself as a man holding the king's
commission.

If any man can arrive at this consciousness of being despatched by God, a new splendour enters into life. However humble his part may be in it, he is on royal service.

> "Life can never be dull again
>   When once we've thrown our windows open wide
>   And seen the mighty world that lies outside,
>   And whispered to ourselves this wondrous thing,
>   'We're wanted for the business of the King!' "

It is always a privilege to do even the most menial things for someone whom we love and respect and admire. All his life the Christian is on the business of the King.

Paul goes on to give to God and to Jesus two great titles.

He speaks of God, *our Saviour*. This is a new way of speaking. We do not find this title for God in any of Paul's earlier letters. There are two backgrounds from which it comes.

(*a*) It comes from an Old Testament background. It is Moses's charge against Israel that Jeshurun "forsook God who made him, and scoffed at *the Rock of his Salvation*" (*Deuteronomy* 32: 15). The Psalmist sings of how the good man will receive righteousness from *the God of his salvation* (*Psalm* 24: 5). It is Mary's song, "My soul magnifies the Lord, and my spirit rejoices in *God my Saviour*" (*Luke* 1: 46, 47). When Paul called God *Saviour*, he was going back to an idea which had always been dear to Israel.

(*b*) There is a pagan background. It so happened that just at this time the title *sōtēr,* Saviour, was much in use. Men had always used it. In the old days the Romans had called Scipio, their great general, "our hope and our salvation." But at this very time it was the title which the Greeks gave to Aesculapius, the god of healing. And it was one of the titles which Nero, the Roman Emperor, had taken to himself. So in this opening sentence Paul is taking the title which was much on the lips of a seeking and a wistful world and giving it to the only person to whom it belonged by right.

We must never forget that Paul called God Saviour. It is possible to take a quite wrong idea of the Atonement.

Sometimes people speak of it in a way which indicates that
something Jesus did pacified the anger of God. The idea
they give is that God was bent on our destruction and that
somehow his wrath was turned to love by Jesus. Nowhere in
the New Testament is there any support for that. It was
because God so *loved* the world that he sent Jesus into the
world (*John* 3: 16). God is Saviour. We must never think
or preach or teach of a God who had to be pacified and
persuaded into loving us, for everything begins from his love.

THE HOPE OF THE WORLD

1 *Timothy* 1: 1, 2 (*continued*)

PAUL uses a title which was to become one of the great titles
of Jesus—"Christ Jesus, *our hope*." Long ago the Psalmist had
demanded of himself: "Why are you cast down, O my soul?"
And he had answered: "Hope in God" (*Psalm* 43: 5). Paul
himself speaks of "Christ in you, the hope of glory"
(*Colossians* 1: 27). John speaks of the dazzling prospect which
confronted the Christian, the prospect of being like Christ;
and goes on to say: "Every one who thus hopes purifies
himself as he is pure" (1 *John* 3: 2, 3).

In the early Church this was to become one of the most
precious titles of Christ. Ignatius of Antioch, when on his way
to execution in Rome, writes to the Church in Ephesus:
"Be of good cheer in God the Father and in Jesus Christ
our common hope" (Ignatius: *To the Ephesians* 21: 2).
Polycarp writes: "Let us therefore persevere in our hope and
the earnest of our righteousness, who is Jesus Christ"
(*Epistle of Polycarp* 8).

(i) Men found in Christ *the hope of moral victory and of
self-conquest*. The ancient world knew its sin. Epictetus had
spoken wistfully of "our weakness in necessary things."
Seneca had said that "we hate our vices and love them at the
same time." He said, "We have not stood bravely enough by

our good resolutions; despite our will and resistance we have lost our innocence. Nor is it only that we have acted amiss; we shall do so to the end." Persius, the Roman poet, wrote poignantly: "Let the guilty see virtue, and pine that they have lost her for ever." Persius talks of "filthy Natta benumbed by vice." The ancient world knew its moral helplessness only too well; and Christ came, not only telling men what was right, but giving them the power to do it. Christ gave to men who had lost it the hope of moral victory instead of defeat.

(ii) Men found in Christ *the hope of victory over circumstances.* Christianity came into the world in an age of the most terrible personal insecurity. When Tacitus, the Roman historian, came to write the history of that very age in which the Christian Church came into being, he began by saying, "I am entering upon the history of a period rich in disaster, gloomy with wars, rent with seditions; nay, savage in its very hours of peace. Four emperors perished by the sword; there were three civil wars; there were more with foreigners, and some had the character of both at once . . . Rome wasted by fires; its oldest temples burned; the very capitol set in flames by Roman hands; the defilement of sacred rites; adultery in high places; the sea crowded with exiles; island rocks drenched with murder; yet wilder was the frenzy in Rome; nobility, wealth, the refusal of office, its acceptance, everything was a crime, and virtue was the surest way to ruin. Nor were the rewards of the informers less odious than their deeds. One found his spoils in a priesthood or a consulate; another in a provincial governorship, another behind the throne. All was one delirium of hate and terror; slaves were bribed to betray their masters, freedmen their patrons; and he who had no foe was betrayed by his friend." (Tacitus: *Histories* 1, 2). As Gilbert Murray said, the whole age was suffering from "the failure of nerve." Men were longing for some ring-wall of defence against "the advancing chaos of the world." It was Christ who in such times gave men the strength to live, and the courage, if need be, to die. In the certainty that nothing on earth could separate them from the love of God in Christ Jesus, men found victory over the terrors of the age.

(iii) Men found in Christ *the hope of victory over death.* They found in him, at one and the same time, strength for mortal things and the immortal hope. Christ, our hope, was—and still should be—the battle-cry of the Church.

TIMOTHY, MY SON

1 *Timothy* 1: 1, 2 (*continued*)

IT is to Timothy that this letter is sent, and Paul was never able to speak of him without affection in his voice.

Timothy was a native of Lystra in the province of Galatia. It was a Roman colony; it called itself "the most brilliant colony of Lystra," but in reality it was a little place at the ends of the civilized earth. Its importance was that there was a Roman garrison quartered there to keep control of the wild tribes of the Isaurian mountains which lay beyond. It was on the first missionary journey that Paul and Barnabas arrived there (*Acts* 14: 8–21). At that time there is no mention of Timothy; but it has been suggested that, when Paul was in Lystra, he found a lodging in Timothy's home, in view of the fact that he knew well the faith and devotion of Timothy's mother Eunice and of his grandmother Lois (2 *Timothy* 1: 5).

On that first visit Timothy must have been very young, but the Christian faith laid hold upon him, and Paul became his hero. It was at Paul's visit to Lystra on the second missionary journey that life began for Timothy (*Acts* 16: 1–3). Young as he was, he had become one of the ornaments of the Christian Church in Lystra. There was such a charm and enthusiasm in the lad that all men spoke well of him. To Paul, he seemed the very man to be his assistant. Maybe even then he had dreams that this lad was the very person to train to take up his work when his day was over.

Timothy was the child of a mixed marriage; his mother was

a Jewess, and his father a Greek (*Acts* 16: 1). Paul circumcised him. It was not that Paul was a slave of the law, or that he saw in circumcision any special virtue; but he knew well that if Timothy was to work amongst the Jews, there would be an initial prejudice against him if he was uncircumcised, and so he took this step as a practical measure to increase Timothy's usefulness as an evangelist.

From that time forward Timothy was Paul's constant companion. He was left behind at Beroea with Silas when Paul escaped to Athens, and later joined him there (*Acts* 17: 14, 15, *Acts* 18: 5). He was sent as Paul's emissary to Macedonia (*Acts* 19: 22). He was there when the collection from the Churches was being taken to Jerusalem (*Acts* 20: 4). He was with Paul in Corinth when Paul wrote his letter to Rome (*Romans* 16: 21). He was Paul's emissary to Corinth when there was trouble in that unruly Church (1 *Corinthians* 4: 17; 16: 10). He was with Paul when he wrote 2 *Corinthians* (2 *Corinthians* 1: 1, 19). It was Timothy whom Paul sent to see how things were going in Thessalonica and he was with Paul when he wrote his letter to that Church (1 *Thessalonians* 1: 1; 3: 2, 6). He was with Paul in prison when he wrote to Philippi, and Paul was planning to send him to Philippi as his representative (*Philippians* 1: 1; 2: 19). He was with Paul when he wrote to the Church at Colossae and to Philemon (*Colossians* 1: 1; *Philemon* 1: 1). Constantly Timothy was by Paul's side, and when Paul had a difficult job to do Timothy was the man sent to do it.

Over and over again Paul's voice vibrates with affection when he speaks of Timothy. When he is sending him to that sadly divided Church at Corinth, he writes: "I have sent to you Timothy, my beloved and faithful child in the Lord" (1 *Corinthians* 4: 17). When he is planning to send him to Philippi, he writes: "I have no one like him. . . . As a son with a father he has served with me in the gospel" (*Philippians* 2: 20, 22). Here he calls him "his true son." The word that he uses for *true* is *gnēsios*. It has two meanings. It was the normal word for a *legitimate* child in contradistinction to illegitimate. It was the word for *genuine,* as opposed to counterfeit.

Timothy was the man whom Paul could trust and could send anywhere, knowing that he would go. Happy indeed is the leader who possesses a lieutenant like that. Timothy is our example of how we should serve in the faith. Christ and his Church need servants like that.

GRACE, MERCY AND PEACE

1 *Timothy* 1 : 1, 2 (*continued*)

PAUL always began his letters with a blessing (*Romans* 1: 7; 1 *Corinthians* 1: 3; 2 *Corinthians* 1: 2; *Galatians* 1: 3; *Ephesians* 1: 2; *Philippians* 1: 2; *Colossians* 1: 2; 1 *Thessalonians* 1: 1; 2 *Thessalonians* 1: 2; *Philemon* 3). In all these other letters only Grace and Peace occur. It is only in the letters to Timothy that Mercy is used (2 *Timothy* 1: 2; *Titus* 1: 4). Let us look at these three great words.

(i) In *Grace* there are always three dominant ideas.

(*a*) In classical Greek the word means outward grace or favour, beauty, winsomeness, sweetness. Usually, although not always, it is applied to persons. The English word *charm* comes near to expressing its meaning. Grace is characteristically a lovely and a winsome thing.

(*b*) In the New Testament there is always the idea of sheer generosity. Grace is something unearned and undeserved. It is opposed to that which is a *debt*. Paul says that if it is a case of earning things, the reward is not a matter of grace, but of debt (*Romans* 4: 4). It is opposed to *works*. Paul says that God's election of his chosen people is not the consequence of works, but of grace (*Romans* 11: 6).

(*c*) In the New Testament there is always the idea of sheer *universality*. Again and again Paul uses the word grace in connection with the reception of the Gentiles into the family of God. He thanks God for the grace given to the

Corinthians in Jesus Christ (1 *Corinthians* 1: 4). He talks of the grace of God bestowed on the Churches of Macedonia (2 *Corinthians* 8: 1). He talks of the Galatians being called into the grace of Christ (*Galatians* 1: 6). The hope which came to the Thessalonians came through grace (2 *Thessalonians* 2: 16). It was God's grace which made Paul an apostle to the Gentiles (1 *Corinthians* 15: 10). It was by the grace of God that he moved amongst the Corinthians (2 *Corinthians* 1: 12). It was by grace that God called him and separated him from his mother's womb (*Galatians* 1: 15). It is the grace given to him by God which enables him to write boldly to the Church at Rome (*Romans* 15: 15). To Paul the great demonstration of the grace of God was the reception of the Gentiles into the Church and his apostleship to them.

Grace is a lovely thing; it is a free thing; and it is a universal thing. As F. J. Hort wrote so beautifully: "Grace is a comprehensive word, gathering up all that may be supposed to be expressed in the smile of a heavenly king, looking down upon his people."

(ii) *Peace* was the normal Jewish word of greeting, and, in Hebrew thought, it expresses, not simply the negative absence of trouble, but "the most comprehensive form of well-being." It is everything which makes for a man's highest good. It is the state a man is in when he is within the love of God. F. J. Hort writes: "Peace is the antithesis to every kind of conflict and war and molestation, to enmity without and distraction within."

> "Bowed down beneath a load of sin,
>   By Satan sorely pressed,
> By war without and fears within,
>   I come to thee for rest."

(iii) *Mercy* is the new word in the apostolic blessing. In Greek the word is *eleos,* and in Hebrew *chesedh.* Now *chesedh* is the word which is often in the Old Testament translated *loving-kindness;* and when Paul prayed for *mercy* on Timothy, he is saying, to put it very simply, "Timothy, may God be good to you." But there is more to it than that. *Chesedh* is used in the *Psalms* no fewer than one hundred and twenty-seven times. And time and time again it has the meaning of *help in time of need*. It denotes, as Parry puts it, "God's active intervention to help." As Hort puts it, "It is the coming down of the Most High to help the helpless." In *Psalm* 40 : 11 the Psalmist rejoices, "Thy steadfast love and thy faithfulness ever preserve me." In *Psalm* 57 : 3 he says, "He will send from heaven and save me . . . God will send forth his steadfast love and his faithfulness." In *Psalm* 86 : 14–16 he thinks of the forces of the evil men which are arrayed against him, and comforts himself with the thought that God is "abounding in steadfast love and faithfulness." It is by God's abundant mercy that he has given us the living hope of the resurrection (1 *Peter* 1 : 3). The Gentiles should glorify God for that mercy which has rescued them from sin and hopelessness (*Romans* 15 : 9). God's mercy is God active to save. It may well be that Paul added Mercy to his two usual words, Grace and Peace, because Timothy was up against it and he wanted in one word to tell him that the Most High was the help of the helpless.

ERROR AND HERESY

1 *Timothy* 1 : 3–7

I am writing to you now to reinforce the plea that I already made to you, when I urged you to stay in Ephesus while I went to Macedonia, that you might pass on the order to some of the people there, not to teach erroneous novelties, nor to give their attention to idle tales and endless genealogies, which only succeed in producing empty speculations rather than the effective admin- istration of God's people, which should be based on faith. The instruction which I gave you is designed to produce love which issues from a pure heart, a good conscience and an undissembling faith. But some of these people of whom I am talking have never

even tried to find the right road, and have turned aside out of it
to empty and useless discussions, in their claim to become
teachers of the law, although they do not know what they are
talking about, nor do they realize the real meaning of the things
about which they dogmatize.

It is clear that at the back of the Pastoral Epistles there is
some heresy which is endangering the Church. Right at the
beginning it will be well to try to see what this heresy is. We
will therefore collect the facts about it now.

This very passage brings us face to face with two of its
great characteristics. It dealt in *idle tales* and *endless genealogies*.
These two things were not peculiar to this heresy but were
deeply engrained in the thought of the ancient world.

First, the *idle tales*. One of the characteristics of the
ancient world was that the poets and even the historians loved
to work out romantic and fictitious tales about the foundation
of cities and of families. They would tell how some god came
to earth and founded the city or took in marriage some
mortal maid and founded a family. The ancient world was
full of stories like that.

Second, the *endless genealogies*. The ancient world had a
passion for genealogies. We can see that even in the Old
Testament with its chapters of names and in the New
Testament with the genealogies of Jesus with which Matthew
and Luke begin their gospels. A man like Alexander the Great
had a completely artificial pedigree constructed in which he
traced his lineage back on the one side to Achilles and
Andromache and on the other to Perseus and Hercules.

It would be the easiest thing in the world for Christianity to
get lost in endless and fabulous stories about origins and in
elaborate and imaginary genealogies. That was a danger which
was inherent in the situation in which Christian thought was
developing.

It was peculiarly threatening from two directions.

It was threatening from the *Jewish* direction. To the Jews
there was no book in the world like the Old Testament.
Their scholars spent a lifetime studying it and expounding it.

In the Old Testament many chapters and many sections are long genealogies; and one of the favourite occupations of the Jewish scholars was to construct an imaginary and edifying biography for every name in the list! A man could go on for ever doing that; and it may be that that was what was partly in Paul's mind. He may be saying, "When you ought to be working at the Christian life, you are working out imaginary biographies and genealogies. You are wasting your time on elegant fripperies, when you should be getting down to life and living." This may be a warning to us never to allow Christian thinking to get lost in speculations which do not matter.

THE SPECULATIONS OF THE GREEKS

1 *Timothy* 1 : 3–7 (*continued*)

BUT this danger came with an even greater threat from the *Greek* side. At this time in history there was developing a Greek line of thought which came to be known as *Gnosticism*. We find it specially in the background of the Pastoral Epistles, the Letter to the Colossians and the Fourth Gospel.

Gnosticism was entirely speculative. It began with the problem of the origin of sin and of suffering. If God is altogether good, he could not have created them. How then did they get into the world? The Gnostic answer was that creation was not creation out of nothing; before time began *matter* existed. They believed that this matter was essentially imperfect, an evil thing; and out of this essentially evil matter the world was created.

No sooner had they got this length than they ran into another difficulty. If matter is essentially evil and God is essentially good, God could not himself have touched this matter. So they began another set of speculations. They said that God put out an emanation, and that this emanation put out another emanation, and the second emanation put out a

third emanation and so on and on until there came into
being an emanation so distant from God that he could
handle matter; and that it was not God but this emanation
who created the world.

They went further. They held that each successive emanation
knew less about God so that there came a stage in the
series of emanations when the emanations were completely
ignorant of him and, more, there was a final stage when the
emanations were not only ignorant of God but actively
hostile to him. So they arrived at the thought that the god
who created the world was quite ignorant of and hostile to the
true God. Later on they went even further and identified the
God of the Old Testament with this creating god, and the God
of the New Testament with the true God.

They further provided each one of the emanations with a
complete biography. And so they built up an elaborate
mythology of gods and emanations, each with his story and
his biography and his genealogy. There is no doubt that the
ancient world was riddled with that kind of thinking; and
that it even entered the Church itself. It made Jesus merely the
greatest of the emanations, the one closest to God. It classed
him as the highest link in the endless chain between God and
man.

This Gnostic line of thought had certain characteristics
which appear all through the Pastoral Epistles as the
characteristics of those whose heresies were threatening the
Church and the purity of the faith.

(i) Gnosticism was obviously highly speculative, and it was
therefore intensely intellectually snobbish. It believed that all
this intellectual speculation was quite beyond the mental grasp
of ordinary people and was for a chosen few, the elite of
the Church. So Timothy is warned against "godless chatter
and contradictions of what is falsely called knowledge"
(1 *Timothy* 6: 20). He is warned against a religion of
speculative questions instead of humble faith (1 *Timothy* 1: 4).
He is warned against the man who is proud of his
intellect but really knows nothing and dotes about questions

and strifes of words (1 *Timothy* 6: 4). He is told to shun "godless chatter," for they can produce only ungodliness (2 *Timothy* 2: 16). He is told to avoid "stupid, senseless controversies" which in the end can only engender strife (2 *Timothy* 2: 23). Further, the Pastoral Epistles go out of their way to stress the fact that this idea of an intellectual aristocracy is quite wrong, for God's love is universal. God wants *all* men to be saved and *all* men to come to a knowledge of the truth (1 *Timothy* 2: 4). God is the Saviour of *all* men, especially those who believe (1 *Timothy* 4: 10). The Christian Church would have nothing to do with any kind of faith which was founded on intellectual speculation and set up an arrogant intellectual aristocracy.

(ii) Gnosticism was concerned with this long series of emanations. It gave to each of them a biography and a pedigree and an importance in the chain between God and men. These gnostics were concerned with "endless genealogies" (1 *Timothy* 1: 4). They went in for "godless and silly myths" about them (1 *Timothy* 4: 7). They turned their ears away from the truth to myths (2 *Timothy* 4: 4). They dealt in fables like the Jewish myths (*Titus* 1: 14). Worst of all, they thought in terms of two gods and of Jesus as one of a whole series of mediators between God and man; whereas "there is one God, and one mediator between God and men, the man Christ Jesus" (1 *Timothy* 2: 5). There is only one King of ages, immortal, invisible, there is only one God (1 *Timothy* 1: 17). Christianity had to repudiate a religion which took their unique place from God and from Jesus Christ.

THE ETHICS OF HERESY

1 *Timothy* 1: 3–7 (*continued*)

THE danger of Gnosticism was not only intellectual. It had serious moral and ethical consequences. We must remember that its basic belief was that matter was essentially evil and spirit alone was good. That issued in two opposite results.

(i) If matter is evil, the body is evil; and the body must be despised and held down. Therefore Gnosticism could and did issue in a rigid asceticism. It forbade men to marry, for the instincts of the body were to be suppressed. It laid down strict food laws, for the needs of the body must as far as possible be eliminated. So the Pastorals speak of those who forbid to marry and who command to abstain from meats (1 *Timothy* 4: 3). The answer to these people is that everything which God has created is good and is to be received with thanksgiving (1 *Timothy* 4: 4). The Gnostic looked on creation as an evil thing, the work of an evil god; the Christian looks on creation as a noble thing, the gift of a good God. The Christian lives in a world where all things are pure; the Gnostic lived in a world where all things were defiled (*Titus* 1: 15).

(ii) But Gnosticism could issue in precisely the opposite ethical belief. If the body is evil, it does not matter what a man does with it. Therefore, let him sate his appetites. These things are of no importance, therefore a man can use his body in the most licentious way and it makes no difference. So the Pastorals speak of those who lead away weak women until they are laden with sin and the victims of all kinds of lusts (2 *Timothy* 3: 6). Such men profess to know God, but they deny him by their deeds (*Titus* 1: 16). They used their religious beliefs as an excuse for immorality.

(iii) Gnosticism had still another consequence. The Christian believes in the resurrection of the body. That is not to say that he ever believed that we are resurrected with this mortal, human body; but he always believed that after resurrection from the dead a man would have a spiritual body, provided by God. Paul discusses this whole question in 1 *Corinthians* 15. The Gnostic held that there was no such thing as the resurrection of the body (2 *Timothy* 2: 18). After death a man would be a kind of disembodied spirit. The basic difference is that the Gnostic believed in the body's destruction; the Christian believes in its redemption. The Gnostic believed in what he would call *soul salvation;* the Christian believes in *whole salvation.*

So behind the Pastoral Epistles there are these dangerous heretics, who gave their lives to intellectual speculations, who saw this as an evil world and the creating god as evil, who put between the world and God an endless series of emanations and lesser gods and spent their time equipping each of them with endless fables and genealogies, who reduced Jesus to the position of a link in a chain and took away his uniqueness, who lived either in a rigorous asceticism or an unbridled licentiousness, who denied the resurrection of the body. It was their heretical beliefs that the Pastorals were written to combat.

THE MIND OF THE HERETIC

1 *Timothy* 1: 3–7 (*continued*)

IN this passage there is a clear picture of the mind of the dangerous heretic. There is a kind of heresy in which a man differs from orthodox belief because he has honestly thought things out and cannot agree with it. He does not take any pride in being different; he is different simply because he has to be. Such a heresy does not spoil a man's character; it may in fact enhance his character, because he has really thought out his faith and is not living on a second-hand orthodoxy. But that is not the heretic whose picture is drawn here. Here are distinguished five characteristics of the dangerous heretic.

(i) He is driven by the desire for novelty. He is like someone who must be in the latest fashion and must undergo the latest craze. He despises old things for no better reason than that they are old, and desires new things for no better reason than that they are new. Christianity has always the problem of presenting old truth in a new way. The truth does not change, but every age must find its own way of presenting it. Every teacher and preacher must talk to men in language which they understand. The old truth and the new presentation go ever hand in hand.

(ii) He exalts the mind at the expense of the heart. His conception of religion is speculation and not experience. Christianity has never demanded that a man should stop thinking for himself, but it does demand that his thinking should be dominated by a personal experience of Jesus Christ.

(iii) He deals in argument instead of action. He is more interested in abstruse discussion than in the effective administration of the household of the faith. He forgets that the truth is not only something which a man accepts with his mind, but is also something which he translates into action. Long ago the distinction between the Greek and the Jew was drawn. The Greek loved argument for the sake of argument; there was nothing that he liked better than to sit with a group of friends and indulge in a series of mental acrobatics and enjoy "the stimulus of a mental hike." But he was not specially interested in reaching conclusions, and in evolving a principle of *action*. The Jew, too, liked argument; but he wished every argument to end in a decision which demanded action. There is always a danger of heresy when we fall in love with words and forget deeds, for deeds are the acid test by which every argument must be tested.

(iv) He is moved by arrogance rather than by humility. He looks down with a certain contempt on simple-minded people who cannot follow his flights of intellectual speculation. He regards those who do not reach his own conclusions as ignorant fools. The Christian has somehow to combine an immovable certainty with a gentle humility.

(v) He is guilty of dogmatism without knowledge. He does not really know what he is talking about nor really understand the significance of the things about which he dogmatizes. The strange thing about religious argument is that everyone thinks that he has a right to express a dogmatic opinion. In all other fields we demand that a person should have a certain knowledge before he lays down the law. But there are those who dogmatize about the Bible and its teaching although they have never even tried to find out what the experts in language and history have said. It may well be that the Christian cause has suffered more from ignorant dogmatism than from anything else.

When we think of the characteristics of those who were troubling the Church at Ephesus we can see that their descendants are still with us.

THE MIND OF THE CHRISTIAN THINKER

1 *Timothy* 1: 3–7 (*continued*)

As this passage draws the picture of the thinker who disturbs the Church, it also draws the picture of the really Christian thinker. He, too, has five characteristics.

(i) His thinking is based on *faith*. Faith means taking God at his word; it means believing that he is as Jesus proclaimed him to be. That is to say, the Christian thinker begins from the principle that Jesus Christ has given the full revelation of God.

(ii) His thinking is motivated by *love*. Paul's whole purpose is to produce love. To think in love will always save us from certain things. It will save us from *arrogant* thinking. It will save us from *contemptuous* thinking. It will save us from *condemning* either that with which we do not agree, or that which we do not understand. It will save us from expressing our views in such a way that we hurt other people. Love saves us from *destructive thinking* and *destructive speaking*. To think in love is always to think in sympathy. The man who argues in love argues not to defeat his opponent, but to win him.

(iii) His thinking comes from a *pure heart*. Here the word used is very significant. It is *katharos,* which originally simply meant *clean* as opposed to *soiled* or *dirty.* Later it came to have certain most suggestive uses. It was used of corn that has been winnowed and cleansed of all chaff. It was used of an army which had been purified of all cowardly and un-disciplined soldiers until there was nothing left but first-class fighting men. It was used of something which was without any debasing admixture. So, then, a pure heart is a heart whose motives are absolutely pure and absolutely unmixed. In the heart of the Christian thinker there is no desire to show how clever he is, no desire to win a purely debating victory, no desire to show up the ignorance of his opponent. His only desire is to help and to illumine and to lead nearer to God. The Christian thinker is moved only by love of truth and love for men.

(iv) His thinking comes from a *good conscience*. The Greek word for *conscience* is *suneidēsis*. It literally means a *knowing with*. The real meaning of conscience is a *knowing with oneself*. To have a good conscience is to be able to look in the face the knowledge which one shares with no one but oneself and not be ashamed. Emerson remarked of Seneca that he said the loveliest things, if only he had the right to say them. The Christian thinker is the man whose thoughts and whose deeds give him the right to say what he does—and that is the most acid test of all.

(v) The Christian thinker is the man of *undissembling faith*. The phrase literally means the faith *in which there is no hypocrisy*. That simply means that the great characteristic of the Christian thinker is *sincerity*. He is sincere both in his desire to find the truth—and in his desire to communicate it.

THOSE WHO NEED NO LAW

1 *Timothy* 1: 8–11

We know that the law is good, if a man uses it legitimately, in the awareness that the law was not instituted to deal with good men, but with the lawless and the undisciplined, the irreverent and the sinners, the impious and the polluted, those who have sunk so low that they strike their fathers and their mothers, murderers, fornicators, homosexuals, slave-dealers and kidnappers, liars, perjurers, and all those who are guilty of anything which is the reverse of sound teaching, that teaching which is in accordance with the glorious gospel of the blessed God, that gospel which has been entrusted to me.

THIS passage begins with what was a favourite thought in the ancient world. The place of the law is to deal with evil-doers. The good man does not need any law to control his actions or to threaten him with punishments; and in a world of good men there would be no need for laws at all.

Antiphanes, the Greek, had it: "He who does no wrong needs no law." It was the claim of Aristotle that "philosophy enables a man to do without external control that which others do because of fear of the laws." Ambrose, the great Christian bishop, wrote: "The just man has the law of his own mind, of his own equity and of his own justice as his standard; and therefore he is not recalled from fault by terror of punishment, but by the rule of honour." Pagan and Christian alike regarded true goodness as something which had its source in a man's heart; as something which was not dependent on the rewards and punishments of the law.

But in one thing the pagan and the Christian differed. The pagan looked back to an ancient golden time when all things were good and no law was needed. Ovid, the Roman poet, drew one of the most famous pictures of that ancient golden time (*Metamorphoses* 1 : 90–112). "Golden was that first age, which with no one to compel, without a law, of its own will, kept faith and did the right. There was no fear of punishment, no threatening words were to be read on brazen tablets; no suppliant throng gazed fearfully upon the judge's face; but without judges men lived secure. Not yet had the pine tree, felled on its native mountains, descended thence into the watery plain to visit other lands; men knew no shores except their own. Nor, yet were cities begirt with steep moats; there were no trumpets of straight, no horns of curving brass, no swords or helmets. There was no need at all of armed men, for nations, secure from war's alarms, passed

the years in gentle peace." Tacitus, the Roman historian, had
the same picture (*Annals* 3: 26). "In the earliest times,
when men had as yet no evil passions, they led blameless,
guiltless lives, without either punishment or restraint. Led by
their own nature to pursue none but virtuous ends, they
required no rewards; and as they desired nothing contrary to
the right, there was no need for pains and penalties." The
ancient world looked back and longed for the days that were
gone. But the Christian faith does not look back to a lost
golden age; it looks forward to the day when the only law
will be the love of Christ within a man's heart, for it is
certain that the day of law cannot end until the day of love
dawns.

There should be only one controlling factor in the lives of
every one of us. Our goodness should come, not from fear of
the law, not even from fear of judgment, but from fear of
disappointing the love of Christ and of grieving the fatherly
heart of God. The Christian's dynamic comes from the fact
that he knows sin is not only breaking God's law but also
breaking his heart. It is not the law of God but the love of
God which constrains us.

THOSE WHOM THE LAW CONDEMNS

1 *Timothy* 1: 8–11 (*continued*)

IN an ideal state, when the Kingdom comes, there will be no
necessity for any law other than the love of God within a
man's heart; but as things are, the case is very different.
And here Paul sets out a catalogue of sins which the law
must control and condemn. The interest of the passage is that
it shows us the background against which Christianity grew up.
This list of sins is in fact a description of the world in which
the early Christians lived and moved and had their being.
Nothing shows us so well how the Christian Church was a
little island of purity in a vicious world. We talk about it being

hard to be a Christian in modern civilization; we have only to read a passage like this to see how infinitely harder it must have been in the circumstances in which the Church first began. Let us take this terrible list and look at the items on it.

There are the *lawless (anomoi)*. They are those who know the laws of right and wrong and break them open-eyed. No one can blame a man for breaking a law he does not know exists; but the *lawless* are those who deliberately violate the laws in order to satisfy their own ambitions and desires.

There are the *undisciplined (anhupotaktoi)*. They are the unruly and the insubordinate, those who refuse to obey any authority. They are like soldiers who mutinously disobey the word of command. They are either too proud or too unbridled to accept any control.

There are the *irreverent (asebeis)*. *Asebēs* is a terrible word. It describes not indifference nor the lapse into sin. It describes "positive and active irreligion," the spirit which defiantly withholds from God that which is his right. It describes human nature "in battle array against God."

There are the *sinners (hamartōloi)*. In its commonest usage this word describes character. It can be used, for instance, of a slave who is of lax and useless character. It describes the person who has no moral standards left.

There are the *impious (anosioi)*. *Hosios* is a noble word; it describes, as Trench puts it, "the everlasting ordinances of right, which no law or custom of man has constituted, for they are anterior to all law and custom." The things which are *hosios* are part of the very constitution of the universe, the everlasting sanctities. The Greek, for instance, shudderingly declared that the Egyptian custom where brother could marry sister and the Persian custom where son could marry mother, were *anosia, unholy*. The man who is *anosios* is worse than a mere lawbreaker. He is the man who violates the ultimate decencies of life.

There are the *polluted (bebēloi)*. *Bebēlos* is an ugly word with a queer history. It originally meant simply *that which can be trodden upon,* in contradistinction to that which is sacred to some god and therefore inviolable. It then came to mean *profane* in opposition to *sacred*, then the man who profanes the sacred things, who desecrates God's day, disobeys his laws and belittles his worship. The man who is *bebēlos* soils everything he touches.

There are *those who strike or even kill their parents (patralōai* and *mētralōai)*. Under Roman law a son who struck his parents was liable to death. The words describe sons or daughters who are lost to gratitude, lost to respect and lost to shame. And it must ever be remembered that this most cruel of blows can be one, not upon the body, but upon the heart.

There are the *murderers (androphonoi)*, literally *man-slayers*. Paul is thinking of the Ten Commandments and of how breach after breach of them characterizes the heathen world. We must not think that this at least has nothing to do with us, for Jesus widened the commandment to include not only the act of murder, but also the feeling of anger against a brother.

There are the *fornicators and the homosexuals (pornoi* and *arsenokoitai)*. It is difficult for us to realize the state of the ancient world in matters of sexual morality. It was riddled with unnatural vice. One of the extraordinary things was the actual connection of immorality and religion. The Temple of Aphrodite, goddess of love, at Corinth had attached to it a thousand priestesses who were sacred prostitutes and who at evening came down to the city streets and plied their trade. It is said that Solon was the first law-maker in Athens to legalize prostitution and that with the profits of the public brothels he instituted a new temple was built to Aphrodite, the goddess of love.

E. F. Brown was a missionary in India, and in his commentary on the Pastoral Epistles he quotes an extraordinary section from the Penal Code of India. A section of that code forbade obscene representations and then went on to say: "This section does not extend to any representation or sculpture, engraved, painted or otherwise represented on or in any temple, or any car used for the conveyance of idols, or kept or used for any religious purpose." It is an extraordinary thing that in the non-Christian religions time and time again immorality and obscenity flourish under the very protection of religion. It has often been said and said truly that chastity was the one completely new virtue which Christianity brought into this world. It was no easy thing in the early days to endeavour to live according to the Christian ethic in a world like that.

There are the *andrapodistai.* The word may either mean *slave-dealers* or *slave-kidnappers.* Possibly both meanings are involved here. It is true that slavery was an integral part of the ancient world. It is true that Aristotle declared that civilization was founded on slavery, that certain men and women existed only to perform the menial tasks of life for the convenience of the cultured classes. But even in the ancient world voices were raised against slavery. Philo spoke of slave-dealers as those "who despoil men of their most precious possession, their freedom."

But this more probably refers to kidnappers of slaves. Slaves were valuable property. An ordinary slave with no special gifts fetched from £16 to £20. A specially accomplished slave would fetch three or four times as much. Beautiful youths were in special demand as pages and cupbearers and would fetch as much as £800 or £900. Marcus Antonius is said to have paid £2,000 for two well-matched youths who were wrongly represented to be twins. In the days when Rome was specially eager to learn the arts of Greece and slaves who were skilled in Greek literature and music and art were specially valuable, a certain Lutatius Daphnis was sold for £3,500. The result was that frequently valuable slaves were either seduced from their masters or kidnapped. The kidnapping of specially beautiful or specially accomplished slaves was a common feature of ancient life.

Finally, there are *liars (pseustai)* and *perjurers (epiorkoi),* men who did not hesitate to twist the truth to gain dishonourable ends.

Here is a vivid picture of the atmosphere in which the ancient Church grew up. It was against an infection like that that the writer of the Pastorals sought to protect the Christians in his charge.

THE CLEANSING WORD

1 *Timothy* 1: 8–11 (*continued*)

INTO this world came the Christian message, and this passage tells us four things about it.

(i) It is *sound* teaching. The word used for sound (*hugiainein*) literally means *health-giving*. Christianity is an ethical religion. It demands from a man not only the keeping of certain ritual laws, but the living of a good life. E. F. Brown draws a comparison between it and Islam; a Mohammedan may be regarded as a very holy man if he observes certain ceremonial rituals, even though his moral life is quite unclean. He quotes a writer on Morocco: "The great blot on the creed of Islam is that precept and practice are not expected to go together, except as regards the ritual, so that a man may be notoriously wicked yet esteemed religious, having his blessing sought as that of one who has power with God, without the slightest sense of incongruity. The position of things was very well put to me one day by a Moor in Fez, who remarked: 'Do you want to know what our religion is? We purify ourselves with water while we contemplate adultery; we go to the mosque to pray and as we do so we think how best to cheat our neighbours; we give alms at the door and go back to our shop to rob; we read our Korans and go out to commit unmentionable sins; we fast and go on pilgrimage and yet we lie and kill.'" It must always be remembered that Christianity does not mean observing a ritual, even if that ritual consists of bible-reading and church-going; it means living a good life. Christianity, if it is real, is health-giving; it is the moral antiseptic which alone can cleanse life.

(ii) It is a *glorious gospel;* that is to say, it is *glorious good news*. It is good news of forgiveness for past sins and of power to conquer sin in the days to come, good news of God's mercy, God's cleansing and God's grace.

(iii) It is good news *which comes from God*. The Christian gospel is not a discovery made by man; it is something revealed by God. It does not offer only the help of man; it offers the power of God.

(iv) That good news *comes through men*. It was entrusted to Paul to bring it to others. God makes his offer and he needs his messengers. The real Christian is the person who has himself closed with the offer of God and has realized that he cannot keep such good news to himself but must share it with others who have not yet found it.

SAVED TO SERVE

1 *Timothy* 1 : 12–17

I give thanks to Jesus Christ, our Lord, who has filled me with his power, that he showed that he believed that he could trust me, by appointing me to his service, although I was formerly an insulter, a persecutor and a man of insolent and brutal violence. But I received mercy from him, because it was in ignorance that I acted thus, in the days when I did not believe. But the grace of our Lord rose higher than my sin, and I found it in the faith and love of those whose lives are lived in Jesus Christ. This is a saying on which we can rely, and which we are completely bound to accept, that Christ Jesus came into the world to save sinners—of whom I am chief. This was why I received mercy—so that in me Jesus Christ might display all that patience of his, so that I might be the first outline sketch of those who would one day come to believe in him, that they might find eternal life. To the King, eternal, immortal, invisible, to the only God, be honour and glory for ever and ever. Amen.

THIS passage begins with a very paean of thanksgiving. There were four tremendous things for which Paul wished to thank Jesus Christ.

(i) He thanked him because he *chose* him. Paul never had the feeling that he had chosen Christ, but always that Christ had chosen him. It was as if, when he was heading straight for destruction, Jesus Christ had laid his hand upon his shoulder and arrested him in the way. It was as if, when he was busy throwing away his life, Jesus Christ had suddenly brought him to his senses. In the days of the war I knew a Polish airman. He had crowded more thrilling hairbreadth escapes from death and from worse into a few years than the vast majority of men do into a lifetime. Sometimes he would tell the story of escape from occupied Europe, of parachute descents from the air, of rescue from the sea, and at the end of this amazing odyssey, he would always say, with a look of wonder in his eyes: "And now I am God's man." That is how Paul felt; he was Christ's man for Christ had chosen him.

(ii) He thanked him because he *trusted* him. It was to Paul an amazing thing, that he, the arch-persecutor, had been chosen as the missionary of Christ. It was not only that Jesus Christ had forgiven him; it was that Christ trusted him. Sometimes we forgive a man who has committed some mistake or been guilty of some sin, but we make it very clear that his past makes it impossible for us to trust him again with any responsibility. But Christ had not only forgiven Paul; he entrusted him with work to do. The man who had been Christ's persecutor had been made his ambassador.

(iii) He thanked him because he had *appointed* him. We must be very careful to note that to which Paul felt himself appointed. He was appointed to *service*. Paul never thought of himself as appointed to honour, or to leadership within the Church. He was saved to serve. Plutarch tells that when a Spartan won a victory in the games, his reward was that he might stand beside his king in battle. A Spartan wrestler at the Olympic games was offered a very considerable bribe to abandon the struggle; but he refused. Finally, after a terrific effort, he won his victory. Someone said to him: "Well,

Spartan, what have you got out of this costly victory you have won?" He answered: "I have won the privilege of standing in front of my king in battle." His reward was to serve and, if need be, to die for his king. It was for service, not honour, that Paul knew himself to be chosen.

(iv) He thanked him because he had *empowered* him. Paul had long since discovered that Jesus Christ never gives a man a task to do without also giving him the power to do it. Paul would never have said, "See what I have done," but always, "See what Jesus Christ has enabled me to do." No man is good enough, or strong enough, or pure enough, or wise enough to be the servant of Christ. But if he will give himself to Christ, he will go, not in his own strength, but in the strength of his Lord.

THE MEANS OF CONVERSION

1 *Timothy* 1: 12–17 (*continued*)

THERE are two further interesting things in this passage.

Paul's Jewish background comes out. He says that Jesus Christ had mercy on him because he committed his sins against Christ and his Church in the days of his ignorance. We often think that the Jewish viewpoint was that sacrifice atoned for sin; a man sinned, his sin broke his relationship with God, then sacrifice was made and God's anger was appeased and the relationship restored.

It may well have been that that was in fact the popular, debased view of sacrifice. But the highest Jewish thought insisted on two things. First, it insisted that sacrifice could never atone for deliberate sin, but only for the sins a man committed in ignorance or when swept away in a moment of passion. Second, the highest Jewish thought insisted that no sacrifice could atone for any sin unless there was contrition in the heart of the man who brought it. Here Paul is speaking out of his Jewish background. His heart had been broken by the mercy of Christ; his sins had been committed in the days before he knew Christ and his love. And for these reasons he felt that there was mercy for him.

There is a still more interesting matter, which is pointed out by E. F. Brown. Verse 14 is difficult. In the Revised Standard Version it runs: "The grace of our Lord overflowed for me with the faith and love that are in Christ Jesus." The first part is not difficult; it simply means that the grace of God rose higher than Paul's sin. But what exactly is the meaning of the phrase "with the faith and love that are in Christ Jesus"? E. F. Brown suggests that it is that the work of the grace of Christ in Paul's heart was helped by the faith and the love he found in the members of the Christian Church, things like the sympathy and the understanding and the kindness he received from men like Ananias, who opened his eyes and called him brother (*Acts* 9: 10–19), and Barnabas, who stood by him when the rest of the Church regarded him with bleak suspicion (*Acts* 9: 26–28). That is a very lovely idea. And if it be correct, we can see that there are three factors which co-operate in the conversion of any man.

(i) First, there is God. It was the prayer of Jeremiah: "Restore us to thyself, O Lord" (*Lamentations* 5: 21). As Augustine had it, we would never even have begun to seek for God unless he had already found us. The prime mover is God; at the back of a man's first desire for goodness there is his seeking love.

(ii) There is a man's own self. The Authorized Version renders *Matthew* 18: 3 entirely passively: "Except ye *be converted* and become as little children, ye shall not enter into the Kingdom of Heaven." The Revised Standard Version gives a much more active rendering: "Unless you *turn* and become like children, you will never enter the kingdom of heaven." There must be human response to divine appeal. God gave men free will and they can use it either to accept or to refuse his offer.

(iii) There is the agency of some Christian person. It is Paul's conviction that he is sent "to open the eyes of the Gentiles, that they may turn from darkness to light, and from the power of Satan to God, that they may receive forgiveness of sins" (*Acts* 26: 18). It is James's belief that any man who converts the sinner from the error of his way "will save a soul from death and will cover a multitude of sins" (*James* 5: 19, 20). So then there is a double duty laid upon us. It has been said that a saint is someone who makes it easier to believe in God, and that a saint is someone in whom Christ lives again. We must give thanks for those who showed us Christ, whose words and example brought us to him; and we must strive to be the influence which brings others to him.

In this matter of conversion the initiative of God, the response of man, and the influence of the Christian all combine.

THE UNFORGOTTEN SHAME AND THE UNDYING INSPIRATION

1 *Timothy* 1: 12–17 (*continued*)

THE thing which stands out in this passage is Paul's insistence upon remembering his own sin. He heaps up a very climax of words to show what he did to Christ and the Church. He was an *insulter* of the Church; he had flung hot and angry words at the Christians, accusing them of crimes against God. He was a *persecutor;* he had taken every means open to him under the Jewish law to annihilate the Christian Church. Then comes a terrible word; he had been *a man of insolent and brutal violence.* The word in Greek is *hubristēs.* It indicates a kind of arrogant sadism; it describes the man who is out to inflict pain for the sheer joy of inflicting it. The corresponding abstract noun is *hubris* which Aristotle defines: "*Hubris* means to hurt and to grieve people, in such a way that shame comes to the man who is hurt and grieved, and that not that the person who inflicts the hurt and injury may gain anything else in addition to what he already possesses, but simply that he may find delight in his own cruelty and in the suffering of the other person."

That is what Paul was once like in regard to the Christian Church. Not content with words of insult, he went to the limit of legal persecution. Not content with legal persecution, he went to the limit of sadistic brutality in his attempt to stamp out the Christian faith. He remembered that; and to the end of the day he regarded himself as the chief of sinners. It is not that he *was* the chief of sinners; he still *is*. True, he could never forget that he was a forgiven sinner; but neither could he ever forget that he was a sinner. Why should he remember his sin with such vividness?

(i) The memory of his sin was the surest way to keep him from pride. There could be no such thing as spiritual pride for a man who had done the things that he had done. John Newton was one of the great preachers and the supreme hymn-writers of the Church; but he had sunk to the lowest depths to which a man can sink, in the days when he sailed the seas in a slave-trader's ship. So when he became a converted man and a preacher of the gospel, he wrote a text in great letters, and fastened it above the mantlepiece of his study where he could not fail to see it: "Thou shalt remember that thou wast a bondman in the land of Egypt and the Lord thy God redeemed thee." He also composed his own epitaph: "John Newton, Clerk, once an Infidel and Libertine, a Servant of Slaves in Africa, was by the Mercy of our Lord and Saviour Jesus Christ, Preserved, Restored, Pardoned, and Appointed to Preach the Faith he had so long laboured to destroy." John Newton never forgot that he was a forgiven sinner; neither did Paul. Neither must we. It does a man good to remember his sins; it saves him from spiritual pride.

(ii) The memory of his sin was the surest way to keep his gratitude aflame. To remember what we have been forgiven is the surest way to keep awake our love to Jesus Christ. F. W. Boreham tells of a letter which the old Puritan, Thomas Goodwin, wrote to his son. "When I was threatening to become cold in my ministry, and when I felt Sabbath morning coming and my heart not filled with amazement at the grace of God, or when I was making ready to dispense the Lord's Supper, do you know what I used to do? I used to take a turn up and down among the sins of my past life, and I always came down again with a broken and a contrite heart, ready to preach, as it was preached in the beginning, the forgiveness of sins." "I do not think," he said, "I ever went up the pulpit stair that I did not stop for a moment at the foot of it and take a turn up and down among the sins of my past years. I do not think that I ever planned a sermon that I did not take a turn round my study table and look back at the sins of my youth and of all my life down to the present; and many a Sabbath morning, when my soul had been cold and dry, for the lack of prayer during the week, a turn up and down in my past life before I went into the pulpit always broke my hard heart and made me close with the gospel for my own soul before I began to preach." When we remember how we have hurt God and hurt those who love us and hurt our fellow-men and when we remember how God and men have forgiven us, that memory must awake the flame of gratitude within our hearts.

(iii) The memory of his sin was the constant urge to greater effort. It is quite true that a man can never earn the approval of God, or deserve his love; but it is also true that he can never stop trying to do something to show how much he appreciates the love and the mercy which have made him what he is. Whenever we love anyone we cannot help trying always to demonstrate our love. When we remember how much God loves us and how little we deserve it, when we remember that it was for us that Jesus Christ hung and suffered on Calvary, it must compel us to effort that will tell God we realize what he has done for us and will show Jesus Christ that his sacrifice was not in vain.

(iv) The memory of his sin was bound to be a constant encouragement to others. Paul uses a vivid picture. He says that what happened to him was a kind of outline-sketch of what was going to happen to those who would accept Christ in the days to come. The word he uses is *hupotupōsis* which means an outline, a sketch-plan, a first draft, a preliminary model. It is as if Paul were saying, "Look what Christ has done for me! If someone like me can be saved, there is hope for everyone." Suppose a man was seriously ill and had to go through a dangerous operation, it would be the greatest encouragement to him if he met and talked with someone who had undergone the same operation and had emerged completely cured. Paul did not shrinkingly conceal his record; he blazoned it abroad, that others might take courage and be filled with hope that the grace which had changed him could change them too.

Greatheart said to Christian's boys: "You must know that Forgetful Green is the most dangerous place in all these parts." Paul's sin was something which he refused to forget, for every time he remembered the greatness of his sin, he remembered the still greater greatness of Jesus Christ. It was not that he brooded unhealthily over his sin; it was that he remembered it to rejoice in the wonder of the grace of Jesus Christ.

THE SUMMONS WHICH CANNOT BE DENIED

1 *Timothy* 1: 18–20

I entrust this charge to you, Timothy lad, because it is the natural consequence of the messages which came to the prophets from God, and which marked you out as the very man for this work, so that, in obedience to these messages, you may wage a fine campaign, maintaining your faith and a good conscience all the time; and there are some who, in matters of the faith, have repelled the guidance of conscience, and have come to shipwreck. Amongst them are Hymenaeus and Alexander, whom I have handed over to Satan, that they may be disciplined out of their insults to God and his Church.

THE first section of this passage is highly compressed. What lies behind it is this. There must have been a meeting of the prophets of the Church. They were men known to be within the confidence and the counsels of God. "Surely the Lord does nothing without revealing his secret to his servants the prophets" (*Amos* 3: 7). This meeting thought about the situation which was threatening the Church and came to the conclusion that Timothy was the man to deal with it. We can see the prophets acting in exactly the same way in *Acts* 13: 1–3. The Church was faced with the great decision whether or not to take the gospel out to the Gentiles; and it was to the prophets that there came the message of the Holy Spirit, saying: "Set apart for me Barnabas and Saul for the work to which I have called them" (*Acts* 13: 2). That was what had happened to Timothy. He had been marked out by the prophets as the man to deal with the situation in the Church. It may well have been that he shrank from the greatness of the task which faced him, and here Paul encourages him with certain considerations.

(i) Paul says to him: "You are a man who has been chosen and you cannot refuse your task." Something like that happened to John Knox. He had been teaching in St. Andrews. His teaching was supposed to be private but many came to it, for he was obviously a man with a message. So the people urged him "that he would take the preaching place upon him. But he utterly refused, alleging that he would not run where God had not called him. . . . Whereupon they privily among themselves advising, having with them in council Sir David Lindsay of the Mount, they concluded that they would give a charge to the said John, and that publicly by the mouth of their preacher."

So Sunday came and Knox was in Church and John Rough was preaching. "The said John Rough, preacher, directed his words to the said John Knox, saying: 'Brother, ye shall not be offended, albeit that I speak unto you that which I have in charge, even from all those that are here present, which is this: In the name of God, and of his Son

Jesus Christ, and in the name of these that presently call you by my mouth, I charge you that you refuse not this holy vocation, but . . . that you take upon you the public office and charge of preaching, even as you look to avoid God's heavy displeasure, and desire that he shall multiply his graces with you.' And in the end he said to those that were present: 'Was not this your charge to me? And do ye not approve this vocation?' They answered: 'It was: and we approve it.' Whereat the said John, abashed, burst forth in most abundant tears, and withdrew himself to his chamber. His countenance and behaviour, from that day till the day that he was compelled to present himself to the public place of preaching, did sufficiently declare the grief and trouble of his heart; for no man saw any sign of mirth in him, neither yet had he pleasure to accompany any man, many days together."

John Knox was chosen; he did not want to answer the call; but he had to, for the choice had been made by God. Years afterwards the Regent Morton uttered his famous epitaph by Knox's graveside: "In respect that he bore God's message, to whom he must make account for the same, he (albeit he was weak and an unworthy creature, and a fearful man) feared not the faces of men." The consciousness of being chosen gave him courage.

So Paul says to Timothy: "You have been chosen; you cannot let down God and man." To every one of us there comes God's choosing; and when we are summoned to some work for him, we dare not refuse it.

(ii) It may be that Paul was saying to Timothy: "Be true to your name." *Timothy*—its full form is *Timotheos*—is composed of two Greek words, *timē* which means *honour* and *theos* which means *God,* and so means *honour to God.* If we are called by the name *Christian*, one of Christ's folk, to that name we must be true.

(iii) Finally, Paul says to Timothy: "I entrust this charge to you". The word which he uses for *to entrust* is *paratithesthai,* which is the word used of entrusting something valuable to someone's safe keeping. It is used, for instance, of making a deposit in a bank, or of entrusting someone to another's care. It always implies that a trust has been reposed in someone for which he will be called to account. So Paul says: "Timothy, into your hands I am placing a sacred trust. See that you do not fail." God reposes his trust in us; into our hands he puts his honour and his Church. We too must see to it that we do not fail.

DESPATCHED ON GOD'S CAMPAIGN

1 *Timothy* 1: 18–20 (*continued*)

WHAT then is entrusted to Timothy? He is despatched to fight a *good campaign*. The picture of life as a campaign is one which has always fascinated men's thoughts. Maximus of Tyre said: "God is the general; life is the campaign; man is the soldier." Seneca said: "For me to live, my dear Lucilius, is to be a soldier." When a man became a follower of the goddess Isis and was initiated into the Mysteries connected with the goddess's name, the summons to him was: "Enrol yourself in the sacred soldiery of Isis."

There are three things to be noted.

(i) It is not to a *battle* that we are summoned; it is to a *campaign*. Life is one long campaign, a service from which there is no release, not a short, sharp struggle after which a man can lay aside his arms and rest in peace. To change the metaphor, life is not a sprint; it is a marathon race. It is there that the danger enters in. It is necessary to be for ever on the watch. "Eternal vigilance is the price of liberty." The temptations of life never cease their search for a chink in the armour of the Christian. It is one of the commonest dangers in life to proceed in a series of spasms. We must remember that we are summoned to a campaign which goes on as long as life does.

(ii) It is to a *fine* campaign that Timothy is summoned. Here again we have the word *kalos* of which the Pastorals are so fond. It does not mean only something which is good and strong; it means something which is also winsome and lovely. The soldier of Christ is not a conscript who serves grimly and grudgingly; he is a volunteer who serves with a certain knightly chivalry. He is not the slave of duty, but the servant of joy.

(iii) Timothy is commanded to take with him two weapons of equipment. (*a*) He is to take *faith*. Even when things are at their darkest, he must have faith in the essential rightness of his cause and in the ultimate triumph of God. It was faith which kept up John Knox when he was in despair. Once when he was a slave on the galleys, the ship came in sight of St. Andrews. He was so weak that he had to be lifted up bodily in order to see. They showed him the church steeple and asked if he knew it. "Yes," he said, "I know it well: and I am fully persuaded, how weak that ever I now appear, that I shall not depart this life till that my tongue shall glorify his godly name in the same place." He describes his feelings in 1554 when he had to flee the country to escape the vengeance of Mary Tudor. "Not only the ungodly, but even my faithful brethren, yea, and my own self, that is, all natural understanding, judged my cause to be irremediable. The frail flesh, oppressed with fear and pain, desireth deliverance, ever abhorring and drawing back from obedience giving. O Christian brethren, I write by experience. . . . I know the grudging and murmuring complaints of the flesh; I know the anger, wrath, and indignation which it conceiveth against God, calling all his promises in doubt, and being ready every hour utterly to fall from God. *Against which remains only faith.*" The Christian soldier needs in the darkest hour the faith that will not shrink. (*b*) He is to take the defence of a *good conscience*. That is to say, the Christian soldier must at least try to live in accordance with his own doctrine. The virtue is gone out of a man's message when his conscience condemns him as he speaks.

A STERN REBUKE

1 *Timothy* 1: 18–20 (*continued*)

THE passage closes with a stern rebuke to two members of the Church who have injured the Church, grieved Paul, and made shipwreck of their own lives. Hymenaeus is mentioned again in 2 *Timothy* 2: 17; and Alexander may well be the Alexander who is referred to in 2 *Timothy* 4: 14. Paul has three complaints against them.

(i) They had rejected the guidance of conscience. They had allowed their own desires to speak with more persuasiveness than the voice of God.

(ii) They had relapsed into evil practices. Once they had abandoned God, life had become soiled and debased. When God went from life, beauty went along with him.

(iii) They had taken to false teaching. Again it was almost inevitable. When a man takes the wrong way, his first instinct is to find excuses for himself. He takes the Christian teaching and twists it to suit himself. Out of the right he finds perverted arguments to justify the wrong. He finds arguments in the words of Christ to justify the ways of the devil. The moment a man disobeys the voice of conscience, his conduct becomes debased and his thinking twisted.

So Paul goes on to say that he has "handed them over to Satan." What is the meaning of this terrible phrase? There are three possibilities.

(i) He may be thinking of the Jewish practice of excommunication. According to synagogue practice, if a man was an evil-doer he was first publicly rebuked. If that was ineffective, he was banished from the synagogue for a period of thirty days. If he was still stubbornly unrepentant, he was put under the ban, which made him a person accursed, debarred from the society of men and the fellowship of God. In such a case a man might well be said to be handed over to Satan.

(ii) He may be saying that he has barred them from the Church and turned them loose in the world. In a heathen society it was inevitable that men should draw a hard and fast

line between the Church and the world. The Church was
God's territory; the world was Satan's; and to be debarred
from the Church was to be handed over to that territory
which was under the sway of Satan. The phrase may mean
that these two troublers of the Church were abandoned to
the world.

(iii) The third explanation is the most likely of the three.
Satan was held to be responsible for human suffering and pain.
A man in the Corinthian Church had been guilty of the
terrible sin of incest. Paul's advice was that he should be
delivered to Satan "for the destruction of the flesh, that the
spirit may be saved in the day of the Lord Jesus"
(1 *Corinthians* 5: 5). The idea is that the Church should pray
for some physical chastisement to fall on that man so that,
by the pain of his body, he might be brought to the
senses of his mind. In Job's case it was Satan who brought
the physical suffering upon him (*Job* 2: 6, 7). In the New
Testament itself we have the terrible end of Ananias and
Sapphira (*Acts* 5: 5, 10), and the blindness which fell upon
Elymas because of his opposition to the gospel (*Acts* 13: 11).
It may well be that it was Paul's prayer that these two men
should be subjected to some painful visitation which would be
a punishment and a warning.

That is all the more likely because it is Paul's hope that
they will be, not obliterated and destroyed, but disciplined
out of their evil ways. To him, as it ought to be to us,
punishment was never mere vindictive vengeance but always
remedial discipline, never meant simply to hurt but always to
cure.

THE UNIVERSALITY OF THE GOSPEL

1 *Timothy* 2: 1–7

So then the first thing I urge you to do is to offer your requests,
your prayers, your petitions, your thanksgivings for all men.
Pray for kings and for all who are in authority, that they may

enjoy a life that is tranquil and undisturbed, and that they may act in all godliness and reverence. That is the fine way to live, the way which meets with the approval of God, our Saviour, who wishes all men to be saved, and to come to a full knowledge of the truth. For there is one God, and one Mediator, between God and man, the man Jesus Christ, who gave himself a ransom for all. It was thus he bore his witness to God in his own good times, a witness to which I have been appointed a herald and an envoy (I am speaking the truth: I do not lie), a teacher to the Gentiles, a teacher whose message is based on faith and truth.

BEFORE we study this passage in detail we must note one thing which shines out from it in a way that no one can fail to see. Few passages in the New Testament so stress the universality of the gospel. Prayer is to be made for *all* men; God is the Saviour who wishes *all* men to be saved; Jesus gave his life a ransom for *all*. As Walter Lock writes: "God's will to save is as wide as his will to create."

This is a note which sounds in the New Testament again and again. Through Christ God was reconciling the *world* to himself (2 *Corinthians* 5: 18, 19). God so loved the *world* that he gave his Son (*John* 3: 16). It was Jesus's confidence that, if he was lifted up on his Cross, soon or late he would draw *all* men to him (*John* 12: 32).

E. F. Brown calls this passage "the charter of missionary work." He says that it is the proof that all men are *capax dei,* capable of receiving God. They may be lost, but they can be found; they may be ignorant, but they can be enlightened; they may be sinners, but they can be saved. George Wishart, the forerunner of John Knox, writes in his translation of the First Swiss Confession: "The end and intent of the Scripture is to declare that God is benevolent and friendly-minded to mankind; and that he hath declared that kindness in and through Jesus Christ, his only Son; the which kindness is received by faith." That is why prayer must be made for all. God wants all men, and so, therefore, must his Church.

(i) The gospel includes *high and low*. Both the Emperor in his power and the slave in his helplessness were included in the sweep of the gospel. Both the philosopher in his wisdom and the simple man in his ignorance need the grace and truth that the gospel can bring. Within the gospel there are no class distinctions. King and commoner, rich and poor, aristocrat and peasant, master and man are all included in its limitless embrace.

(ii) The gospel includes *good and bad*. A strange malady has sometimes afflicted the Church in modern times, causing it to insist that a man be respectable before he is allowed in, and to look askance at sinners who seek entry to its doors. But the New Testament is clear that the Church exists, not only to edify the good, but to welcome and save the sinner. C. T. Studd used to repeat four lines of doggerel:

> "Some want to live within the sound
> Of Church or Chapel bell;
> I want to run a rescue shop
> Within a yard of hell."

One of the great saints of modern times, and indeed of all time, was Toyohiko Kagawa. It was to Shinkawa that he went to find men and women for Christ and he lived there in the filthiest and most depraved slums in the world. W. J. Smart describes the situation: "His neighbours were unregistered prostitutes, thieves who boasted of their power to outwit all the police in the city, and murderers who were not only proud of their murder record but always ready to add to their local prestige by committing another. All the people, whether sick, or feeble-minded or criminal, lived in conditions of abysmal misery, in streets slippery with filth, where rats crawled out of open sewers to die. The air was always filled with stench. An idiot girl who lived next door to Kagawa had vile pictures painted on her back to decoy lustful men to her den. Everywhere human bodies rotted with syphilis." Kagawa wanted people like that, and so does Jesus Christ, for he wants *all* men, good and bad alike.

(iii) The gospel embraces *Christian and non-Christian*. Prayer is to be made for *all* men. The Emperors and rulers for whom this letter bids us pray were not Christians; they were in fact hostile to the Church; and yet they were to be borne to the throne of grace by the prayers of the Church. For the true Christian there is no such thing as an enemy in all this world. None is outside his prayers, for none is outside the love of Christ, and none is outside the purpose of God, who wishes *all* men to be saved.

THE WAY OF PRAYER

1 *Timothy* 2: 1–7 (*continued*)

FOUR different words for prayer are grouped together. It is true that they are not to be sharply distinguished; nevertheless each has something to tell us of the way of prayer.

(i) The first is *deēsis,* which we have translated *request.* It is not exclusively a religious word; it can be used of a request made either to a fellow-man or to God. But its fundamental idea is a sense of need. No one will make a request unless a sense of need has already wakened a desire. Prayer begins with a sense of need. It begins with the conviction that we cannot deal with life ourselves. That sense of human weakness is the basis of all approach to God.

> "Let not conscience make you linger,
>   Nor of fitness fondly dream;
>   All the fitness he requireth
>   Is to feel your need of him."

(ii) The second is *proseuchē,* which we have translated *prayer.* The basic difference between *deēsis* and *proseuchē* is that *deēsis* may be addressed either to man or God, but *proseuchē* is never used of anything else but approach to God. There are certain needs which only God can satisfy. There is a strength which he alone can give; a forgiveness which he alone can grant; a certainty which he alone can bestow. It may well be that our weakness haunts us because we so often take our needs to the wrong place.

(iii) The third is *enteuxis,* which we have translated *petition.*

Of the three words this is the most interesting. It has a most interesting history. It is the noun from the verb *entugchanein.* This originally meant simply *to meet,* or *to fall in* with a person; it went on to mean *to hold intimate conversation with a person;* then it acquired a special meaning and meant *to enter into a king's presence and to submit a petition to him.* That tells us much about prayer. It tells us that the way to God stands open and that we have the right to bring our petitions to one who is a king.

> "Thou art coming to a King;
>   Large petitions with thee bring;
>   For his grace and power are such,
>   None can ever ask too much."

It is impossible to ask too great a boon from this King.

(iv) The fourth is *eucharistia,* which we have translated *thanksgiving.* Prayer does not mean only asking God for things; it also means thanking God for things. For too many of us prayer is an exercise in complaint, when it should be an exercise in thanksgiving. Epictetus, not a Christian but a Stoic philosopher, used to say: "What can I, who am a little old lame man, do, except give praise to God?" We have the right to bring our needs to God; but we have also the duty of bringing our thanksgivings to him.

PRAYER FOR THOSE IN AUTHORITY

1 *Timothy* 2: 1–7 (*continued*)

THIS passage distinctly commands prayer for kings and emperors and all who are set in authority. This was a cardinal principle of communal Christian prayer. Emperors might be persecutors and those in authority might be determined to stamp out Christianity. But the Christian Church never, even in the times of bitterest persecution, ceased to pray for them.

It is extraordinary to trace how all through its early days, those days of bitter persecution, the Church regarded it as an absolute duty to pray for the Emperor and his subordinate kings and governors. "Fear God," said Peter. "Honour the Emperor" (1 *Peter* 2: 17), and we must remember that that Emperor was none other than Nero, that monster of cruelty. Tertullian insists that for the Emperor the Christian pray for "long life, secure dominion, a safe home, a faithful senate, a righteous people, and a world at peace" (*Apology* 30). "We pray for our rulers," he wrote, "for the state of the world, for the peace of all things and for the postponement of the end" (*Apology* 39). He writes: "The Christian is the enemy of no man, least of all of the Emperor, for we know that, since he has been appointed by God, it is necessary that we should love him, and reverence him, and honour him, and desire his safety, together with that of the whole Roman Empire. Therefore we sacrifice for the safety of the Emperor" (*Ad Scapulam* 2). Cyprian, writing to Demetrianus, speaks of the Christian Church as "sacrificing and placating God night and day for your peace and safety" (*Ad Demetrianum* 20). In A.D. 311 the Emperor Galerius actually asked for the prayers of the Christians, and promised them mercy and indulgence if they prayed for the state. Tatian writes: "Does the Emperor order us to pay tribute? We willingly offer it. Does the ruler order us to render service or servitude? We acknowledge our servitude. But a man must be honoured as befits a man, but only God is to be reverenced" (*Apology* 4). Theophilus of Antioch writes: "The honour that I will give the Emperor is all the greater, because I will not worship him, but I will pray for him. I will worship no one but the true and real God, for I know that the Emperor was appointed by him. . . . Those give real honour to the Emperor who are well-disposed to him, who obey him, and who pray for him" (*Apology* 1: 11). Justin Martyr writes: "We worship God alone, but in all other things we gladly serve you, acknowledging kings and rulers of men, and praying that they may be found to have pure reason with kingly power" (*Apology* 1: 14, 17).

The greatest of all the prayers for the Emperor is in Clement of Rome's First Letter to the Church at Corinth which was written about A.D. 90 when the savagery of Domitian was still fresh in men's minds: "Thou, Lord and Master, hast given our rulers and governors the power of sovereignty through thine excellent and unspeakable might, that we, knowing the glory and honour which thou hast given them, may submit ourselves unto them, in nothing resisting thy will. Grant unto them, therefore, O Lord, health, peace, concord, stability, that they may administer the government which thou hast given them without failure. For thou, O heavenly Master, King of the Ages, givest to the sons of men glory and honour and power over all things that are upon the earth. Do thou, Lord, direct their counsel according to that which is good and well-pleasing in thy sight, that, administering the power which thou hast given them in peace and gentleness with godliness, they may obtain thy favour. O thou, who alone art able to do these things, and things far more exceeding good than these for us, we praise thee through the High Priest and Guardian of our souls, Jesus Christ, through whom be the glory and the majesty unto thee both now and for all generations, and for ever and ever. Amen" (1 *Clement* 61).

The Church always regarded it as a bounden duty to pray for those set in authority over the kingdoms of the earth; and brought even its persecutors before the throne of grace.

THE GIFTS OF GOD

1 *Timothy* 2: 1–7 (*continued*)

THE Church prayed for certain things for those in authority.

(i) It prayed for "a life that is tranquil and undisturbed." That was the prayer for freedom from war, from rebellion and from anything which would disturb the peace of the realm. That is the good citizen's prayer for his country.

(ii) But the Church prayed for much more than that. It

prayed for "a life that is lived in godliness and reverence." Here we are confronted with two great words which are keynotes of the Pastoral Epistles and describe qualities which not only the ruler but every Christian must covet.

First, there is *godliness, eusebeia*. This is one of the great and almost untranslatable Greek words. It describes reverence both towards God and man. It describes that attitude of mind which respects man and honours God. Eusebius defined it as "reverence towards the one and only God, and the kind of life that he would wish us to lead." To the Greek, the great example of *eusebeia* was Socrates whom Xenophon describes in the following terms: "So pious and devoutly religious that he would take no step apart from the will of heaven; so just and upright that he never did even a trifling injury to any living soul; so self-controlled, so temperate, that he never at any time chose the sweeter in place of the bitter; so sensible and wise and prudent that in distinguishing the better from the worse he never erred" (Xenophon: *Memorabilia,* 4, 8, 11). *Eusebeia* comes very near to that great Latin word *pietas,* which Warde Fowler describes thus: "The quality known to the Romans as *pietas* rises, in spite of trial and danger, superior to the enticements of individual passion and selfish ease. Aeneas's *pietas* became a sense of duty to the will of the gods, as well as to his father, his son and his people; and this duty never leaves him." Clearly *eusebeia* is a tremendous thing. It never forgets the reverence due to God; it never forgets the rights due to men; it never forgets the respect due to self. It describes the character of the man who never fails God, man or himself.

Second, there is reverence, *semnotēs*. Here again we are in the realm of the untranslatable. The corresponding adjective *semnos* is constantly applied to the gods. R. C. Trench says that the man who is *semnos* "has on him a grace and a dignity, not lent by earth." He says that he is one who "without demanding it challenges and inspires reverence." Aristotle was the great ethical teacher of the Greeks. He had a way of describing every virtue as the mean between two extremes. On the one side there was an extreme of excess and on the other an extreme of defect, and in between there was the mean, the happy medium, in which virtue lay. Aristotle says that *semnotēs* is the mean between *areskeia, subservience*, and *authadeia, arrogance*. It may be said that for the man who is *semnos* all life is one act of worship; all life is lived in the presence of God; he moves through the world, as it has been put, as if it was the temple of the living God. He never forgets the holiness of God or the dignity of man.

These two great qualities are regal qualities which every man must covet and for which every man must pray.

ONE GOD AND ONE SAVIOUR

1 *Timothy* 2: 1-7 (*continued*)

PAUL concludes with a statement of the greatest truths of the Christian faith.

(i) There is one God. We are not living in a world such as the Gnostics produced with their theories of two gods, hostile to each other. We are not living in a world such as the heathen produced with their horde of gods, often in competition with one another. Missionaries tell us that one of the greatest reliefs which Christianity brings to the heathen is the conviction that there is only one God. They live for ever terrified of the gods and it is an emancipation to discover that there is one God only whose name is Father and whose nature is Love.

(ii) There is one Mediator. Even the Jews would have said that there are many mediators between God and man. A mediator is one who stands between two parties and acts as go-between. To the Jews the angels were mediators. *The Testament of Dan* (6: 2) has it: "Draw near unto God, and unto the angel who intercedes for you, for he is a mediator between God and man." To the Greeks there were all kinds of mediators. Plutarch said it was an insult to God to conceive that he was in any way directly involved in the world; he was involved in the world only through angels and demons and demi-gods who were, so to speak, his liaison officers.

Neither in Jewish nor in Greek thought had a man *direct* access to God. But, through Jesus Christ, the Christian has direct that access, with nothing to bar the way between. Further, there is only *one* Mediator. E. F. Brown tells us that that is, for instance, what the Hindus find so hard to believe. They say: "Your religion is good for you, and ours for us." But unless there is one God and one Mediator there can be no such thing as the brotherhood of man. If there are many gods and many mediators competing for their allegiance and their love, religion becomes something which divides men instead of uniting them. It is because there is one God and one Mediator that men are brethren one of another.

Paul goes on to call Jesus the one who gave his life a ransom for all. That simply means that it cost God the life and death of his Son to bring men back to himself. There was a man who lost a son in the war. He had lived a most careless and even a godless life; but his son's death brought him face to face with God as never before. He became a changed man. One day he was standing before the local war memorial, looking at his son's name upon it. And very gently he said: "I guess he had to go down to lift me up." That is what Jesus did; it cost his life and death to tell men of the love of God and to bring men home to him.

Then Paul claims to himself four offices.

(i) He is a *herald* of the story of Jesus Christ. A herald is a man who makes a statement and who says: "This is true." He is a man who brings a proclamation that is not his own, but which comes from the king.

(ii) He is a *witness* to the story of Christ. A witness is a man who says: "This is true, and I know it" and says also "It works." He is a man who tells, not only the story of Christ, but also the story of what Christ has done for him.

(iii) He is an *envoy.* An envoy is one whose duty is to commend his country in a foreign land. An envoy in the

Christian sense is therefore one who commends the story of Christ to others. He wishes to communicate that story to others, so that it will mean as much to them as it does to him.

(iv) He is a *teacher*. The *herald* is the person who proclaims the facts; the *witness* is the person who proclaims the power of the facts; the *envoy* is the person who commends the facts; the *teacher* is the person who leads men into the meaning of the facts. It is not enough to know that Christ lived and died; we must think out what that meant. A man must not only feel the wonder of the story of Christ; he must think out its meaning for himself and for the world.

BARRIERS TO PRAYER

1 *Timothy* 2: 8–15

So, then, it is my wish that men should pray everywhere, lifting up holy hands, with no anger in their hearts and no doubts in their minds. Even so it is my wish that women should modestly and wisely adorn themselves in seemly dress. This adornment should not consist in braided hair, and ornaments of gold, and pearls, but—as befits women who profess to reverence God—they should adorn themselves with good works. Let a woman learn in silence and with all submission. I do not allow a woman to teach or to dictate to a man. Rather, it is my advice that she should be silent. For Adam was formed first, and then Eve; and Adam was not deceived, but the woman was deceived, and so became guilty of transgression. But women will be saved through child-bearing, if they continue in faith and love, and if they wisely walk the road that leads to holiness.

THE early Church took over the Jewish attitude of prayer, which was to pray standing, with hands outstretched and the palms upwards. Later Tertullian was to say that this depicted the attitude of Jesus upon the Cross.

The Jews had always known about the barriers which kept a man's prayers from God. Isaiah heard God say to the people: "When you spread forth your hands, I will hide my eyes from you; even though you make many prayers, I will not listen; your hands are full of blood" (*Isaiah* 1: 15). Here, too, certain things are demanded.

(i) He who prays must stretch forth holy hands. He must hold up to God hands which do not touch the forbidden things. This does not mean for one moment that the sinner is debarred from God; but it does mean that there is no reality in the prayers of the man who then goes out to soil his hands with forbidden things, as if he had never prayed. It is not thinking of the man who is helplessly in the grip of some passion and desperately fighting against it, bitterly conscious of his failure. It is thinking of the man whose prayers are a sheer formality.

(ii) He who prays must have no anger in his heart. It has been said that "forgiveness is indivisible." Human and divine forgiveness go hand in hand. Again and again Jesus stresses the fact that we cannot hope to receive the forgiveness of God so long as we are at enmity with our fellow-men. "So if you are offering your gift at the altar, and there remember that your brother has something against you, leave your gift there before the altar and go; first be reconciled to your brother, and then come and offer your gift" (*Matthew* 5: 23, 24). "If you do not forgive men their trespasses, neither will your Father forgive your trespasses" (*Matthew* 6: 15). Jesus tells how the unforgiving servant himself found no forgiveness, and ends: "So also my heavenly Father will do to every one of you, if you do not forgive your brother from your heart" (*Matthew* 18: 35). To be forgiven, we must be forgiving. The *Didachē*, the earliest Christian book on public worship, which dates from about A.D. 100, has it: "Let no one who has a quarrel with his neighbour come to us, until they are reconciled." The bitterness in a man's heart is a barrier which hinders his prayers from reaching God.

(iii) He who prays must have no doubts in his mind. This phrase can mean two things. The word used is *dialogismos*, which can mean both an *argument* and a *doubt*. If we take it in the sense of *argument*, it simply repeats what has gone before and restates the fact that bitterness and quarrels and venomous debates are a hindrance to prayer. It is better to take it in the sense of *doubt*. Before prayer is answered there must be belief that God will answer. If a man prays pessimistically and with no real belief that it is any use, his prayer falls wingless to the ground. Before a man can be cured, he must believe that he can be cured; before a man can lay hold on the grace of God, he must believe in that grace. We must take our prayers to God in the complete confidence that he hears and answers prayer.

WOMEN IN THE CHURCH

1 *Timothy* 2: 8–15 (*continued*)

THE second part of this passage deals with the place of women in the Church. It cannot be read out of its historical context, for it springs entirely from the situation in which it was written.

(i) It was written against a Jewish background. No nation ever gave a bigger place to women in home and in family things than the Jews did; but officially the position of a woman was very low. In Jewish law she was not a person but a thing; she was entirely at the disposal of her father or of her husband. She was forbidden to learn the law; to instruct a woman in the law was to cast pearls before swine. Women had no part in the synagogue service; they were shut apart in a section of the synagogue, or in a gallery, where they could not be seen. A man came to the synagogue to *learn;* but, at the most, a woman came to *hear.* In the synagogue the lesson from Scripture was read by members of the congregation; but not by women, for that would have been to lessen "the honour of the congregation." It was absolutely forbidden for a woman to teach in a school; she might not even teach the youngest children. A woman was exempt from the stated demands of the Law. It was not obligatory on her to attend the sacred feasts and festivals. Women, slaves and children were classed together. In the Jewish morning prayer a man thanked God that God had not made him "a Gentile, a slave or a woman." In the *Sayings of the Fathers* Rabbi Josē ben Johanan is quoted as saying: " 'Let thy house be opened wide, and let the poor be thy household, and talk not much with a woman.' Hence the wise have said: 'Everyone that talketh much with a woman causes evil to himself, and desists from the works of the Law, and his end is that he inherits Gehenna.' " A strict Rabbi would never greet a woman on the street, not even his own wife or daughter or mother or sister. It was said of woman: "Her work is to send her children to the synagogue; to attend to domestic concerns; to leave her husband free to study in the schools; to keep house for him until he returns."

(ii) It was written against a Greek background. The Greek background made things doubly difficult. The place of women in Greek religion was low. The Temple of Aphrodite in Corinth had a thousand priestesses who were sacred prostitutes and every evening plied their trade on the city streets. The Temple of Diana in Ephesus had its hundreds of priestesses called the *Melissae*, which means the *bees*, whose function was the same. The respectable Greek woman led a very confined life. She lived in her own quarters into which no one but her husband came. She did not even appear at meals. She never at any time appeared on the street alone; she never went to any public assembly. The fact is that if in a Greek town Christian women had taken an active and a speaking part in its work, the Church would inevitably have gained the reputation of being the resort of loose women.

Further, in Greek society there were women whose whole life consisted in elaborate dressing and braiding of the hair. In Rome, Pliny tells us of a bride, Lollia Paulina, whose bridal dress cost the equivalent of £432,000. Even the Greeks and the Romans were shocked at the love of dress and of adornment which characterized some of their women. The great Greek religions were called the Mystery religions, and they had precisely the same regulations about dress as Paul has here. There is an inscription which reads: "A consecrated woman shall not have gold ornaments, nor rouge, nor face-whitening, nor a head-band, nor braided hair, nor shoes, except those made of felt or of the skins of sacrificed animals." The early Church did not lay down these regulations as in any sense permanent, but as things which were necessary in the situation in which it found itself.

In any event there is much on the other side. In the old story it was the woman who was created second and who fell to the seduction of the serpent tempter; but it was Mary of Nazareth who bore and who trained the child Jesus; it was Mary of Magdala who was first to see the risen Lord; it was four women who of all the disciples stood by the Cross. Priscilla with her husband Aquila was a valued teacher in the early Church, who led Apollos to a knowledge of the truth (*Acts* 18: 26). Euodia and Syntyche, in spite of their quarrel, were women who laboured in the gospel (*Philippians* 4: 2, 3). Philip, the evangelist, had four daughters who were prophetesses (*Acts* 21: 9). The aged women were to teach (*Titus* 2: 3). Paul held Lois and Eunice in the highest honour (2 *Timothy* 1: 5), and there is many a woman's name held in honour in *Romans* 16.

All the things in this chapter are mere temporary regulations to meet a given situation. If we want Paul's permanent view on this matter, we get it in *Galatians* 3: 28: "There is neither Jew nor Greek, there is neither slave nor free, there is neither male nor female: for you are all one in Christ Jesus." In Christ the differences of place and honour and function within the Church are all wiped out.

And yet this passage ends with a real truth. Women, it says, will be saved in child-bearing. There are two possible meanings here. It is just possible that this is a reference to the fact that Mary, a woman, was the mother of Jesus and that it means that women will be saved—as all others will—by that supreme act of child-bearing. But it is much more likely that the meaning is much simpler; and that it means that women will find salvation, not in addressing meetings, but in motherhood, which is their crown. Whatever else is true, a woman is queen within her home.

We must not read this passage as a barrier to all women's service within the Church, but in the light of its Jewish and its Greek background. And we must look for Paul's permanent views in the passage where he tells us that the differences are wiped out, and that men and women, slaves and freemen, Jews and Gentiles, are all eligible to serve Christ.

THE LEADERS OF THE CHURCH

1 *Timothy* 3: 1–7

There is a saying which everyone must believe—if a man aspires to the office of overseer in the Church, it is a fine work on which his heart is set. An overseer must be a man against whom no criticism can be made; he must have been married only once; he must be sober, prudent, well-behaved, hospitable and possessed of an aptitude for teaching. He must not over-indulge in wine, nor must he be the kind of man who assaults others, but he must be gentle and peaceable, and free from the love of money. He must manage his own house well, keeping his children under control with complete dignity. (If a man does not know how to manage his own house, how can he take charge of the congregation of God?) He must not be a recent convert, in case he becomes inflated with a sense of his own importance, and so fall into the same condemnation as the devil did. He must have earned the respect of those outside the Church, that he may not fall into reproach and into the snare of the devil.

THIS is a very important passage from the point of view of Church government. It deals with the man whom the Authorized and Revised Standard Versions call the *bishop*, and whom we have translated *overseer*.

In the New Testament there are two words which describe the principal office-bearers of the Church, the office-bearers who were to be found in every congregation, and on whose conduct and administration its welfare depended.

(i) There was the man who was called the *elder (presbuteros)*. The eldership is the most ancient of all offices within the Church. The Jews had their elders, and they traced their origin to the occasion when Moses, in the desert wanderings, appointed seventy men to help him in the task of controlling and caring for the people (*Numbers* 11: 16). Every synagogue had its elders, and they were the real leaders of the Jewish community. They presided over the worship of the synagogue; they administered rebuke and discipline where these were necessary; they settled the disputes which other nations would have taken to the law-courts. Amongst the Jews the elders were the respected men who exercised a fatherly oversight over the spiritual and material affairs of every Jewish community. But more nations than the Jews had an eldership. The presiding body of the Spartans was called the *gerousia*, which means *the board of the elder men*. The Parliament of Rome was called the *senate*, which comes from *senex*, which means *an old man*. In England the men who looked after the affairs of the community were called the *aldermen*, which means the *elder men*. In New Testament times every Egyptian village had its village elders who looked after the affairs of the community. The elders had a long history, and they had a place in the life of almost every community.

(ii) But sometimes the New Testament uses another word, *episkopos*, which the Authorized and Revised Standard Versions translate *bishop*, and which literally means *overseer*, or *superintendent*. This word, too, has a long and honourable history. The Septuagint, the Greek version of the Hebrew scriptures, uses it to describe those who were the *taskmasters*, who were over the public works and public building schemes (2 *Chronicles* 34: 17). The Greeks use it to describe the men appointed to go out from the mother city to regulate the affairs of a newly founded colony in some distant place. They use it to describe what we might call *commissioners* appointed to regulate the affairs of a city. The Romans use it to describe the magistrates appointed to oversee the sale of food within the city of Rome. It is used of the special delegates appointed by a king to see that the laws he had laid down were carried out. *Episkopos* always implies two things; first, *oversight* over some area or sphere of work and second, *responsibility* to some higher power and authority.

The great question is: What was the relationship in the early Church between the elder, the *presbuteros,* and the overseer, the *episkopos?*

Modern scholarship is practically unanimous in holding that in the early Church the *presbuteros* and the *episkopos* were one and the same. The grounds for that identification are: (*a*) Elders were everywhere appointed. After the first missionary journey, Paul and Barnabas appointed elders in all the Churches they had founded (*Acts* 14: 23). Titus is instructed to appoint and ordain elders in all the cities of Crete (*Titus* 1: 5). (*b*) The qualifications of a *presbuteros* and of an *episkopos* are to all intents and purposes identical (1 *Timothy* 3: 2–7; *Titus* 1: 6–9). (*c*) At the beginning of *Philippians,* Paul's greetings are to the *bishops and the deacons* (*Philippians* 1: 1). It is quite impossible that Paul would have sent no greetings at all to the *elders,* who, as we have already seen, were in every Church; and therefore the *bishops* and the *elders* must be one and the same body of people. (*d*) When Paul was on his last journey to Jerusalem, he sent for the *elders* of Ephesus to meet him at Miletus (*Acts* 20: 17), and in the course of his talk to them he says that God has made them *episkopoi* to feed the Church of God (*Acts* 20: 28). That is to say, he addresses precisely the same body of men first as *elders* and second as bishops or overseers. (*e*) When Peter is writing to his people, he talks to them as an *elder* to *elders* (1 *Peter* 5: 1), and then he goes on to say that their function is *oversight* of the flock of God (1 *Peter* 5: 2), and the word he uses for *oversight,* is the verb *episkopein* from which *episkopos* comes. All the evidence from the New Testament goes to prove that the *presbuteros* and the *episkopos,* the elder and the bishop or overseer, were one and the same person.

Two questions arise. First, if they were the same, why were there two names for them? The answer is that *presbuteros* described these leaders of the Church as they personally were. They were the elder men, the older and respected members of the community. *Episkopos*, on the other hand, described *their function,* which was to oversee the life and the work of the Church. The one word described the man; the other described his task.

The second question is—if the elder and the bishop were originally the same, how did the bishop become what he did? The answer is simple. Inevitably the body of the elders would acquire a leader. Someone to lead would be essential and would inevitably emerge. The more organized the Church became, the more such a figure would be bound to arise. And the elder who stood out as leader came to be called the *episkopos*, the *superintendent* of the Church. But it is to be noted that he was simply a leader amongst equals. He was in fact the elder whom circumstances and personal qualities had combined to make a leader for the work of the Church.

It will be seen that to translate *episkopos* by the word *bishop* in the New Testament now gives the word a misleading meaning. It is better to translate it *overseer* or *superintendent*.

THE APPOINTMENT AND THE DUTIES OF THE LEADERS OF THE CHURCH

1 *Timothy* 3: 1-7 (*continued*)

THIS passage is further interesting in that it tells us something of the appointment and the duties of the leaders of the Church.

(i) They were formally set apart for their office. Titus was to ordain elders in every Church (*Titus* 1: 5). The office-bearer of the Church is not made an office-bearer in secret; he is set apart before the eyes of men; the honour of the Church is publicly delivered into his hands.

(ii) They had to undergo a period of testing. They had first to be proved (1 *Timothy* 3: 10). No one builds a bridge or a piece of machinery with metal which has not been tested. The

Church might do well to be more strict than she is in the testing of those chosen for leadership.

(iii) They were paid for the work which they had to do. The labourer was worthy of his hire (1 *Timothy* 5: 18). The Christian leader does not work for pay, but, on the other hand, the duty of the Church which chose him for the work is to supply him with the means to live.

(iv) They were liable to censure (1 *Timothy* 5: 19–22). In the early Church the office-bearer had a double function. He was a leader of the Church; but he was also the servant of the Church. He had to answer for his stewardship. No Christian office-bearer must ever consider himself answerable to no one; he is answerable to God and to the people over whom God gave him the task of presiding.

(v) They had the duty of *presiding* over the Christian assembly and of *teaching* the Christian congregation (1 *Timothy* 5: 17). The Christian office-bearer has the double duty of *administration* and *instruction*. It may well be that one of the tragedies of the modern Church is that the administrative function of the office-bearer has usurped the teaching function almost entirely. It is, for instance, sad to see how few elders of the Church are actively engaged in the teaching work of Sunday schools.

(vi) The office-bearer was not to be *a recent convert*. Two reasons are given for this advice. The first is quite clear. It is "in case he becomes inflated with a sense of his own importance." The second is not so clear. It is, as the Revised Standard Version has it, "lest he fall into the condemnation of the devil." There are three possible explanations of that strange phrase. (*a*) It was through his pride that Lucifer rebelled against God and was expelled from heaven. And this may simply be a second warning against the danger of pride. (*b*) It may mean that, if the too quickly advanced convert becomes guilty of pride, he gives the devil a chance to level his charges against him. A conceited Church office-bearer gives the devil a chance to say to critics of the Church: "Look! There's your Christian! There's your Church member! That's what an office-bearer is like!" (c) The word *diabolos* has two meanings. It means *devil,* and that is the way in which the Revised Standard Version has taken it here; but it also means *slanderer.* It is in fact the word used for *slanderer* in verse 11, where the women are forbidden to be slanderers. So then this phrase may mean that the recent convert, who has been appointed to office, and has acquired, as we say, a swelled head, gives opportunity to the slanderers. His unworthy conduct is ammunition for those who are ill-disposed to the Church. No matter how we take it, the point is that the conceited Church official is a bad debt to the Church.

But, as the early Church saw it, the responsibility of the office-bearer did not begin and end in the Church. He had two other spheres of responsibility, and if he failed in them, he was bound also to fail in the Church.

(i) His first sphere of duty was his own home. If a man did not know how to rule his own household, how could he engage upon the task of ruling the congregation of the Church? (1 *Timothy* 3: 5). A man who had not succeeded in making a Christian home could hardly be expected to succeed in making a Christian congregation. A man who had not instructed his own family could hardly be the right man to instruct the family of the Church.

(ii) The second sphere of responsibility was the world. He must be "well thought of by outsiders" (1 *Timothy* 3: 7). He must be a man who has gained the respect of his fellow-men in the day-to-day business of life. Nothing has hurt the Church more than the sight of people who are active in it, whose business and social life belies the faith which they profess and the precepts which they teach. The Christian office-bearer must first of all be a good man.

THE CHARACTER OF THE CHRISTIAN LEADER

1 *Timothy* 3: 1–7 (*continued*)

WE have just seen that the Christian leader must be a man

who has won the respect of all. In this passage there is a great series of words and phrases describing his character; and it will be worth while to look at each in turn. Before we do that it will be interesting to set beside them two famous descriptions by great heathen thinkers of the good leader's character. Diogenes Laertius (7: 116–126) hands down to us the Stoic description. He must be married; he must be without pride; he must be temperate; and he must combine prudence of mind with excellence of outward behaviour. A writer called Onosander gives us the other. He must be prudent, self-controlled, sober, frugal, enduring in toil, intelligent, without love of money, neither young nor old, if possible the father of a family, able to speak competently, and of good reputation. It is interesting to see how the pagan and the Christian descriptions coincide.

The Christian leader must be *a man against whom no criticism can be made (anepilēptos)*. *Anepilēptos* is used of a position which is not open to attack, of a life which is not open to censure, of an art or technique which is so perfect that no fault can be found with it, of an agreement which is inviolable. The Christian leader must not only be free from such faults as can be assailed by definite charges; he must be of such fine character as to be even beyond criticism. The Rheims version of the New Testament translates this Greek word by the very unusual English word *irreprehensible*, unable to be found fault with. The Greeks themselves defined the word as meaning "affording nothing of which an adversary can take hold." Here is the ideal of perfection. We will not be able fully to attain to it; but the fact remains that the Christian leader must seek to offer to the world a life of such purity that he leaves no loophole even for criticism of himself.

The Christian leader must have been married only once. The Greek literally means that he must be "the husband of one wife." Some take this to mean that the Christian leader must be a married man, and it is possible that the phrase could mean that. It is certainly true that a married man can be a

recipient of confidences and a bringer of help in a way that a
single man cannot be, and that he can bring a special
understanding and sympathy to many a situation. Some few
take it to mean that the Christian leader cannot marry a
second time, even after his wife's death. In support they
quote Paul's teaching in 1 *Corinthians* 7. But in its context
here we can be quite certain that the phrase means that the
Christian leader must be a loyal husband, preserving
marriage in all its purity. In later days the *Apostolic Canons*
laid it down: "He who is involved in two marriages, after his
baptism, or he who has taken a concubine, cannot be an
episkopos, a bishop."

We may well ask why it should be necessary to lay down
what looks obvious. We must understand the state of the
world in which this was written. It has been said, and with
much truth, that the only totally new virtue which Christianity
brought into this world was chastity. In many ways the
ancient world was in a state of moral chaos, even the
Jewish world. Astonishing as it may seem, certain Jews still
practised polygamy. In the *Dialogue with Trypho*, in which
Justin Martyr discusses Christianity with a Jew, it is said that
"it is possible for a Jew even now to have four or five wives"
(*Dialogue with Trypho,* 134). Josephus can write: "By
ancestral custom a man can live with more than one wife"
(*Antiquities of the Jews*, 17: 1, 2).

Apart altogether from these unusual cases, divorce was
tragically easy in the Jewish world. The Jews had the highest
ideals of marriage. They said that a man must surrender his
life rather than commit murder, idolatry or adultery. They had
the belief that marriages are made in heaven. In the story of
the marriage of Isaac and Rebecca it is said: "The thing
comes from the Lord" (*Genesis* 24: 50). This was taken to
mean that the marriage was arranged by God. So it is said in
Proverbs 19: 14: "A prudent wife is from the Lord." In the
story of Tobit, the angel says to Tobit: "Fear not for she
was prepared for thee from the beginning" (*Tobit* 6: 17).
The Rabbis said: "God sits in heaven arranging marriages."

"Forty days before the child is formed a heavenly voice proclaims its mate."

For all that, the Jewish law allowed divorce. Marriage was indeed the ideal but divorce was permitted. Marriage was "inviolable but not indissoluble." The Jews held that once the marriage ideal had been shattered by cruelty or infidelity or incompatibility, it was far better to allow a divorce and to permit the two to make a fresh start. The great tragedy was that the wife had no rights whatsoever. Josephus says: "With us it is lawful for a husband to dissolve a marriage, but a wife, if she departs from her husband, cannot marry another, unless her former husband put her away" (*Antiquities of the Jews*, 15: 8, 7). In a case of divorce by consent, in the time of the New Testament, all that was required was two witnesses, and no court case at all. A husband could send his wife away for any cause; at the most a wife could petition the court to urge her husband to write her a bill of divorcement, but it could not compel him even to do that.

In face of that situation, things came to such a pass that "women refused to contract marriages, and men grew grey and celibate." A brake was put upon this process by legislation introduced by Simon ben Shetah. A Jewish wife always brought her husband a dowry which was called *Kethubah*. Simon enacted that a man had unrestricted use of the *Kethubah*, so long as he remained married to his wife, but on divorce he was absolutely liable to repay it, even if he had "to sell his hair" to do so. This checked divorce; but the Jewish system was always vitiated by the fact that the wife had no rights.

In the heathen world things were infinitely worse. There, too, according to Roman law, the wife had no rights. Cato said: "If you were to take your wife in adultery, you could kill her with impunity, without any court judgment; but if you were involved in adultery, she would not dare to lift a finger against you, for it is unlawful." Things grew so bad, and marriage grew so irksome, that in 131 B.C. a well-known Roman called Metellus Macedonicus made a statement which

Augustus was afterwards to quote: "If we could do without wives, we would be rid of that nuisance. But since nature has decreed that we can neither live comfortably with them, nor live at all without them, we must look rather to our permanent interests than to passing pleasure."

Even the Roman poets saw the dreadfulness of the situation. "Ages rich in sin," wrote Horace, "were the first to taint marriage and family life. From this source the evil has overflowed." "Sooner will the seas be dried up," said Propertius, "and the stars be reft from heaven, than our women reformed." Ovid wrote his famous, or infamous, book *The Art of Love*, and never from beginning to end mentions married love. He wrote cynically: "These women alone are pure who are unsolicited, and a man who is angry at his wife's love affair is nothing but a rustic boor." Seneca declared: "Anyone whose affairs have not become notorious, and who does not pay a married woman a yearly fee, is despised by women as a mere lover of girls; in fact husbands are got as a mere decoy for lovers." "Only the ugly," he said, "are loyal." "A woman who is content to have only two followers is a paragon of virtue." Tacitus commended the supposedly barbarian German tribes for "not laughing at evil, and not making seduction the spirit of the age." When a marriage took place, the home to which the couple were going was decorated with green bay leaves. Juvenal said that there were those who entered on divorce before the bays of welcome had faded. In 19 B.C. a man named Quintus Lucretius Vespillo erected a tablet to his wife which said: "Seldom do marriages last until death undivorced; but ours continued happily for forty-one years." The happy marriage was the astonishing exception.

Ovid and Pliny had three wives; Caesar and Antony had four; Sulla and Pompey had five; Herod had nine; Cicero's daughter Tullia had three husbands. The Emperor Nero was the third husband of Poppaea and the fifth husband of Statilla Messalina.

It was not for nothing that the Pastorals laid it down that

the Christian leader must be the husband of one wife. In a world where even the highest places were deluged with immorality, the Christian Church must demonstrate the chastity, the stability and the sanctity of the Christian home.

THE CHARACTER OF THE CHRISTIAN LEADER

1 *Timothy* 3: 1–7 (*continued*)

THE Christian leader must be *sober (nēphalios)* and he must not *over-indulge in wine, (paroinos)*. In the ancient world wine was continually used. Where the water supply was very inadequate and sometimes dangerous, wine was the most natural drink of all. It is wine which cheers the hearts of gods and men (*Judges* 9: 13). In the restoration of Israel she will plant her vineyards and drink her wine (*Amos* 9: 14). Strong drink is given to those who are ready to perish, and wine to those whose hearts are heavy (*Proverbs* 31: 6).

This is not to say that the ancient world was not fully alive to the dangers of strong drink. *Proverbs* speaks of the disaster which comes to the man who looks on the wine when it is red (*Proverbs* 23: 29–35). Wine is a mocker, strong drink a brawler (*Proverbs* 20: 1). There are terrible stories of what happened to people through over-indulgence in wine. There is the case of Noah (*Genesis* 9: 18–27); of Lot (*Genesis* 19: 30–38); of Amnon (2 *Samuel* 13: 28, 29). Although the ancient world used wine as the commonest of all drinks, it used it most abstemiously. When wine was drunk, it was drunk in the proportion of two parts of wine to three parts of water. A man who was drunken would be disgraced in ordinary heathen society, let alone in the Church.

The interesting thing is the double meaning that both words in this section possess. *Nēphalios* means *sober*, but it also means *watchful* and *vigilant;* paroinos means *addicted to wine,* but it also means *quarrelsome* and *violent*. The point that the

Pastorals make here is that the Christian must allow himself no indulgence which would lessen his Christian vigilance or soil his Christian conduct.

There follow two Greek words which describe two great qualities which must characterize the Christian leader. He must be *prudent (sōphrōn)* and *well-behaved (kosmios)*.

We have translated *sōphrōn* by *prudent*, but it is virtually untranslatable. It is variously translated *of sound mind, discreet, prudent, self-controlled, chaste, having complete control over sensual desires.* The Greeks derived it from two words which mean *to keep one's mind safe and sound.* The corresponding noun is *sōphrosunē*, and the Greeks wrote and thought much about it. It is the opposite of intemperance and lack of self-control. Plato defined it as "the mastery of pleasure and desire." Aristotle defined it as "that power by which the pleasures of the body are used as law commands." Philo defined it as "a certain limiting and ordering of the desires, which eliminates those which are external and excessive, and which adorns those which are necessary with timeliness and moderation." Pythagoras said that it was "the foundation on which the soul rests." Iamblichus said that "it is the safeguard of the most excellent habits in life." Euripides said that it was "the fairest gift of God." Jeremy Taylor called it "reason's girdle and passion's bridle." Trench describes *sōphrosunē* as "the condition of entire command over the passions and desires, so that they receive no further allowance than that which law and right reason admit and approve." Gilbert Murray wrote of *sōphrōn:* "There is a way of thinking which destroys and a way which saves. The man or woman who is *sōphrōn* walks among the beauties and perils of the world, feeling love, joy, anger, and the rest; and through all he has that in his mind which saves. Whom does it save? Not him only, but, as we should say, the whole situation. It saves the imminent evil from coming to be." E. F. Brown quotes in illustration of *sōphrosunē* a prayer of Thomas Aquinas which asks for "a quieting of all our impulses, fleshly and spiritual."

The man who is *sōphrōn* has every part of his nature under perfect control, which is to say that the man who is *sōphrōn* is the man in whose heart Christ reigns supreme.

The companion word is *kosmios*, which we have translated *well-behaved*. If a man is *kosmios* in his outer conduct it is because he is *sōphrōn* in his inner life. *Kosmios* means *orderly, honest, decorous*. In Greek it has two special usages. It is common in tributes and in inscriptions to the dead. And it is commonly used to describe the man who is a good citizen. Plato defines the man who is *kosmios* as "the citizen who is quiet in the land, who duly fulfils in his place and order the duties which are incumbent upon him as such." This word has more in it than simply good behaviour. It describes the man whose life is beautiful and in whose character all things are harmoniously integrated.

The leader of the Church must be a man who is *sōphrōn*, his every instinct and desire under perfect control; he must be a man who is *kosmios*, his inner control issuing in outward beauty. The leader must be one in whose heart Christ's power reigns and on whose life Christ's beauty shines.

THE CHARACTER OF THE CHRISTIAN LEADER

1 *Timothy* 3: 1–7 (*continued*)

THE Christian leader must be *hospitable (philoxenos)*. This is a quality on which the New Testament lays much stress. Paul bids the Roman Church to "practise hospitality" (*Romans* 12: 13). "Practise hospitality ungrudgingly to one another," says Peter (1 *Peter* 4: 9). In the *Shepherd of Hermas,* one of the very early Christian writings, it is laid down: "The *episkopos* must be hospitable, a man who gladly and at all times welcomes into his house the servants of God." The Christian leader must be a man with an open heart and an open house.

The ancient world was very careful of the rights of the guest. The stranger was under the protection of Zeus Xenios, the

Protector of Strangers. In the ancient world, inns were notoriously bad. In one of Aristophanes's plays Heracles asks his companion where they will lodge for the night; and the answer is: "Where the fleas are fewest." Plato speaks of the inn-keeper being like a pirate who holds his guests to ransom. Inns tended to be dirty and expensive and, above all, immoral. The ancient world had a system of what were called *Guest Friendships*. Over generations families had arrangements to give each other accommodation and hospitality. Often the members of the families came in the end to be unknown to each other by sight and identified themselves by means of what were called *tallies*. The stranger seeking accommodation would produce one half of some object; the host would possess the other half of the tally; and when the two halves fitted each other the host knew that he had found his guest, and the guest knew that the host was indeed the ancestral friend of his household.

In the Christian Church there were wandering teachers and preachers who needed hospitality. There were also many slaves with no homes of their own to whom it was a great privilege to have the right of entry to a Christian home. It was of the greatest blessing that Christians should have Christian homes ever open to them in which they could meet people like-minded to themselves. We live in a world where there are still many who are far from home, many who are strangers in a strange place, many who live in conditions where it is hard to be a Christian. The door of the Christian home and the welcome of the Christian heart should be open to all such.

The Christian leader must be possessed of an *aptitude for teaching (didaktikos)*. It has been said that his duty is "to preach to the unconverted and to teach the converted." There are two things to be said about this. It is one of the disasters of modern times that the teaching ministry of the Church is not being exercised as it should. There is any amount of topical preaching and any amount of exhortation; but there is little use in exhorting a man to be a Christian when he does not know what being a Christian means.

Instruction is a primary duty of the Christian preacher and leader. The second thing is this. The finest and the most effective teaching is done not by *speaking* but by *being*. Even the man with no gift of words can teach, by living in such a way that in him men see the reflection of the Master. A saint has been defined as someone "in whom Christ lives again."

The Christian leader *must not be a man who assaults others (plēktēs, a striker)*. That this instruction was not unnecessary is seen in one of the very early regulations of the *Apostolic Canons:* "A bishop, priest or deacon who smites the faithful when they err, or the unbelievers when they commit injury, and desires by such means as this to terrify them, we command to be deposed; for nowhere hath the Lord taught us this. When he was reviled, he reviled not again, but the contrary. When he was smitten, he smote not again; when he suffered, he threatened not." It will not be likely that any Christian leader will nowadays strike another Christian, but the fact remains that blustering, bullying, irritable, bad-tempered speech or action is forbidden to the Christian.

The Christian leader must be *gentle*. The Greek is *epieikēs*, another of these completely untranslatable words. The noun is *epieikeia*. and Aristotle describes it as "that which corrects justice" and as that which "is just and better than justice." He said that it was that quality which corrects the law when the law errs because of its generality. What he means is that sometimes it may actually be unjust to apply the strict letter of the law. Trench said that *epieikeia* means "retreating from the letter of right better to preserve the spirit of right" and is "the spirit which recognizes the impossibility of cleaving to all formal law . . . that recognizes the danger that ever waits upon the assertion of legal rights, lest they should be pushed into moral wrongs . . . the spirit which rectifies and redresses the injustice of justice." Aristotle describes in full the action of *epieikeia:* "To pardon human failings; to look to the law-giver, not to the law; to the intention, not to the action; to the whole, not to the part; to the character of the actor in the long run and not in the present moment; to remember good rather than evil, and the good that one has received rather than the good that one has done; to bear being injured; to wish to settle a matter by words rather than deeds." If there is a matter under dispute, it can be settled by consulting a book of practice and procedure, or it can be settled by consulting Jesus Christ. If there is a matter of debate, it can be settled in law, or it can be settled in love. The atmosphere of many a Church would be radically changed if there was more *epieikeia* within it.

The Christian leader must be *peaceable (amachos)*. The Greek word means *disinclined to fight*. There are people who, as we might put it, are "trigger-happy" in their relationships with other people. But the real Christian leader wants nothing so much as he wants peace with his fellow-men.

The Christian leader must be *free from the love of money*. He will never do anything simply for profit's sake. He will know that there are values which are beyond all money price.

THE MEN OF CHRISTIAN SERVICE

1 *Timothy* 3: 8–10, 12, 13

> In the same way, the deacons must be men of dignity, men who are straight, men who are not given to over-indulgence in wine, men who are not prepared to stoop to disgraceful ways of making money; they must hold the secret of the faith which has been revealed to them with a clear conscience. The deacons too must first of all be put upon probation, and, if they emerge blameless from the test, let them become deacons. . . . Deacons must be married only once; they must manage their own children and their own homes well. For those who make a fine job of the office of deacon win for themselves a fine degree of honour, and they gain much boldness in their faith in Christ Jesus.

IN the early Church the function of the deacons lay much more in the sphere of practical service. The Christian Church inherited a magnificent organization of charitable help from the Jews. No nation has ever had such a sense of responsibility for the poorer brother and sister as the Jews. The synagogue had a regular organization for helping such people. The Jews rather discouraged the giving of individual help to individual people. They preferred that help should be given through the community and especially through the synagogue.

Each Friday in every community two official collectors went round the markets and called on each house, collecting donations for the poor in money and in goods. The material so collected was distributed to those in need by a committee of two, or more if necessary. The poor of the community were given enough food for fourteen meals, that is for two meals a day for the week; but no one could receive from this fund if he already possessed a week's food in the house. This fund for the poor was called the *Kuppah*, or the *basket*. In addition to this there was a daily collection of food from house to house for those who were actually in emergency need that day. This fund was called the *Tamhui,* or the *tray*. The Christian Church inherited this charitable organization, and no doubt it was the task of the deacons to attend to it.

Many of the qualifications of the deacon are the same as for the *episkopos*. They are to be men of dignified character; they are to be abstemious; they are not to soil their hands with disreputable ways of making money; they have to undergo a test and a time of probation; they must practise what they preach, so that they can hold the Christian faith with a clear conscience.

One new qualification is added; they are to be *straight*. The Greek is that they must not be *dilogos* and *dilogos* means *speaking with two voices*, saying one thing to one and another to another. In *The Pilgrim's Progress* John Bunyan puts into By-ends mouth a description of the people who live in the town of Fair-speech. There is my Lord Turn-about, my Lord Time-Server, my Lord Fair-speech, after whose ancestors the town was named, Mr. Smooth man, Mr. Facing-both-ways, Mr. Any-thing; and the parson of the parish, Mr. Two-tongues. A deacon, in his going from house to house, and in his dealing with those who needed charity, had to be a straight man. Again and again he would be tempted to evade issues by a little timely hypocrisy and smooth speaking. But the man who would do the work of the Christian Church must be straight.

It is clear that the man who performs well the office of deacon can look for promotion to the high office of elder, and will gain such a confidence in the faith that he can look any man in the face.

WOMEN WHO SERVE THE CHURCH

1 *Timothy* 3: 11

> In the same way, the women must be dignified; they must not be given to slanderous gossip; they must be sober; they must be in all things reliable.

As far as the Greek goes, this could refer to the wives of the deacons, or to women engaged in a similar service. It seems far more likely that it refers to women who are also engaged upon this work of charity. There must have been acts of kindness and of help which only a woman could properly do for another woman. Certainly in the early Church there were deaconesses. They had the duty of instructing female converts and in particular of presiding and attending at their baptism, which was by total immersion.

It was necessary that such women workers should be warned against slanderous gossip and bidden to be absolutely reliable. When a young doctor graduates and before he begins to practise, he takes the Hippocratic oath, and part of that oath is a pledge never to repeat anything that he has heard in the house of a patient, or anything that he has heard about a patient, even if he has heard it on the street. In the work of helping the poor, things might easily be heard and be repeated and infinite damage done. It is not any insult to women that the Pastorals specially forbid gossip to them. In the nature of things a woman runs more risk of gossip than a man. A man's work takes him out into the world; a woman of necessity lives in a narrower sphere and for that very reason has fewer things to talk about. This increases the danger of talking about the personal relationships from which slanderous gossip arises. Whether man or woman, a tale-bearing, confidence-repeating Christian is a monstrous thing.

In Greek civilization it was essential that the women workers of the Church should preserve their dignity. The respectable Greek woman lived in the greatest seclusion; she never went out alone; she never even shared meals with her men folk. Pericles said that the duty of an Athenian mother was to live so retired a life that her name should never be mentioned among men for praise or blame. Xenophon tells how a country gentleman who was a friend of his said about the young wife whom he had just married and whom he dearly loved. "What was she likely to know when I married her? Why, she was not yet fifteen when I introduced her to my house, and she had been brought up always under the strictest supervision; as far as could be managed, she had not been allowed to see anything, hear anything or ask any questions." That is the way in which respectable Greek girls were brought up. Xenophon gives a vivid picture of one of these girl-wives gradually "growing accustomed to her husband and becoming sufficiently tame to hold conversation with him."

Christianity emancipated women; it liberated them from a kind of slavery. But there were dangers. She who was liberated might misuse her new-found freedom; the respectable world might be shocked by such an emancipation; and so the Church had to lay down its regulations. It was by wisely using freedom, and not misusing it, that women came to hold the proud position in the Church which they hold today.

THE PRIVILEGE AND THE RESPONSIBILITY OF
LIFE WITHIN THE CHURCH

1 *Timothy* 3: 14, 15

> I am writing these things to you, hoping, as I write, to come to you soon. But I am writing, so that, if I am delayed, you may know how to behave yourselves in the household of God, which is the assembly of the living God, and the pillar and buttress of the truth.

HERE in one phrase is the reason why the Pastoral Epistles were written; they were written to tell men how to behave within the Church. The word for *to behave* is *anastrephesthai;* it describes what we might call a man's *walk and conversation*. It describes his whole life and character; but it specially describes him in his relationships with other people. As it has been said, the word in itself lays it down that a church member's personal character must be excellent and that his personal relationships with other people should be a true fellowship. A church congregation is a body of people who are friends with God and friends with each other. Paul goes on to use four words which describe four great functions of the Church.

(i) The Church is the *household (oikos)* of God. First and foremost it must be a family. In a despatch written after one of his great naval victories, Nelson ascribed his victory to the fact that he "had the happiness to command a band of brothers." Unless a church is a band of brothers it is not a true church at all. Love of God can exist only where brotherly love exists.

(ii) The Church is the assembly *(ekklēsia)* of the living God. The word *ekklēsia* literally means a company of people who have been called out. It does not mean that they have been *selected* or *picked out*. In Athens the *ekklēsia* was the governing body of the city; and its membership consisted of *all* the citizens met in assembly. But, very naturally, at no time did all attend. The summons went out to come to the Assembly of the City, but only some citizens answered it and came. God's call has gone out to every man; but only some have accepted it; and they are the *ekklēsia*, the Church. It is not that God has been selective. The invitation comes to all; but to an invitation there must be a response.

(iii) The Church is the *pillar* of the truth (*stulos*). In Ephesus, to which these letters were written, the word *pillar* would have a special significance. The greatest glory of Ephesus was the Temple of Diana or Artemis. "Great is Diana of the Ephesians" (*Acts* 19: 28). It was one of the seven wonders of the world. One of its features was its pillars. It contained one hundred and twenty-seven pillars, every one of them the gift of a king. All were made of marble, and some were studded with jewels and overlaid with gold. The people of Ephesus knew well how beautiful a thing a pillar could be. It may well be that the idea of the word *pillar* here is not so much *support*—that is contained in *buttress*—as *display*. Often the statue of a famous man is set on the top of a pillar that it may stand out above all ordinary things and so be clearly seen, even from a distance. The idea here is that the Church's duty is to hold up the truth in such a way that all men may see it.

(iv) The Church is the *buttress (hedraiōma)* of the truth. The buttress is the support of the building. It keeps it standing intact. In a world which does not wish to face the truth, the Church holds it up for all to see. In a world which would often gladly eliminate unwelcome truth, the Church supports it against all who would seek to destroy it.

A HYMN OF THE CHURCH

1 *Timothy* 3: 16

> As everyone must confess, great is the secret which God has revealed to us in our religion:
>> He who was manifested in the flesh:
>> He who was vindicated by the Spirit:
>> He who was seen by angels:
>> He who has been preached among the nations:
>> He in whom men have believed all over the world:
>> He who was taken up into glory.

THE great interest of this passage is that here we have a fragment of one of the hymns of the early Church. It is a setting of belief in Christ to poetry and to music, a hymn in which men sang their creed. We cannot expect in poetry the precision of statement for which we would look in a creed; but we must try to see what each line in this hymn is saying to us.

(i) *He who was manifested in the flesh.* Right at the beginning it stresses the real humanity of Jesus. It says: "Look at Jesus, and you will see the mind and the heart and the action of God, in a form that men can understand."

(ii) *He who was vindicated by the Spirit.* This is a difficult line. There are three things it may mean. (*a*) It may mean that all through his earthly days Jesus was kept sinless by the power of the Spirit. It is the Spirit who gives a man guidance; our error is that we so often refuse his guidance. It was Jesus's perfect submission to the Spirit of God which kept him without sin. (*b*) It may mean that Jesus's claims were vindicated by the action of the Spirit who dwelt in him. When Jesus was accused by the scribes and Pharisees of effecting cures by the power of the devil, his answer was: "If I cast out devils *by the Spirit of God,* then the kingdom of God is come upon you" (*Matthew* 12: 28). The power that was in Jesus was the power of the Spirit, and the mighty acts he performed were the vindication of the tremendous claims which he made. (*c*) It may be that this is a reference to the Resurrection. Men took Jesus and crucified him as a criminal upon a cross; but through the power of the Spirit he rose again; the verdict of men was demonstrated to be false, and he was vindicated. No matter how we take this line, its meaning is that the Spirit is the power who proved Jesus to be what he claimed to be.

(iii) *He who was seen by angels.* Again there are three possible meanings. (*a*) It may be a reference to Jesus's life before he came to earth. (*b*) It may be a reference to his life on earth. Even on earth the hosts of heaven were looking on at his tremendous contest with evil. (*c*) It may connect with the belief of all men in the time of Jesus that the air was full of demonic and angelic powers. Many of these powers were hostile to God and to man, and bent on the destruction of Jesus. Paul at least once argued that they were bent on the destruction of Jesus through ignorance, and that Jesus brought to them and to men the wisdom which had been hidden since the world began (1 *Corinthians* 2: 7, 8). This phrase may mean that Jesus brought the truth even to the angelic and demonic powers who had never known it. However we take it, it means that the work of Jesus is so tremendous that it includes both heaven and earth.

(iv) *He who has been preached among the nations.* Here we have the great truth that Jesus was the exclusive possession of no race. He was not the Messiah who had come to raise the Jews to earthly greatness, but the Saviour of the whole wide world.

(v) *He in whom men have believed all over the world.* Here is an almost miraculous truth stated with utter simplicity. After Jesus had died and risen again and ascended to his glory, the number of his followers was one hundred and twenty (*Acts* 1: 15). All that his followers had to offer was the story of a Galilaean carpenter who had been crucified on a hilltop in Palestine as a criminal. And yet before seventy years had passed that story had gone out to the ends of the earth and men of every nation accepted this crucified Jesus as Saviour and Lord. In this simple phrase there is the whole wonder of the expansion of the Church, an expansion which on any human grounds is incredible.

(vi) *He who was taken up into glory.* This is a reference to the Ascension. The story of Jesus begins in heaven and ends in heaven. He lived as a servant; he was branded as a criminal; he was crucified on a cross; he rose with the nailprints still upon him; but the end is glory.

THE SERVICE OF GOD OR THE SERVICE OF SATAN

1 *Timothy* 4: 1–5

The Spirit clearly says that in the later times some will desert from the faith, through paying attention to spirits who can do nothing but lead them astray, and to teachings which come from the demons, teachings of false men whose characteristic is insincerity, teachings of men whose conscience has been branded with the mark of Satan, teachings of those who forbid marriage, and who order men to abstain from foods which God created in order that men might gratefully take their share of them in the company of those who believe and who really know the truth; for everything that God has made is good, and nothing is to be rejected, but it is to be gratefully received; for it is hallowed by the word of God and by prayer.

THE Christian Church had inherited from the Jews the belief that in this world things would be a great deal worse before they were better. The Jews always thought of time in terms of two ages. There was *this present age,* which was altogether bad and in the grip of the evil powers; there was *the age to come,* which was to be the perfect age of God and of goodness. But the one age would not pass into the other without a last convulsive struggle. In between the two ages would come *The Day of the Lord.* On that day the world would be shaken to its foundations; there would be a last supreme battle with evil, a last universal judgment, and then the new day would dawn.

The New Testament writers took over that picture. Being Jews, they had been brought up in it. One of the expected features of the last age was heresies and false teachers. "Many false prophets will arise, and lead many astray" (*Matthew* 24: 11). "False Christs and false prophets will arise, and show signs and wonders, to lead astray, if possible, the elect" (*Mark* 13: 22). In these last days Paul looks for the emergence of "the man of sin, the son of perdition," who would set himself up against God (2 *Thessalonians* 2: 3).

Into the Church at Ephesus such false teachers had come. The way in which their false teaching is regarded in this passage should make us think very seriously. At that time men believed in evil spirits who haunted the air and were out to ruin men. It was from them that this false teaching came. But though it came *from* the demons, it came *through* men. It came through men whose characteristic was a smooth hypocrisy and whose consciences had been branded by Satan. It sometimes happened that a slave was branded with a mark identifying him as belonging to a certain owner. These false teachers bear upon their consciences the very brand of Satan, marking them out as his property.

Here is the threatening and the terrible thing. God is always searching for men who will be his instruments in the world; but the terrible fact is that the forces of evil are also looking for men to use. Here is the terrible responsibility of manhood. Men may accept the service of God or the service of the devil. Whose service are they to choose?

ENSLAVERS OF MEN AND INSULTERS OF GOD

1 *Timothy* 4: 1–5 (*continued*)

THE heretics of Ephesus were propagating a heresy with very definite consequences for life. As we have already seen, these heretics were Gnostics; and the essence of Gnosticism was that spirit is altogether good and matter altogether evil. One of the consequences was that there were men who preached that everything to do with the body was evil and that everything in the world was evil. In Ephesus this issued in two definite errors. The heretics insisted that men must, as far as possible, abstain from food, for food was material and therefore evil; food ministered to the body and the body was evil. They also insisted that a man must abstain from marriage, for the instincts of the body were evil and must be entirely suppressed.

This was an ever-recurring heresy in the Church; in every generation men arose who tried to be stricter than God. When the *Apostolic Canons* came to be written, it was necessary to set it down in black and white: "If any overseer, priest or deacon, or anyone on the priestly list, abstains from marriage and flesh and wine, not on the ground of asceticism (that is, for the sake of discipline), but through abhorrence of them as evil in themselves, forgetting that all things are very good,

and that God made man male and female, but blaspheming
and slandering the workmanship of God, either let him
amend, or be deposed and cast out of the Church.
Likewise a layman also" (*Apostolic Canons* 51). Irenaeus,
writing towards the end of the second century, tells how
certain followers of Saturninus "declare that marriage and
generation are from Satan. Many likewise abstain from
animal food, and draw away multitudes by a feigned
temperance of this kind" (Irenaeus, *Against Heresies*, 1, 24, 2).
This kind of thing came to a head in the monks and
hermits of the fourth century. They went away and lived in
the Egyptian desert, entirely cut off from men. They spent
their lives mortifying the flesh. One never ate cooked food
and was famous for his "fleshlessness." Another stood all night
by a jutting crag so that it was impossible for him to sleep.
Another was famous because he allowed his body to become
so dirty and neglected that vermin dropped from him as he
walked. Another deliberately ate salt in midsummer and then
abstained from drinking water. "A clean body," they said,
"necessarily means an unclean soul."

The answer to these men was that by doing things like
that they were insulting God, for he is the creator of the
world and repeatedly his creation is said to be good. "And
God saw everything that he had made and behold it was
very good" (*Genesis* 1: 31). "Every moving thing that lives
shall be meat for you" (*Genesis* 9: 3). "God created man in
his own image . . . male and female he created them. And
God blessed them, and God said to them, Be fruitful and
multiply and fill the earth" (*Genesis* 1: 27, 28).

But all God's gifts have to be used in a certain way.

(i) They have to be used *in the memory that they are gifts
of God*. There are things which come to us so unfailingly that
we begin to forget that they are gifts and begin to take them as
rights. We are to remember that all that we have is a gift
from God and that there is not a living thing which could
have life apart from him.

(ii) They have to be used *in sharing*. All selfish use is

forbidden. No man can monopolize God's gifts; every man must share them.

(iii) They are to be used *with gratitude*. Always there is to be grace before meat. The Jew always said his grace. He had a grace for different things. When he ate fruits he said: "Blessed art thou, King of the Universe, who createst the fruit of the tree." When he drank wine he said: "Blessed art thou, King of the Universe, who createst the fruit of the vine." When he ate vegetables he said: "Blessed art thou, King of the Universe, who createst the fruit of the earth." When he ate bread he said: "Blessed art thou, King of the Universe, who bringest forth bread from the ground." The very fact that we thank God for it makes a thing sacred. Not even the demons can touch it when it has been touched by the Spirit of God.

The true Christian does not serve God by enslaving himself with rules and regulations and insulting his creation; he serves him by gratefully accepting his good gifts and remembering that this is a world where God made all things well and by never forgetting to share God's gifts with others.

ADVICE TO AN ENVOY OF CHRIST

1 *Timothy* 4: 6-10

If you lay these things before the brothers, you will be a fine servant of Jesus Christ, if you feed your life on the words of faith, and of the fine teaching of which you have been a student and a follower. Refuse to have anything to do with irreligious stories like the tales of old women tell to children. Train yourself towards the goal of true godliness. The training of the body has only a limited value; but training in godliness has a universal value for mankind, because it has the promise of life in this present age, and life in the age to come. This is a saying which deserves to be accepted by all. The reason why we toil and struggle so hard is that we have set our hopes on the living God, who is the Saviour of all men, and especially of those who believe.

THIS passage is close-packed with practical advice, not only for Timothy, but for any servant of the Church who is charged with the duty of work and leadership.

(i) It tells us *how to instruct others*. The word used for *laying these things* before the brothers is most suggestive *(hupotithesthai)*. It does not mean *to issue orders* but rather to advise, to suggest. It is a gentle, humble, and modest word. It means that the teacher must never dogmatically and pugnaciously lay down the law. It means that he must act rather as if he was reminding men of what they already knew or suggesting to them, not that they should learn from him, but that they should discover from their own hearts what is right. Guidance given in gentleness will always be more effective than bullying instructions laid down with force. Men may be led when they will refuse to be driven.

(ii) It tells us *how to face the task of teaching*. Timothy is told that he must feed his life on the words of faith. No man can give out without taking in. He who would teach must be continually learning. It is the reverse of the truth that when a man becomes a teacher he ceases to be a learner; he must daily know Jesus Christ better before he can bring him to others.

(iii) It tells us *what to avoid*. Timothy is to avoid profitless tales like those which old women tell to children. It is easy to get lost in side-issues and to get entangled in things which are at best embroideries. It is on the great central truths that a man must ever feed his mind and nourish his faith.

(iv) It tells us *what to seek*. Timothy is told that as an athlete trains his body, so the Christian must train his soul. It is not that bodily fitness is despised. The Christian faith believes that the body is the temple of the Holy Spirit. But there are certain things in Paul's mind. First, in the ancient world, especially in Greece, the gymnasia were dangerous places. Every town had its gymnasium; for the Greek youth between the ages of sixteen and eighteen, gymnastics were the main part of education. But the ancient world was riddled with homosexuality and the gymnasia were notorious as hotbeds of that particular sin. Second, Paul is pleading for a sense of proportion. Physical training is good, and even essential; but its use is limited. It develops only part of a man; and it produces only results which last for so short a time, for the body passes away. Training in godliness develops the whole man in body, mind and spirit, and its results affect not only time, but eternity as well. The Christian is not the athlete of the gymnasium, he is the athlete of God. The greatest of the Greeks well recognized this. Isocrates wrote: "No ascetic ought to train his body as a king ought to train his soul." "Train yourself by submitting willingly to toils, so that when they come on you unwillingly you will be able to endure them."

(v) It shows us *the basis of the whole matter*. No one has ever claimed that the Christian life is an easy way; *but its goal is God*. It is because life is lived in the presence of God and ends in his still nearer presence, that the Christian is willing to endure as he does. The greatness of the goal makes the toil worth while.

THE ONLY WAY TO SILENCE CRITICISM

1 *Timothy* 4: 11–16

Make it your business to hand on and to teach these commandments. Do not give anyone a chance to despise you because you are young; but in your words and in your conduct, in love, in loyalty and in purity, show yourself an example of what believing people should be. Until I come, devote your attention to the public reading of the scriptures, to exhortation and to teaching. Do not neglect the special gift which was given to you, when the voices of the prophets picked you out for the charge which has been given to you, when the body of the elders laid their hands upon you. Think about these things; find your whole life in them, that your progress may be evident to all. Take heed to yourself and to your teaching; stick to them; for if you do, you will save yourself and those who hear you.

ONE of the difficulties Timothy had to overcome was that he was young. We are not to think of him as a mere stripling. After all, it was fifteen years since he had first become Paul's helper. The word used for *youth (neotēs)* can in Greek describe anyone of military age, that is up to the age of forty. But the Church has generally liked its office-bearers to be men of maturity. *The Apostolic Canons* laid it down that a man was not to become a bishop until he was over fifty, for by then "he will be past youthful disorders." Timothy was young in comparison with Paul, and there would be many who would watch him with a critical eye. When the elder William Pitt was making a speech in the House of Commons at the age of thirty-three, he said: "The atrocious crime of being a young man . . . I will neither attempt to palliate or deny." The Church has always regarded youth with a certain suspicion, and under that suspicion Timothy inevitably fell.

The advice given to Timothy is the hardest of all to follow, and yet it was the only possible advice. It was that he must silence criticism by conduct. Plato was once falsely accused of dishonourable conduct. "Well," he said, "we must live in such a way that all men will see that the charge is false." Verbal defences may not silence criticism; conduct will. What then were to be the marks of Timothy's conduct?

(i) First, there was to be *love. Agapē,* the Greek word for the greatest of the Christian virtues, is largely untranslatable. Its real meaning is unconquerable benevolence. If a man has *agapē*, no matter what other people do to him or say of him, he will seek nothing but their good. He will never be bitter, never resentful, never vengeful; he will never allow himself to hate; he will never refuse to forgive. Clearly this is the kind of love which takes the whole of a man's personality to achieve. Ordinarily love is something which we cannot help. Love of our nearest and dearest is an instinctive thing. The love of a man for a maid is an experience unsought. Ordinarily love is a thing of the *heart;* but clearly this Christian love is a thing of the *will.* It is that conquest of self whereby we develop an unconquerable caring for other people.

So then the first authenticating mark of the Christian leader
is that he cares for others, no matter what they do to him.
That is something of which any Christian leader quick
to take offence and prone to bear grudges should constantly
think.

(ii) Second, there was to be *loyalty*. Loyalty is an unconquerable fidelity to Christ, no matter what it may cost.
It is not difficult to be a good soldier when things are going
well. But the really valuable soldier is he who can fight well
when his body is weary and his stomach empty, when the
situation seems hopeless and he is in the midst of a campaign
the movements of which he cannot understand. The second
authenticating mark of the Christian leader is a loyalty to
Christ which defies circumstances.

(iii) Third, there was to be *purity*. Purity is unconquerable
allegiance to the standards of Christ. When Pliny was
reporting back to Trajan about the Christians in Bithynia,
where he was governor, he wrote: "They are accustomed to
bind themselves by an oath to commit neither theft, nor
robbery, nor adultery; never to break their word; never to
deny a pledge that has been made when summoned to
answer for it." The Christian pledge is to a life of purity. The
Christian ought to have a standard of honour and honesty,
of self-control and chastity, of discipline and consideration,
far above the standards of the world. The simple fact is that
the world will never have any use for Christianity, unless
it can prove that it produces the best men and women. The
third authenticating mark of the Christian leader is a life
lived on the standards of Jesus Christ.

THE DUTIES OF THE CHRISTIAN LEADER
WITHIN THE CHURCH

1 *Timothy* 4: 11–16 (*continued*)

CERTAIN duties are laid upon Timothy, the young leader

designate of the Church. He is to devote himself to the public reading of scripture, to exhortation and to teaching. Here we have the pattern of the Christian Church service.

The very first description of a church service which we possess is in the works of Justin Martyr. About the year A.D. 170 he wrote a defence of Christianity to the Roman government, and in it (Justin Martyr: *First Apology,* 1: 67) he says: "On the day called the day of the Sun a gathering takes place of all who live in the towns or in the country in one place. The Memoirs of the Apostles or the writings of the prophets are read as long as time permits. Then the reader stops, and the leader by word of mouth impresses and urges to the imitation of these good things. Then we all stand together and send forth prayers." So then in the pattern of any Christian service there should be four things.

(i) There should be *the reading and exposition of scripture.* Men ultimately do not gather together to hear the opinions of a preacher; they gather together to hear the word of God. The Christian service is Bible-centred.

(ii) There should be *teaching.* The Bible is a difficult book, and therefore it has to be explained. Christian doctrine is not easy to understand, but a man must be able to give a reason for the hope that is in him. There is little use in exhorting a man to be a Christian, if he does not know what being a Christian is. The Christian preacher has given many years of his life to gain the necessary equipment to explain the faith to others. He has been set free from the ordinary duties of life in order to think, to study and to pray that he may better expound the word of God. There can be no lasting Christian faith in any Church without a teaching ministry.

(iii) There should be *exhortation.* The Christian message must always end in Christian action. Someone has said that every sermon should end with the challenge: "What about it, chum?" It is not enough to present the Christian message as something to be studied and understood; it has to be presented as something to be done. Christianity is truth, but it is truth in action.

(iv) There should be *prayer*. The gathering meets in the presence of God; it thinks in the Spirit of God; it goes out in the strength of God. Neither the preaching nor the listening during the service, nor the consequent action in the world, is possible without the help of the Spirit of God.

It would do us no harm sometimes to test our modern services against the pattern of the first services of the Christian Church.

THE PERSONAL DUTY OF THE CHRISTIAN LEADER

1 *Timothy* 4: 11–16 (*continued*)

HERE in this passage is set out in the most vivid way the personal duty of the Christian leader.

(i) He must remember that he is *a man set apart for a special task by the Church*. The Christian leader does not make sense apart from the Church. His commission came from it; his work is within its fellowship; his duty is to build others into it. That is why the really important work of the Christian Church is never done by any itinerant evangelist but always by its settled ministry.

(ii) He must remember *the duty to think about these things*. His great danger is intellectual sloth and the shut mind, neglecting to study and allowing his thoughts to continue in well-worn grooves. The danger is that new truths, new methods and the attempt to restate the faith in contemporary terms may merely annoy him. The Christian leader must be a Christian thinker or he fails in his task; and to be a Christian thinker is to be an adventurous thinker so long as life lasts.

(iii) He must remember *the duty of concentration*. The danger is that he may dissipate his energies on many things which are not central to the Christian faith. He is presented with the invitation to many duties and confronted with the claims of many spheres of service. There was a prophet who confronted Ahab with a kind of parable. He said that in a battle a man brought him a prisoner to guard, telling him that if the prisoner escaped his own life would be forfeit; but he allowed his attention to wander, and "as your servant was busy here and there he was gone" (1 *Kings* 20: 35–43). It is easy for the Christian leader to be busy here and there, and to let the central things go. Concentration is a prime duty of the Christian leader.

(iv) He must remember *the duty of progress*. His progress must be evident to all men. It is all too true of most of us that the same things conquer us year in and year out; that as year succeeds year, we are no further on. The Christian leader pleads with others to become more like Christ. How can he do so with honesty unless he himself from day to day becomes more like the Master whose he is and whom he seeks to serve? When Kagawa decided to become a Christian, his first prayer was: "God, make me like Christ." The Christian leader's prayer must first be that he may grow more like Christ, for only thus will he be able to lead others to him.

THE DUTY TO REPRIMAND

1 *Timothy* 5: 1, 2

> If you have occasion to reprimand an older man, do not do so sharply, but appeal to him as you would to a father. Treat the younger men like brothers; the older women as mothers; the younger women as sisters, in complete purity.

IT is always difficult to reprimand anyone with graciousness; and to Timothy there would sometimes fall a duty that was doubly difficult—that of reprimanding a man older than himself. Chrysostom writes: "Rebuke is in its own nature offensive particularly when it is addressed to an old man; and when it proceeds from a young man too, there is a threefold show of forwardness. By the manner and mildness of it, therefore, he would soften it. For it is possible to reprove without offence, if one will only make a point of this; it requires great discretion, but it may be done."

Rebuke is always a problem. We may so dislike the task of speaking a warning word that we may shirk it altogether. Many a person would have been saved from sorrow and shipwreck, if someone had only spoken a warning word in time. There can be no more poignant tragedy than to hear someone say: "I would never have come to this, if you had only spoken in time." It is always wrong to shirk the word that should be spoken.

We may reprimand a person in such a way that there is clearly nothing but anger in our voice and nothing but bitterness in our minds and hearts. A rebuke given solely in anger may produce fear; and may cause pain; but it will almost inevitably arouse resentment; and its ultimate effect may well be to confirm the mistaken person in the error of his ways. The rebuke of anger and the reprimand of contemptuous dislike are seldom effective, and far more likely to do harm than good.

It was said of Florence Allshorn, the great missionary teacher, that, when she was Principal of a women's college, she always rebuked her students, when need arose, as it were with her arm around them. The rebuke which clearly comes from love is the only effective one. If we ever have cause to reprimand anyone, we must do so in such a way as to make it clear that we do this, not because we find a cruel pleasure in it, not because we wish to do it, but because we are under the compulsion of love and seek to help, not to hurt.

THE RELATIONSHIPS OF LIFE

1 *Timothy* 5: 1, 2 (*continued*)

THESE two verses lay down the spirit which the different age relationships should display.

(i) To older people we must show *affection and respect*. An older man is to be treated like a father and an older woman like a mother. The ancient world knew well the deference and respect which were due to age. Cicero writes: "It is, then, the duty of a young man to show deference to his elders, and to attach himself to the best and most approved of them, so as to receive the benefit of their counsel and influence. For the inexperience of youth requires the practical wisdom of age to strengthen and direct it. And this time of life is above all to be protected against sensuality and trained to toil and endurance of both mind and body, so as to be strong for active duty in military and civil service. And even when they wish to relax their minds and give themselves up to enjoyment, they should beware of excesses and bear in mind the rules of modesty. And this will be easier, if the young are not unwilling to have their elders join them, even in their pleasures" (Cicero: *De Officiis,* 1: 34). Aristotle writes: "To all older persons too one should give honour appropriate to their age, by rising to receive them and finding seats for them and so on" (Aristotle: *Nicomachean Ethics,* 9: 2). It is one of the tragedies of life that youth is so often apt to find age a nuisance. A famous French phrase says with a sigh: "If youth but had the knowledge, if age but had the power." But when there is mutual respect and affection, then the wisdom and experience of age can co-operate with the strength and enthusiasm of youth, to the great profit of both.

(ii) To our contemporaries we must show *brotherliness*. The younger men are to be treated like brothers. Aristotle has it: "To comrades and brothers one should allow freedom of speech and common use of all things" (Aristotle, *Nicomachean Ethics*, 9: 2). With our contemporaries there should be tolerance and sharing.

(iii) To those of the opposite sex our relationships must always be marked with *purity*. The Arabs have a phrase for a man of chivalry; they call him "a brother of girls." There is a famous phrase which speaks of "Platonic friendship." Love must be kept for one; it is a fearful thing when physical things dominate the relationship between the sexes and a man cannot see a woman without thinking in terms of her body.

CHURCH AND FAMILY DUTY

1 *Timothy* 5: 3–8

> Honour widows who are genuinely in a widow's destitute position. But if any widow has children or grandchildren, let such children learn to begin by discharging the duties of religion in their own homes; and let them learn to give a return for all that their parents have done for them; for this is the kind of conduct that meets with God's approval. Now she who is genuinely in the position of a widow, and who is left all alone, has set her hope on God, and night and day she devotes herself to petitions and prayers. But she who lives with voluptuous wantonness is dead even though she is still alive. Pass on these instructions that they may be irreproachable. If anyone fails to provide for his own people, and especially for the members of his own family, he has denied the faith and is worse than an unbeliever.

THE Christian Church inherited a fine tradition of charity to those in need. No people has ever cared more for its needy and its aged than the Jews. Advice is now given for the care of widows. There may well have been two classes of women here. There were certainly widows who had become widows in the normal way by the death of their husbands. But it was not uncommon in the pagan world, in certain places, for a man to have more than one wife. When a man became a Christian, he could not go on being a polygamist, and therefore had to choose which wife he was going to live with. That meant that some wives had to be sent away and they were clearly in a very unfortunate position. It may be that such women as these were also reckoned as widows and given the support of the Church.

Jewish law laid it down that at the time of his marriage a

man ought to make provision for his wife, should she become a widow. The very first office-bearers whom the Christian Church appointed, had this duty of caring fairly for the widows (*Acts* 6: 1). Ignatius lays it down: "Let not widows be neglected. After the Lord be thou their guardian." *The Apostolic Constitutions* enjoin the bishop: "O bishop, be mindful of the needy, both reaching out thy helping hand and making provision for them as the steward of God, distributing the offerings seasonably to every one of them, to the widows, the orphans, the friendless, and those tried with affliction." The same book has an interesting and kindly instruction: "If anyone receives any service to carry to a widow or poor woman . . . let him give it the same day." As the proverb has it: "He gives twice who gives quickly," and the Church was concerned that those in poverty might not have to wait and want while one of its servants delayed.

It is to be noted that the Church did not propose to assume responsibility for older people whose children were alive and well able to support them. The ancient world was very definite that it was the duty of children to support aged parents, and, as E. K. Simpson has well said: "A religious profession which falls below the standard of duty recognised by the world is a wretched fraud." The Church would never have agreed that its charity should become an excuse for children to evade their responsibility.

It was Greek law from the time of Solon that sons and daughters were, not only morally, but also legally bound to support their parents. Anyone who refused that duty lost his civil rights. Aeschines, the Athenian orator, says in one of his speeches: "And whom did our law-giver (Solon) condemn to silence in the Assembly of the people? And where does he make this clear? 'Let there be,' he says, 'a scrutiny of public speakers, in case there be any speaker in the Assembly of the people who is a striker of his father or mother, or who neglects to maintain them or to give them a home'." Demosthenes says: "I regard the man who neglects his parents as unbelieving in and hateful to the gods, as well as to men." Philo, writing of the commandment to honour parents, says: "When old storks become unable to fly, they remain in their nests and are fed by their children, who go to endless exertions to provide their food because of their piety." To Philo it was clear that even the animal creation acknowledged its obligations to aged parents, and how much more must men? Aristotle in the *Nicomachean Ethics* lays it down: "It would be thought in the matter of food we should help our parents before all others, since we owe our nourishment to them, and it is more honourable to help in this respect the authors of our being, even before ourselves." As Aristotle saw it, a man must himself starve before he would see his parents starve. Plato in *The Laws* has the same conviction of the debt that is owed to parents: "Next comes the honour of loving parents, to whom, as is meet, we have to pay the first and greatest and oldest of debts, considering that all which a man has belongs to those who gave him birth and brought him up, and that he must do all that he can to minister to them; first, in his property; secondly, in his person; and thirdly, in his soul; paying the debts due to them for their care and travail which they bestowed upon him of old in the days of his infancy, and which he is now able to pay back to them, when they are old and in the extremity of their need."

It is the same with the Greek poets. When Iphigenia is speaking to her father Agamemnon, in Euripides's *Iphigenia at Aulis,* she says (the translation is that of A. S. Way):

"'Twas I first called thee father, thou me child.
'Twas I first throned my body on thy knees,
And gave thee sweet caresses and received.
And this thy word was: 'Ah, my little maid,
Blest shall I see thee in a husband's halls
Living and blooming worthily of me?'
And as I twined my fingers in thy beard,
Whereto I now cling, thus I answered thee:
'And what of thee? Shall I greet thy grey hairs,
Father, with loving welcome in mine halls,
Repaying all thy fostering toil for me?' "

The child's joy was to look forward to the day when she could repay all that her father had done for her.

When Euripides tells how Orestes discovered that an unkind fate had made him unwittingly slay his own father, he makes him say:

> "He fostered me a babe, and many a kiss
> Lavished upon me. . . .
> O wretched heart and soul of mine!
> I have rendered foul return! What veil of gloom
> Can I take for my face? Before me spread
> What cloud, to shun the old man's searching eye?"

To Euripides the most haunting sin on earth was failure in duty to a parent.

The New Testament ethical writers were certain that support of parents was an essential part of Christian duty. It is a thing to be remembered. We live in a time when even the most sacred duties are pushed on to the state and when we expect, in so many cases, public charity to do what private piety ought to do. As the Pastorals see it, help given to a parent is two things. First, it is an honouring of the recipient. It is the only way in which a child can demonstrate the esteem within his heart. Second, it is an admission of the claims of love. It is repaying love received in time of need with love given in time of need; and only with love can love be repaid.

There remains one thing left to say, and to leave it unsaid would be unfair. This very passage goes on to lay down certain of the qualities of the people whom the Church is called upon to support. What is true of the Church is true within the family. If a person is to be supported, that person must be supportable. If a parent is taken into a home and then by inconsiderate conduct causes nothing but trouble, another situation arises. There is a double duty here; the duty of the child to support the parent and the duty of the parent to be such that that support is possible within the structure of the home.

AN HONOURED AND A USEFUL OLD AGE

1 *Timothy* 5: 9, 10

Let a woman be enrolled as a widow only if she is more than sixty years of age; if she has been the wife of one husband; if she has earned an attested reputation for good works; if she has nourished children; if she has been hospitable to strangers; if she has helped those in trouble; if she has washed the feet of the saints; if she has devoted herself to every good work.

FROM this passage it is clear that the Church had an official register of widows; and it seems that the word widow is being used in a double sense. Women who were aged and whose husbands had died and whose lives were lovely and useful were the responsibility of the Church; but it is also true that, perhaps as early as this, and certainly later in the early Church, there was an official order of widows, an order of elderly women who were set apart for special duties.

In the regulations of the *Apostolic Constitutions*, which tell us what the life and organization of the Church were like in the third century, it is laid down: "Three widows shall be appointed, two to persevere in prayer for those who are in temptation, and for the reception of revelations, when such are necessary, but one to assist women who are visited with sickness; she must be ready for service, discreet, telling the elders what is necessary, not avaricious, not given to much love of wine, so that she may be sober and able to perform the night services, and other loving duties."

Such widows were not ordained as the elders and the bishops were; they were set apart by prayer for the work which they had to do. They were not to be set apart until they were over sixty years of age. That was an age which the ancient world also considered to be specially suited for concentration on the spiritual life. Plato, in his plan for the ideal state, held that sixty was the right age for men and women to become priests and priestesses.

The Pastoral Epistles are always intensely practical; and in this passage we find seven qualifications which the Church's widows must satisfy.

They must have been the wife of one husband. In an age when the marriage bond was lightly regarded and almost universally dishonoured, they must be examples of purity and fidelity.

They must have earned an attested reputation for good works. The office-bearers of the Church, male or female, have within their keeping, not only their personal reputation, but also the good name of the Church. Nothing discredits a church like unworthy office-bearers; and nothing is so good an advertisement for it as an office-bearer who has taken his Christianity into the activity of daily living.

They must have nourished children. This may well mean more than one thing. It may mean that widows must have given proof of their Christian piety by bringing up their own families in the Christian way. But it can mean more than that. In an age when the marriage bond was very lax and men and women changed their partners with bewildering rapidity, children were regarded as a misfortune. This was the great age of child exposure. When a child was born, he was brought and laid before his father's feet. If the father stooped and lifted him, that meant that he acknowledged him and was prepared to accept responsibility for his upbringing. If the father turned and walked away, the child was quite literally thrown out, like an unwanted piece of rubbish. It often happened that such unwanted children were collected by unscrupulous people and, if girls, brought up to stock the public brothels, and, if boys, trained to be slaves or gladiators for the public games. It would be a Christian duty to rescue such children from death and worse than death, and to bring them up in a Christian home. So this may mean that widows must be women who had been prepared to give a home to abandoned children.

They must have been hospitable to strangers. Inns in the ancient world were notoriously dirty, expensive and immoral.

Those who opened their homes to the traveller, or the stranger in a strange place, or to young people whose work and study took them far from home, were doing a most valuable service to the community. The open door of the Christian home is always a precious thing.

They must have washed the feet of the saints. That need not be taken literally, although the literal sense is included. To wash a person's feet was the task of a slave, the most menial of duties. This means that Christian widows must have been willing to accept the humblest tasks in the service of Christ and of his people. The Church needs its leaders who will live in prominence; but no less it needs those who are prepared to do the tasks which receive no prominence and little thanks.

They must have helped those in trouble. In days of persecution it was no small thing to help Christians who were suffering for their faith. This was to identify oneself with them and to accept the risk of coming to a like punishment. The Christian must stand by those in trouble for their faith, even if, in so doing, he brings trouble on himself.

They must have devoted themselves to all good works. Every man concentrates his life on something; the Christian concentrates his on obeying Christ and helping men.

When we study these qualifications for those who were to be enrolled as widows, we see that they are the qualifications of every true Christian.

THE PRIVILEGE AND THE DANGERS OF SERVICE

1 *Timothy* 5: 9, 10 (*continued*)

As we have already said, if not as early as the time of the Pastoral Epistles, certainly in later days, the widows became an accepted order in the Christian Church. Their place and work are dealt with in the first eight chapters of the third book of *The Apostolic Constitutions*, and these chapters reveal the use that such an order could be and the dangers into which it almost inevitably ran.

(i) It is laid down that women who would serve the Church must be women of discretion. Particularly they must be discreet in speech: "Let every widow be meek, quiet, gentle, sincere, free from anger, not talkative, not clamorous, not hasty of speech, not given to evil-speaking, not captious, not double-tongued, not a busybody. If she see or hear anything that is not right, let her be as one that does not see, and as one that does not hear." Such Church officials must be very careful when they discuss the faith with outsiders: "For unbelievers when they hear the doctrine concerning Christ, not explained as it ought to be, but defectively, especially that concerning his Incarnation or his Passion, will rather reject it with scorn, and laugh at it as false, than praise God for it."

There is nothing more dangerous than an official of the Church who talks about things which ought to be kept secret; and a Church office-bearer must be equipped to communicate the gospel in a way that will make men think more and not less of Christian truth.

(ii) It is laid down that women who serve the Church must not be gadabouts: "Let the widow therefore own herself to be the 'altar of God,' and let her sit in her own house, and not enter into the houses of the unfaithful, under any pretence to receive anything; for the altar of God never runs about, but is fixed in one place. Let therefore the virgin and the widow be such as do not run about, or gad to the houses of those who are alien from the faith. For such as these are gadders and impudent." The restless gossip is ill-equipped to serve the Church.

(iii) It is laid down that widows who accept the charity of the Church are not to be greedy. "There are some widows who esteem gain their business; and since they ask without shame, and receive without being satisfied, render other people more backward in giving. . . . Such a woman is thinking in her mind of where she can go to get, or that a

certain woman who is her friend has forgotten her, and she
has something to say to her. . . . She murmurs at the
deaconess who distributed the charity, saying, 'Do you not
see that I am in more distress and need of your charity?
Why therefore have you preferred her before me?' " It is an
ugly thing to seek to live off the Church rather than for the
Church.

(iv) It is laid down that such women must do all they can
to help themselves: "Let her take wool and assist others
rather than herself want from them." The charity of the
Church does not exist to make people lazy and dependent.

(v) Such women are not to be envious and jealous: "We
hear that some widows are jealous, envious calumniators, and
envious of the quiet of others. . . . It becomes them when one
of their fellow-widows is clothed by anyone, or receives
money, or meat, or drink, or shoes, at the refreshment of their
sister, to thank God."

There we have at one and the same time a picture of the
faults of which the Church is all too full, and of the virtues
which should be the marks of the true Christian life.

THE PERILS OF IDLENESS

1 *Timothy* 5: 11–16

Refuse to enrol the younger women as widows, for when they grow
impatient with the restrictions of Christian widowhood, they wish
to marry, and so deserve condemnation, because they have
broken the pledge of their first faith; and, at the same time, they
learn to be idle and to run from house to house. Yes, they can
become more than idle; they can become gossips and busybodies,
saying things which should not be repeated. It is my wish that the
younger widows should marry, and bear children, and run a house
and home, and give our opponents no chance of abuse. For, even
as things are, some of them have turned aside from the way to
follow Satan. If any believing person has widowed relations, let
such a person help them, and let not the Church be burdened

with the responsibility, so that it may care for those who are genuinely in the position of widows.

A PASSAGE like this reflects the situation in society in which the early Church found itself.

It is not that younger widows are condemned for marrying again. What is condemned is this. A young husband dies; and the widow, in the first bitterness of sorrow and on the impulse of the moment, decides to remain a widow all her life and to dedicate her life to the Church; but later she changes her mind and remarries. That woman is regarded as having taken Christ as her bridegroom. So that by marrying again she is regarded as breaking her marriage vow to Christ. She would have been better never to have taken the vow.

What complicated this matter very much was the social background of the times. It was next to impossible for a single or a widowed woman to earn her living honestly. There was practically no trade or profession open to her. The result was inevitable; she was almost driven to prostitution in order to live. The Christian woman, therefore, had either to marry or to dedicate her life completely to the service of the Church; there was no halfway house.

In any event the perils of idleness remain the same in any age. There was the danger of becoming *restless;* because a woman had not enough to do, she might become one of those creatures who drift from house to house in an empty social round. It was almost inevitable that such a woman would become a *gossip;* because she had nothing important to talk about, she would tend to talk scandal, repeating tales from house to house, each time with a little more embroidery and a little more malice. Such a woman ran the risk of becoming a *busybody;* because she had nothing of her own to take up her attention, she would be very apt to be over-interested and over-interfering in the affairs of others.

It was true then, as it is true now, that "Satan finds some mischief still for idle hands to do." The full life is always the safe life, and the empty life is always the life in peril.

So the advice is that these younger women should marry and engage upon the greatest task of all, rearing a family and making a home. Here we have another example of one of the main thoughts of the Pastoral Epistles. They are always concerned with how the Christian appears to the outside world. Does he give opportunity to criticize the Church or reason to admire it? It is always true that "the greatest handicap the Church has is the unsatisfactory lives of professing Christians" and equally true that the greatest argument for Christianity is a genuinely Christian life.

RULES FOR PRACTICAL ADMINISTRATION

1 *Timothy* 5: 17–22

> Let elders who discharge their duties well be judged worthy of double honour, especially those who toil in preaching and in teaching; for Scripture says: "You must not muzzle the ox when he is treading the corn," and, "The workman deserves his pay."
>
> Do not accept an accusation against an elder unless on the evidence of two or three witnesses.
>
> Rebuke those who persist in sin in the presence of all, so that the others may develop a healthy fear of sinning.
>
> I adjure you before God and Christ Jesus and the chosen angels that you keep these regulations impartially, and that you do nothing because of your own prejudices or predilection.
>
> Do not be too quick to lay your hands on any man, and do not share the sins of others. Keep yourself pure.

HERE is a series of the most practical regulations for the life and administration of the Church.

(i) Elders are to be properly honoured and properly paid. When threshing was done in the East, the sheaves of corn were laid on the threshing-floor; then oxen in pairs were driven repeatedly across them; or they were tethered to a post in the middle and made to march round and round on the grain; or a threshing sledge was harnessed to them and the sledge was drawn to and fro across the corn. In all cases the oxen were left unmuzzled and were free to eat as much of the grain as they wished, as a reward for the work they were doing. The actual law that the ox must not be muzzled is in *Deuteronomy* 25: 4.

The saying that the workman deserves his pay is a saying of Jesus (*Luke* 10: 7). It is most likely a proverbial saying which he quoted. Any man who works deserves his support, and the harder he works, the more he deserves. Christianity has never had anything to do with the sentimental ethic which clamours for equal shares for all. A man's reward must always be proportioned to a man's toil.

It is to be noted what kind of elders are to be specially honoured and rewarded. It is those who toil in *preaching* and *teaching*. The elder whose service consisted only in words and discussion and argument is not in question here. He whom the Church really honoured was the man who worked to edify and build it up by his preaching of the truth and his educating of the young and of the new converts in the Christian way.

(ii) It was Jewish law that no man should be condemned on the evidence of a single witness: "A single witness shall not prevail against a man for any crime or for any wrong in connection with any offence that he has committed, only on the evidence of two witnesses, or of three witnesses, shall a charge be sustained" (*Deuteronomy* 19: 15). The *Mishnah*, the codified Rabbinic law, in describing the process of trial says: "The second witness was likewise brought in and examined. If the testimony of the two was found to agree, the case for the defence was opened." If a charge was supported by the evidence of only one witness, it was held that there was no case to answer.

In later times Church regulations laid it down that the two witnesses must be Christian, for it would have been easy for a malicious heathen to fabricate a false charge against a Christian elder in order to discredit him, and through him to discredit the Church. In the early days, the Church authorities did not hesitate to apply discipline, and Theodore of

Mopseuestia, one of the early fathers, points out how necessary this regulation was, because the elders were always liable to be disliked and were specially open to malicious attack "due to the retaliation by some who had been rebuked by them for sin." A man who had been disciplined might well seek to get his own back by maliciously charging an elder with some irregularity or some sin.

This permanent fact remains, that this would be a happier world and the Church, too, would be happier, if people would realize that it is nothing less than sin to spread stories of whose truth they are not sure. Irresponsible, slanderous and malicious talk does infinite damage and causes infinite heartbreak, and such talk will not go unpunished by God.

RULES FOR PRACTICAL ADMINISTRATION

1 Timothy 5: 17–22 (*continued*)

(iii) Those who persist in sin are to be publicly rebuked. That public rebuke had a double value. It sobered the sinner into a consideration of his ways; and it made others have a care that they did not involve themselves in a like humiliation. The threat of publicity is no bad thing, if it keeps a man in the right way, even from fear. A wise leader will know the time to keep things quiet and the time for public rebuke. But whatever happens, the Church must never give the impression that it is condoning sin.

(iv) Timothy is urged to administer his office without favouritism or prejudice. B. S. Easton writes: "The well-being of every community depends on impartial discipline." Nothing does more harm than when some people are treated as if they could do no wrong and others as if they could do no right. Justice is a universal virtue and the Church must surely never fall below the impartial standards which even the world demands.

(v) Timothy is warned not to be too hasty "in laying hands on any man." That may mean one of two things.

(a) It may mean that he is not to be too quick in laying hands on any man to ordain him to office in the Church. Before a man gains promotion in business, or in teaching, or in the army or the navy or the air force, he must give proof that he deserves it. No man should ever start at the top. This is doubly important in the Church; for a man who is raised to high office and then fails in it, brings dishonour, not only on himself, but also on the Church. In a critical world the Church cannot be too careful in regard to the kind of men whom it chooses as its leaders.

(b) In the early Church it was the custom to lay hands on a penitent sinner who had given proof of his repentance and had returned to the fold of the Church. It is laid down: "As each sinner repents, and shows the fruits of repentance, lay hands on him, while all pray for him." Eusebius tells us that it was the ancient custom that repentant sinners should be received back with the laying on of hands and with prayer. If that be the meaning here, it will be a warning to Timothy not to be too quick to receive back the man who has brought disgrace on the Church; to wait until he has shown that his penitence is genuine, and that he is truly determined to mould his life to fit his penitent professions. That is not for a moment to say that such a man is to be held at arms' length and treated with suspicion; he has to be treated with all sympathy and with all help and guidance in his period of probation. But it is to say that membership of the Church is never to be treated lightly, and that a man must show his penitence for the past and his determination for the future, before he is received, not into the *fellowship* of the Church, but into its *membership*. The fellowship of the Church exists to help such people redeem themselves, but its membership is for those who have truly pledged their lives to Christ.

ADVICE FOR TIMOTHY

1 *Timothy* 5: 23

Stop drinking only water, and use a little wine for the sake of your stomach, to help your frequent illnesses.

THIS sentence shows the real intimacy of these letters. Amidst the affairs of the Church and the problems of administration, Paul finds time to slip in a little bit of loving advice to Timothy about his health.

There had always been a strain of asceticism in Jewish religion. When a man took the Nazirite vow (*Numbers* 6: 1–21) he was pledged never to taste any of the product of the vine: "He shall separate himself from wine and strong drink; he shall drink no vinegar made from wine, or strong drink, and shall not drink any juice of grapes or eat grapes, fresh or dried. All the days of his separation he shall eat nothing that is produced by the grapevine, not even the seeds or the skins" (*Numbers* 6: 3, 4). The Rechabites also were pledged to abstain from wine. The *Book of Jeremiah* tells how Jeremiah went and set before the Rechabites wine and cups: "But they answered, We will drink no wine; for Jonadab, the son of Rechab our father, commanded us, You shall not drink wine, neither you nor your sons for ever; you shall not build a house; you shall not sow seed; you shall not plant or have a vineyard" (*Jeremiah* 35: 5–7). Now Timothy was on one side a Jew—his mother was a Jewess (*Acts* 16: 1)—and it may well be that from his mother he had inherited this ascetic way of living. On his father's side he was a Greek. We have already seen that at the back of the Pastorals there is the heresy of gnosticism which saw all matter as evil and often issued in asceticism; and it may well be that Timothy was unconsciously influenced by this Greek asceticism as well.

Here we have a great truth which the Christian forgets at his peril, that we dare not neglect the body, for often spiritual dullness and aridity come from the simple fact that the body is tired and neglected. No machine will run well unless it is cared for; and neither will the body. We cannot do Christ's work well unless we are physically fit to do it. There is no virtue—rather the reverse—in neglect of or contempt for the body. *Mens sana in corpore sano*, a healthy mind in a healthy body, was the old Roman ideal, and it is the Christian ideal too.

This is a text which has much troubled those who are
advocates of total abstinence. It must be remembered that it
does not give any man a licence to indulge in drink to excess;
it simply approves the use of wine where it may be
medicinally helpful. If it does lay down any principle at all,
E. F. Brown has well stated it: "It shows that while total
abstinence may be recommended as a wise counsel, it is never
to be enforced as a religious obligation." Paul is simply saying
that there is no virtue in an asceticism which does the body
more harm than good.

THE IMPOSSIBILITY OF ULTIMATE
CONCEALMENT

1 *Timothy* 5: 24, 25

Some men's sins are plain for all to see, and lead the way to
judgment; the sins of others will duly catch up on them. Even so
there are good deeds which are plain for all to see, and there are
things of a very different quality which cannot be hidden.

THIS saying bids us leave things to God and be content.
There are obvious sinners, whose sins are clearly leading to
their disaster and their punishment; and there are secret
sinners who, behind a front of unimpeachable rectitude, live a
life that is in essence evil and ugly. What man cannot see,
God does. "Man sees the deed, but God sees the intention."
There is no escape from the ultimate confrontation with the
God who sees and knows everything.

There are some whose good deeds are plain for all to see,
and who have already won the praise and thanks and
congratulations of men. There are some whose good deeds
have never been noticed, never appreciated, never thanked,
never praised, never valued as they ought to have been.
They need not feel either disappointed or embittered. God
knows the good deed also, and he will repay, for he is never
in any man's debt.

Here we are told that we must neither grow angry at the apparent escape of others nor embittered at the apparent thanklessness of men, but that we must be content to leave all things to the ultimate judgment of God.

HOW TO BE A SLAVE AND A CHRISTIAN

1 *Timothy* 6: 1, 2

Let all those who are slaves under the yoke hold their own masters to be worthy of all respect, in order that no one may have an opportunity to speak evil of the name of God and the Christian teaching. If they have masters who are believers, let them not try to take advantage of them because they are brothers, but rather let them render even better service, because those who lay claim to that service are believers and beloved.

BENEATH the surface of this passage there are certain supremely important Christian principles for everyday life and work.

The Christian slave was in a peculiarly difficult position. If he was the slave of a heathen master, he might very easily make it clear that he regarded his master as bound for perdition and himself as the heir of salvation. His Christianity might well give him a feeling of intolerant superiority which would create an impossible situation. On the other hand, if his master was a Christian, the slave might be tempted to take advantage of the relationship and to trade upon it, using it as an excuse for producing inefficient work in the expectation of escaping all punishment. He might think that the fact that both he and his master were Christians entitled him to all kinds of special consideration. There was an obvious problem here. We must note two general things.

(i) In those early days the Church did not emerge as the would-be destroyer of slavery by violent and sudden means. And it was wise. There were something like 60,000,000 slaves in the Roman Empire. Simply because of their numbers

they were always regarded as potential enemies. If ever there
was a slave revolt it was put down with merciless force,
because the Roman Empire could not afford to allow the
slaves to rise. If a slave ran away and was caught, he was
either executed or branded on the forehead with the letter F,
which stood for *fugitivus*, which means *runaway*. There was
indeed a Roman law which stated that if a master was
murdered all his slaves could be examined under torture, and
could indeed be put to death in a body. E. K. Simpson
wisely writes: "Christianity's spiritual campaign would have
been fatally compromised by stirring the smouldering embers
of class-hatred into a devouring flame, or opening an asylum
for runaway slaves in its bosom."

For the Church to have encouraged slaves to revolt
against their masters would have been fatal. It would simply
have caused civil war, mass murder, and the complete
discredit of the Church. What happened was that as the
centuries went on Christianity so permeated civilization that in
the end the slaves were freed voluntarily and not by force.
Here is a tremendous lesson. It is the proof that neither men
nor the world nor society can be reformed by force and by
legislation. The reform must come through the slow
penetration of the Spirit of Christ into the human situation.
Things have to happen in God's time, not in ours. In the end
the slow way is the sure way, and the way of violence always
defeats itself.

(ii) There is here the further truth, that "spiritual equality
does not efface civil distinctions." It is a continual danger
that a man may unconsciously regard his Christianity as an
excuse for slackness and inefficiency. Because he and his
master are both Christians, he may expect to be treated
with special consideration. But the fact that both master and
man are Christian does not release the employee from doing
a good day's work and earning his wage. The Christian is
under the same obligation to submit to discipline and to earn
his pay as any other man.

(iii) What then is the duty of the Christian slave as the

Pastorals see it? It is to be a good slave. If he is not, if he is slack and careless, if he is disobedient and insolent, he merely supplies the world with ammunition to criticize the Church. The Christian workman must commend his Christianity by being a better workman than other people. In particular, his work will be done in a new spirit. He will not now think of himself as being unwillingly compelled to work; he will think of himself as rendering service to his master, to God and to his fellow-men. His aim will be, not to see how little can be forced out of him, but how much he can willingly do. As George Herbert had it:

> "A servant with this clause
> Makes drudgery divine:
> Who sweeps a room, as for thy laws,
> Makes that and the action fine."

FALSE TEACHERS AND FALSE TEACHING

1 *Timothy* 6: 3–5

If any man offers a different kind of teaching, and does not apply himself to sound words (it is the words of our Lord Jesus Christ I mean) and to godly teaching, he has become inflated with pride. He is a man of no understanding; rather he has a diseased addiction to subtle speculations and battles of words, which can be only a source of envy, strife, the exchange of insults, evil suspicions, continual altercations of men whose minds are corrupt and who are destitute of the truth, men whose belief is that religion is a means of making gain.

THE circumstances of life in the ancient world presented the false teacher with an opportunity which he was not slow to take. On the Christian side, the Church was full of wandering prophets, whose very way of life gave them a certain prestige. The Christian service was much more informal than it is now. Anyone who felt he had a message was free to give it; and the door was wide open to men who were out to propagate a false and misleading message. On the heathen side, there were men called *sophists, wise men,* who made it their business, so to speak, to sell philosophy. They had two lines. They claimed for a fee to be able to teach men to argue cleverly; they were the men who with their smooth tongues and their adroit minds were skilled in "making the worse appear the better reason." They had turned philosophy into a way of becoming rich. Their other line was to give demonstrations of public speaking. The Greek had always been fascinated by the spoken word; he loved an orator; and these wandering sophists went from town to town, giving their oratorical demonstrations. They went in for advertising on an intensive scale and even went the length of delivering by hand personal invitations to their displays. The most famous of them drew people literally by the thousand to their lectures; they were in their day the equivalent of the modern pop star. Philostratus tells us that Adrian, one of the most famous of them, had such a popular power that, when his messenger appeared with the news that he was to speak, even the senate and the circus emptied, and the whole population flocked to the Athenaeum to hear him. They had three great faults.

Their speeches were quite unreal. They would offer to speak on any subject, however remote and recondite and unlikely, that any member of the audience might propose. This is the kind of question they would argue; it is an actual example. A man goes into the citadel of a town to kill a tyrant who has been grinding down the people; not finding the tyrant, he kills the tyrant's son; the tyrant comes in and sees his dead son with the sword in his body, and in his grief kills himself; the man then claims the reward for killing the tyrant and liberating the people; should he receive it?

Their thirst was for applause. Competition between them was a bitter and a cut-throat affair. Plutarch tells of a travelling sophist called Niger who came to a town in Galatia where a prominent orator resided. A competition was immediately arranged. Niger had to compete or lose his reputation. He was suffering from a fishbone in his throat and had difficulty in speaking; but for the sake of prestige he had to go on. Inflammation set in soon after, and in the end he died. Dio Chrysostom paints a picture of a public place in Corinth with all the different kinds of competitors in full blast: "You might hear many poor wretches of sophists shouting and abusing each other, and their disciples, as they call them, squabbling, and many writers of books reading their stupid compositions, and many poets singing their poems, and many jugglers exhibiting their marvels, and many sooth-sayers giving the meaning of prodigies, and a thousand rhetoricians twisting lawsuits, and no small number of traders driving their several trades." There you have just that inter-change of insults, that envy and strife, that constant wordy altercation of men with decadent minds that the writer of the Pastorals deplores. "A sophist," wrote Philostratus, "is put out in an extempore speech by a serious-looking audience and tardy praise and no clapping." "They are all agape," said Dio Chrysostom, "for the murmur of the crowd. . . . Like men walking in the dark they move always in the direction of the clapping and the shouting." Lucian writes: "If your friends see you breaking down, let them pay the price of the suppers you give them by stretching out their arms and giving you a chance of thinking of something to say in the intervals between the rounds of applause." The ancient world well knew just the kind of false teacher who was invading the Church.

Their thirst was for praise, and their criterion was numbers. Epictetus has some vivid pictures of the sophist talking to his disciples after his performance. " 'Well, what did you think of me today?' 'Upon my life, sir, I thought you were admirable.' 'What did you think of my best passage?' 'Which was that?' 'Where I described Pan and the Nymphs.' 'Oh, it was excessively well done.' " " 'A much larger audience today, I think,' says the sophist. 'Yes, much larger,' responds the disciple. 'Five hundred, I should guess.' 'O, nonsense! It could not have been less than a thousand.' 'Why, that is more than Dio ever had. I wonder why it was? They appreciated what I said, too.' 'Beauty, sir, can move a stone.' " These performing sophists were "the pets of society." They became senators, governors, ambassadors. When they died monuments were erected to them, with inscriptions such as, "The Queen of Cities to the King of Eloquence."

The Greeks were intoxicated with the spoken word. Among them, if a man could speak, his fortune was made. It was against a background like that that the Church was growing up; and it is little wonder that this type of teacher invaded it. The Church gave him a new area in which to exercise his meretricious gifts and to gain a tinsel prestige and a not unprofitable following.

THE CHARACTERISTICS OF THE
FALSE TEACHER

1 *Timothy* 6: 3-5 (*continued*)

HERE in this passage are set out the characteristics of the false teacher.

(i) His first characteristic is conceit. His desire is not to display Christ, but to display himself. There are still preachers and teachers who are more concerned to gain a following for themselves than for Jesus Christ, more concerned to press their own views than to bring to men the word of God. In a lecture on his old teacher A. B. Bruce, W. M. Macgregor said: "One of our own Highland ministers tells how he had been puzzled by seeing Bruce again and again during lectures take up a scrap of paper, look at it and then proceed. One day he caught at the chance of seeing what this paper contained, and discovered on it an indication of the words: 'O, send out thy light and thy truth,' and thus he realized with awe that into his classroom the professor brought the majesty and the hopefulness of worship." The great teacher does not offer men his own farthing candle of illumination; he offers them the light and the truth of God.

(ii) His concern is with abstruse and recondite speculations. There is a kind of Christianity which is more concerned with argument than with life. To be a member of a discussion circle or a Bible study group and spend enjoyable hours in talk about doctrines does not necessarily make a Christian. J. S. Whale in his book *Christian Doctrine* has certain scathing things to say about this pleasant intellectualism: "We have as Valentine said of Thurio, 'an exchequer of words, but no other treasure.' Instead of putting off our shoes from our feet because the place whereon we stand is holy ground, we are taking nice photographs of the Burning Bush from suitable angles: we are chatting about theories of the Atonement with our feet on the mantelpiece, instead of kneeling down before the wounds of Christ." As Luther had it: "He who merely studies the commandments of God *(mandata Dei)* is not greatly moved. But he who listens to God commanding *(Deum mandantem)*, how can he fail to be terrified by majesty so great?" As Melanchthon had it: "To know Christ is not to speculate about the mode of his Incarnation, but to know his saving benefits." Gregory of Nyssa drew a revealing picture of Constantinople in his day: "Constantinople is full of mechanics and slaves, who are all of them profound theologians, preaching in the shops and the streets. If you want a man to change a piece of silver, he informs you wherein the Son differs from the Father; if you ask the price of a loaf, you are told by way of reply that the Son is inferior to the Father; and if you enquire whether the bath is ready, the answer is that the Son is made out of nothing." Subtle argumentation and glib theological statements do not make a Christian. That kind of thing may well be nothing other than a mode of escape from the challenge of Christian living.

(iii) The false teacher is a disturber of the peace. He is instinctively competitive; he is suspicious of all who differ from him; when he cannot win in an argument he hurls insults at his opponent's theological position, and even at his character; in any argument the accent of his voice is bitterness and not love. He has never learned to speak the truth in love. The source of his bitterness is the exaltation of self; for his tendency is to regard any difference from or any criticism of his views as a personal insult.

(iv) The false teacher commercializes religion. He is out for profit. He looks on his teaching and preaching, not as a vocation, but as a career. One thing is certain—there is no place for careerists in the ministry of any Church. The Pastorals are quite clear that the labourer is worthy of his hire; but the motive of his work must be public service and not private gain. His passion is, not to get, but to spend and be spent in the service of Christ and of his fellow-men.

THE CROWN OF CONTENT

1 *Timothy* 6: 6–8

> And in truth godliness with contentment is great gain. We brought nothing into the world, and it is quite clear that we cannot take anything out of it either; but if we have food and shelter, we shall be content with them.

THE word here used for *contentment* is *autarkeia*. This was one of the great watchwords of the Stoic philosophers. By it they meant a complete *self-sufficiency*. They meant a frame of mind which was completely independent of all outward things, and which carried the secret of happiness within itself.

Contentment never comes from the possession of external things. As George Herbert wrote:

> "For he that needs five thousand pounds to live
> Is full as poor as he that needs but five."

Contentment comes from an inward attitude to life. In the Third part of *Henry the Sixth*, Shakespeare draws a picture of the king wandering in the country places unknown. He meets two gamekeepers and tells them that he is a king. One of them asks him:

"But, if thou be a king, where is thy crown?" And the king gives a great answer:

> "My crown is in my heart, not on my head;
> Not deck'd with diamonds and Indian stones,
> Nor to be seen; my crown is call'd content—
> A crown it is that seldom kings enjoy."

Long ago the Greek philosophers had gripped the right end of the matter. Epicurus said of himself: "To whom little is not enough nothing is enough. Give me a barley cake and a glass of water and I am ready to rival Zeus for happiness." And when someone asked him for the secret of happiness, his answer was: "Add not to a man's possessions but take away from his desires."

The great men have always been content with little. One of the sayings of the Jewish Rabbis was: "Who is rich? He that is contented with his lot." Walter Lock quotes the kind of training on which a Jewish Rabbi engaged and the kind of life he lived: "This is the path of the Law. A morsel with salt shalt thou eat, thou shalt drink also water by measure, and shalt sleep upon the ground and live a life of trouble while thou toilest in the Law. If thou doest this, happy shalt thou be, and it shall be well with thee; happy shalt thou be in this world and it shall be well with thee in the world to come." The Rabbi had to learn to be content with enough. E. F. Brown quotes a passage from the great preacher Lacordaire: "The rock of our present day is that no one knows how to live upon little. The great men of antiquity were generally poor. . . . It always seems to me that the retrenchment of useless expenditure, the laying aside of what one may call the relatively necessary, is the high road to Christian disentanglement of heart, just as it was to that of ancient vigour. The mind that has learned to appreciate the moral beauty of life, both as regards God and men, can scarcely be greatly moved by any outward reverse of fortune; and what our age wants most is the sight of a man, who might possess everything, being yet willingly contented with little. For my own part, humanly speaking, I wish for nothing. A great soul in a small house is the idea which has touched me more than any other."

It is not that Christianity pleads for poverty. There is no special virtue in being poor, or in having a constant struggle to make ends meet. But it does plead for two things.

It pleads for the realization that it is never in the power of things to bring happiness. E. K. Simpson says: "Many a millionaire, after choking his soul with gold-dust, has died from melancholia." Happiness always comes from personal relationships. All the things in the world will not make a man happy if he knows neither friendship nor love. The Christian knows that the secret of happiness lies, not in things, but in people.

It pleads for concentration upon the things which are permanent. We brought nothing into the world and we cannot take anything out of it. The wise men of every age and faith have known this. "You cannot," said Seneca, "take anything more out of the world than you brought into it." The poet of the Greek anthology had it: "Naked I set foot on the earth; naked I shall go below the earth." The Spanish proverb grimly puts it: "There are no pockets in a shroud." E. K. Simpson comments: "Whatever a man amasses by the way is in the nature of luggage, no part of his truest personality, but something he leaves behind at the toll-bar of death."

Two things alone a man can take to God. He can, and must, take himself; and therefore his great task is to build up a self he can take without shame to God. He can, and must, take that relationship with God into which he has entered in the days of his life. We have already seen that the secret of happiness lies in personal relationships, and the greatest of all personal relationships is the relationship to God. And the supreme thing that a man can take with him is the utter conviction that he goes to One who is the friend and lover of his soul.

Content comes when we escape the servitude to things, when we find our wealth in the love and the fellowship of men, and when we realize that our most precious possession is our friendship with God, made possible through Jesus Christ.

THE PERIL OF THE LOVE OF MONEY

1 *Timothy* 6: 9, 10

> Those who wish to be rich fall into temptation and a snare, and into many senseless and harmful desires for the forbidden things, desires which swamp men in a sea of ruin and total loss in time and in eternity. For the love of money is a root from which all evils spring; and some, in their reaching out after it, have been sadly led astray, and have transfixed themselves with many pains.

HERE is one of the most misquoted sayings in the Bible. Scripture does not say that *money* is the root of all evil; it says that *the love of money* is the root of all evil. This is a truth of which the great classical thinkers were as conscious as the Christian teachers. "Love of money," said Democritus, "is the metropolis of all evils." Seneca speaks of "the desire for that which does not belong to us, from which every evil of the mind springs." "The love of money," said Phocylides, "is the mother of all evils." Philo spoke of "love of money which is the starting-place of the greatest transgressions of the Law." Athenaeus quotes a saying: "The belly's pleasure is the beginning and root of all evil."

Money in itself is neither good nor bad; but the love of it may lead to evil. With it a man may selfishly serve his own desires; with it he may answer the cry of his neighbour's need. With it he may facilitate the path of wrong-doing; with it he may make it easier for someone else to live as God meant him to do. Money is not itself an evil, but it is a great responsibility. It is powerful to good and powerful to evil. What then are the special dangers involved in the love of money?

(i) The desire for money tends to be a thirst which is insatiable. There was a Roman proverbial saying that wealth is like sea-water; so far from quenching a man's thirst, it intensifies it. The more he gets, the more he wants.

(ii) The desire for wealth is founded on an illusion. It is founded on the desire for security; but wealth cannot buy security. It cannot buy health, nor real love; and it cannot preserve from sorrow and from death. The security which is founded on material things is foredoomed to failure.

(iii) The desire for money tends to make a man selfish. If he is driven by the desire for wealth, it is nothing to him that someone has to lose in order that he may gain. The desire for wealth fixes a man's thoughts upon himself, and others become merely means or obstacles in the path to his own enrichment. True, that *need* not happen; but in fact it often *does*.

(iv) Although the desire for wealth is based on the desire for security, it ends in nothing but anxiety. The more a man has to keep, the more he has to lose and, the tendency is for him to be haunted by the risk of loss. There is an old fable about a peasant who rendered a great service to a king who rewarded him with a gift of much money. For a time the man was thrilled, but the day came when he begged the king to take back his gift, for into his life had entered the hitherto unknown worry that he might lose what he had. John Bunyan was right:

> "He that is down needs fear no fall,
>   He that is low, no pride;
> He that is humble ever shall
>   Have God to be his guide.
>
> I am content with what I have,
>   Little be it or much;
> And, Lord, contentment still I crave,
>   Because Thou savest such.

> Fullness to such a burden is
>   That go on pilgrimage;
> Here little, and hereafter bliss,
>   Is best from age to age."

(v) The love of money may easily lead a man into wrong ways of getting it, and therefore, in the end, into pain and remorse. That is true even physically. He may so drive his body in his passion to get, that he ruins his health. He may discover too late what damage his desire has done to others and be saddled with remorse.

To seek to be independent and prudently to provide for the future is a Christian duty; but to make the love of money the driving-force of life cannot ever be anything other than the most perilous of sins.

CHALLENGE TO TIMOTHY

1 *Timothy* 6: 11–16

> But you, O man of God, flee from these things. Pursue righteousness, godliness, faith, love, endurance, gentleness. Fight the good fight of faith; lay hold on eternal life, to which you are called, now that you have witnessed a noble profession of your faith in the presence of many witnesses. I charge you in the sight of God, who makes all things alive, and in the sight of Christ Jesus, who, in the days of Pontius Pilate, witnessed his noble confession, that you keep the commandment, that you should be without spot and without blame, until the day when our Lord Jesus Christ appears, that appearance which in his own good times the blessed and only Potentate, the King of kings, and the Lord of lords will show, he who alone possesses immortality, he who dwells in the light that no man can approach, he whom no man has seen or ever can see, to whom be honour and everlasting power. Amen.

THE letter comes to an end with a tremendous challenge to Timothy, a challenge all the greater because of the deliberate sonorous nobility of the words in which it is clothed.

Right at the outset Timothy is put upon his mettle. He is addressed as *man of God*. That is one of the great Old Testament titles. It is a title given to Moses. *Deuteronomy* 33: 1 speaks of "Moses, the man of God." The title of *Psalm* 90 is, "A Prayer of Moses the man of God." It is a title of the prophets and the messengers of God. God's messenger to Eli is a man of God (1 *Samuel* 2: 27). Samuel is described as a man of God (1 *Samuel* 9: 6). Shemaiah, God's messenger to Rehoboam, is a man of God (1 *Kings* 12: 22). John Bunyan in *Pilgrim's Progress* calls Great-Grace "God's Champion."

Here is a title of honour. When the charge is given to Timothy, he is not reminded of his own weakness and sin, which might well have reduced him to pessimistic despair; rather he is challenged by the honour which is his, of being God's man. It is the Christian way, not to depress a man by branding him as a lost and helpless sinner, but rather to uplift him by summoning him to be what he has got it in him to be. The Christian way is not to fling a man's humiliating past in his face, but to set before him the splendour of his potential future. The very fact that Timothy was addressed as "Man of God" would make him square his shoulders and throw his head back as one who has received his commission from the King.

The virtues and noble qualities set before Timothy are not just heaped haphazardly together. There is an order in them. First, there comes *righteousness, dikaiosunē*. This is defined as "giving both to men and to God their due." It is the most comprehensive of the virtues; the righteous man is he who does his duty to God and to his fellow-men.

Second, there comes a group of three virtues which look towards God. *Godliness, eusebeia,* is the reverence of the man who never ceases to be aware that all life is lived in the presence of God. *Faith, pistis,* here means *fidelity*, and is the virtue of the man who, through all the chances and the changes of life, down even to the gates of death, is loyal to God. *Love, agapē*, is the virtue of the man who, even if he tried, could not forget what God has done for him nor the love of God to men.

Third, there comes the virtue which looks to the conduct of life. It is *hupomonē*. The Authorized Version translates this *patience;* but *hupomonē* never means the spirit which sits with folded hands and simply bears things, letting the experiences of life flow like a tide over it. It is victorious endurance. "It is unswerving constancy to faith and piety in spite of adversity and suffering." It is the virtue which does not so much accept the experiences of life as conquers them.

Fourthly, there comes the virtue which looks to men. The Greek word is *paupatheia*. It is translated *gentleness* but is really untranslatable. It describes the spirit which never blazes into anger for its own wrongs but can be devastatingly angry for the wrongs of others. It describes the spirit which knows how to forgive and yet knows how to wage the battle of righteousness. It describes the spirit which walks at once in humility and yet in pride of its high calling from God. It describes the virtue by which at all times a man is enabled rightly to treat his fellow-men and rightly to regard himself.

MEMORIES WHICH INSPIRE

1 *Timothy* 6: 11–16 (*continued*)

As Timothy is challenged to the task of the future, he is inspired with the memories of the past.

(i) He is to remember his baptism and the vows he took there. In the circumstances of the early Church, baptism was inevitably adult baptism, for men were coming straight from heathenism to Christ. It was confession of faith and witness to all men that the baptised person had taken Jesus Christ as Saviour, Master and Lord. The earliest of all Christian confessions was the simple creed: "Jesus Christ is Lord"

(*Romans* 10: 9; *Philippians* 2: 11). But it has been suggested that behind these words to Timothy lies a confession of faith which said: "I believe in God the Almighty, Creator of heaven and earth, and in Christ Jesus who suffered under Pontius Pilate and will return to judge; I believe in the Resurrection from the dead and in the life immortal." It may well have been a creed like that to which Timothy gave his allegiance. So, then, first of all, he is reminded that he is a man who has given his pledge. The Christian is first and foremost a man who has pledged himself to Jesus Christ.

(ii) He is to remember that he has made the same confession of his faith as Jesus did. When Jesus stood before Pilate, Pilate said: "Are you the King of the Jews?" and Jesus answered: "You have said so" (*Luke* 23: 3). Jesus had witnessed that he was a King; and Timothy always had witnessed to the lordship of Christ. When the Christian confesses his faith, he does what his Master has already done; when he suffers for his faith, he undergoes what his Master has already undergone. When we are engaged on some great enterprise, we can say: "Brothers, we are treading where the saints have trod," but when we confess our faith before men, we can say even more; we can say: "I stand with Christ"; and surely this must lift up our hearts and inspire our lives.

(iii) He is to remember that Christ comes again. He is to remember that his life and work must be made fit for him to see. The Christian is not working to satisfy men; he is working to satisfy Christ. The question he must always ask himself is not: "Is this good enough to pass the judgment of men?" but: "Is it good enough to win the approval of Christ?"

(iv) Above all he is to remember God. And what a memory that is! He is to remember the One who is King of every king and Lord of every lord; the One who possesses the gift of life eternal to give to men; the One whose holiness and majesty are such that no man can ever dare look upon them. The Christian must ever remember God and say: "If God be for us, who can be against us?"

ADVICE TO THE RICH

1 *Timothy* 6: 17–19

> Charge those who are rich in this world's goods not to be proud, and not set their hopes on the uncertainty of riches, but on God who gives them all things richly to enjoy. Charge them to do good; to find their wealth in noble deeds; to be ready to share all that they have; to be men who never forget that they are members of a fellowship; to lay up for themselves the treasure of a fine foundation for the world to come, that they may lay hold on real life.

SOMETIMES we think of the early Church as composed entirely of poor people and slaves. Here we see that even as early as this it had its wealthy members. They are not condemned for being wealthy nor told to give all their wealth away; but they are told what not to do and what to do with it.

Their riches must not make them proud. They must not think themselves better than other people because they have more money than they. Nothing in this world gives any man the right to look down on another, least of all the possession of wealth. They must not set their hopes on wealth. In the chances and the changes of life a man may be wealthy today and a pauper tomorrow; and it is folly to set one's hopes on what can so easily be lost.

They are told that they must use their wealth to do good; that they must ever be ready to share; and that they must remember that the Christian is a member of a fellowship. And they are told that such wise use of wealth will build for them a good foundation in the world to come. As someone put it: "What I kept, I lost; what I gave I have."

There is a famous Jewish Rabbinic story. A man called Monobaz had inherited great wealth, but he was a good, a kindly and a generous man. In time of famine he gave away all his wealth to help the poor. His brothers came to him and said: "Your fathers laid up treasure, and added to the treasure that they had inherited from their fathers, and are you going to waste it all?" He answered: "My fathers laid up treasure below: I have laid it up above. My fathers laid up treasure of Mammon: I have laid up treasure of souls. My fathers laid up treasure for this world: I have laid up treasure for the world to come."

Every time we could give and do not give lessens the wealth laid up for us in the world to come; every time we give increases the riches laid up for us when this life comes to an end.

The teaching of the Christian ethic is, not that wealth is a sin, but that it is a very great responsibility. If a man's wealth ministers to nothing but his own pride and enriches no one but himself, it becomes his ruination, because it impoverishes his soul. But if he uses it to bring help and comfort to others, in becoming poorer, he really becomes richer. In time and in eternity "it is more blessed to give than to receive."

A FAITH TO HAND ON

1 *Timothy* 6: 20, 21

> O Timothy, guard the trust that has been entrusted to you. Avoid irreligious empty talking; and the paradoxes of that knowledge which has no right to be called knowledge, which some have professed, and by so doing have missed the target of the faith.
> Grace be with you.

IT may well be that the name *Timothy* is here used in the fullness of its meaning. It comes from two words, *timan, to honour,* and *theos, God* and literally means *he who honours God.* It may well be that this concluding passage begins by reminding Timothy of his name and urging him to be true to it.

The passage talks of the *trust* that has been entrusted to him. The Greek word for *trust* is *parathēkē,* which literally means a *deposit.* It is the word for money deposited with a banker or with a friend. When such money was in time demanded back, it was a sacred duty to hand it back entire.

Sometimes children were called a *paratheke*, a sacred trust. If the gods gave a man a child, it was his duty to present that child trained and equipped to the gods.

The Christian faith is like that, something which we received from our forefathers, and which we must pass on to our children. E. F. Brown quotes a famous passage from St. Vincent of Lerins: "What is meant by the *deposit? (paratheke)*. That which is committed to thee, not that which is invented by thee; that which thou hast received, not that which thou hast devised; a thing not of wit, but of learning; not of private assumption, but of public tradition; a thing brought to thee, not brought forth of thee; wherein thou must not be an author, but a keeper; not a leader, but a follower. Keep the deposit. Preserve the talent of the Catholic faith safe and undiminished; let that which is committed to thee remain with thee, and that deliver. Thou hast received gold, render gold."

A man does well to remember that his duty is not only to himself, but also to his children and his children's children. If in our day the Church were to become enfeebled; if the Christian ethic were to be more and more submerged in the world; if the Christian faith were to be twisted and distorted; it would not only be we who were the losers, those of generations still to come would be robbed of something infinitely precious. We are not only the possessors but also the trustees of the faith. That which we have received, we must also hand on.

Finally the Pastorals condemn those who, as the Authorized Version has it, have given themselves to "the oppositions of science falsely so-called." First, we must note that here the word *science* is used in its original sense; it simply means *knowledge (gnosis)*. What is being condemned is a false intellectualism and a false stressing of human knowledge.

But what is meant by *oppositions?* The Greek word is *antitheseis*. Very much later than this there was a heretic called Marcion who produced a book called *The Antitheseis* in which he quoted Old Testament texts and set beside them New

Testament texts which contradicted them. This might very well mean: "Don't waste your time seeking out contradictions in Scripture. Use the Scriptures to live by and not to argue about." But there are two meanings more probable than that.

(i) The word *antithesis* could mean a *controversy;* and this might mean: "Avoid controversies; don't get yourself mixed up in useless and bitter arguments." This would be a very relevant bit of advice to a Greek congregation in Ephesus. The Greek had a passion for going to law. He would even go to law with his own brother, just for the pleasure of it. This may well mean, "Don't make the Church a battle-ground of theological arguments and debates. Christianity is not something to argue about, but something to live by."

(ii) The word *antithesis* can mean a *rival thesis*. This is the most likely meaning, because it suits Jew and Gentile alike. The scholastics in the later days used to argue about questions like: "How many angels can stand on the point of a needle?" The Jewish Rabbis would argue about hair-splitting points of the law for hours and days and even years. The Greeks were the same, only in a still more serious way. There was a school of Greek philosophers, and a very influential school it was, called the Academics. The Academics held that in the case of everything in the realm of human thought, you could by logical argument arrive at precisely opposite conclusions. They therefore concluded that there is no such thing as absolute truth; that always there were two hypotheses of equal weight. They went on to argue that, this being so, the wise man will never make up his mind about anything but will hold himself for ever in a state of suspended judgment. The effect was of course to paralyse all action and to reduce men to complete uncertainty. So Timothy is told: "Don't waste your time in subtle arguments; don't waste your time in 'dialectical fencing.' Don't be too clever to be wise. Listen rather to the unequivocal voice of God than to the subtle disputations of over-clever minds."

So the letter draws to a close with a warning which our own

generation needs. Clever argument can never be made a substitute for Christian action. The duty of the Christian is not to sit in a study and weigh arguments but to live the Christian life in the dust and heat of the world. In the end it is not intellectual cleverness, but conduct and character which count.

Then comes the closing blessing—"Grace be with you." The letter ends with the beauty of the grace of God.

2 TIMOTHY

AN APOSTLE'S GLORY AND AN APOSTLE'S PRIVILEGE

2 *Timothy* 1 : 1–7

This is a letter from Paul, who was made an apostle of Christ Jesus by the will of God, and whose apostleship was designed to make known to all men God's promise of real life in Christ Jesus, to Timothy his own beloved child. Grace, mercy and peace be to you from God, the Father, and from Christ Jesus, our Lord.

I thank God, whom I serve with a clear conscience, as my forefathers did before me, for all that you are to me, just as in my prayers I never cease to remember you, for, remembering your tears when we parted, I never cease to yearn to see you, that I may be filled with joy. And I thank God that I have received a fresh reminder of that sincere faith which is in you, a faith of the same kind as first dwelt in your grandmother Lois and in your mother Eunice, and which, I am convinced, dwells in you too. That is why I send you this reminder to keep at white heat the gift that is in you and which came to you through the laying of my hands upon you; for God did not give us the spirit of craven fear, but of power and love and self-discipline.

WHEN Paul speaks of his own apostleship there are always certain unmistakable notes in his voice. To him it was always certain things.

(*a*) His apostleship was an *honour*. He was chosen to it by the will of God. Every Christian must regard himself as a God-chosen man.

(*b*) His apostleship was a *responsibility*. God chose him because he wanted to do something with him. He wished to make him the instrument by which the tidings of new life went out to men. No Christian is ever chosen entirely for his own sake, but for what he can do for others. A Christian is a man lost in wonder, love and praise at what God has done for him and aflame with eagerness to tell others what God can do for them.

(*c*) His apostleship was a *privilege*. It is most significant to see what Paul conceived it his duty to bring to others—the *promise* of God, not his *threat*. To him, Christianity was not the threat of damnation; it was the good news of salvation. It is worth remembering that the greatest evangelist and missionary the world has ever seen was out, not to terrify men by shaking them over the flames of hell, but to move them to astonished submission at the sight of the love of God. The dynamic of his gospel was love, not fear.

As always when he speaks to Timothy, there is a warmth of loving affection in Paul's voice. "My beloved child," he calls him. Timothy was his child in the faith. Timothy's parents had given him physical life; but it was Paul who gave him eternal life. Many a person who never knew physical parenthood has had the joy and privilege of being a father or a mother in the faith; and there is no joy in all the world like that of bringing one soul to Christ.

THE INSPIRING OF TIMOTHY

2 *Timothy* 1: 1-7 (*continued*)

PAUL'S object in writing is to inspire and strengthen Timothy for his task in Ephesus. Timothy was young and he had a hard task in battling against the heresies and the infections that were bound to threaten the Church. So, then, in order to keep his courage high and his effort strenuous, Paul reminds Timothy of certain things.

(i) He reminds him of his own confidence in him. There is no greater inspiration than to feel that someone believes in us. An appeal to honour is always more effective than a threat of punishment. The fear of letting down those who love us is a cleansing thing.

(ii) He reminds him of his family tradition. Timothy was walking in a fine heritage, and if he failed, not only would he smirch his own name, but he would lessen the honour of his family name as well. A fine parentage is one of the greatest

C6

gifts a man can have. Let him thank God for it and never bring dishonour to it.

(iii) He reminds him of his setting apart to office and of the gift which was conferred upon him. Once a man enters upon the service of any association with a tradition, anything that he does affects not only himself nor has it to be done only in his own strength. There is the strength of a tradition to draw upon and the honour of a tradition to preserve. That is specially true of the Church. He who serves it has its honour in his hands; he who serves it is strengthened by the consciousness of the communion of all the saints.

(iv) He reminds him of the qualities which should characterize the Christian teacher. These, as Paul at that moment saw them, were four.

(*a*) There was *courage*. It was not craven fear but courage that Christian service should bring to a man. It always takes courage to be a Christian, and that courage comes from the continual consciousness of the presence of Christ.

(*b*) There was *power*. In the true Christian there is the power to cope, the power to shoulder the back-breaking task, the power to stand erect in face of the shattering situation, the power to retain faith in face of the soul-searing sorrow and the wounding disappointment. The Christian is characteristically the man who could pass the breaking-point and not break.

(*c*) There was *love*. In Timothy's case this was love for the brethren, for the congregation of the people of Christ over whom he was set. It is precisely that love which gives the Christian pastor his other qualities. He must love his people so much that he will never find any toil too great to undertake for them or any situation threatening enough to daunt him. No man should ever enter the ministry of the Church unless there is love for Christ's people within his heart.

(*d*) There was *self-discipline*. The word is *sōphronismos,* one of these great Greek untranslatable words. Someone has defined it as "the sanity of saintliness." Falconer defines it as "control of oneself in face of panic or of passion." It is Christ alone who can give us that self-mastery which will keep us alike from being swept away and from running away. No man can ever rule others unless he has first mastered himself. *Sōphronismos* is that divinely given self-control which makes a man a great ruler of others because he is first of all the servant of Christ and the master of himself.

A GOSPEL WORTH SUFFERING FOR

2 *Timothy* 1 : 8–11

> So, then, do not be ashamed to bear your witness to our Lord; and do not be ashamed of me his prisoner; but accept with me the suffering which the gospel brings, and do so in the power of God, who saved us, and who called us with a call to consecration, a call which had nothing to do with our own achievements, but which was dependent solely on his purpose, and on the grace which was given to us in Christ Jesus: and all this was planned before the world began, but now it stands full-displayed through the appearance of our Saviour Christ Jesus, who abolished death and brought life and incorruption to light by means of the good news which he brought, good news in the service of which I have been appointed a herald, and an apostle and a teacher.

IT is inevitable that loyalty to the gospel will bring trouble. For Timothy, it meant loyalty to a man who was regarded as a criminal, because as Paul wrote he was in prison in Rome. But here Paul sets out the gospel in all its glory, something worth suffering for. Sometimes by implication and sometimes by direct statement he brings out element after element in that glory. Few passages in the New Testament have in them and behind them such a sense of the sheer grandeur of the gospel.

(i) It is the gospel of *power*. Any suffering which it involves is to be borne in the power of God. To the ancient world the gospel was the power to live. That very age in which Paul was writing was the great age of suicide. The highest-principled of the ancient thinkers were the Stoics; but they had their own way out when life became intolerable. They had a saying: "God gave men life, but God gave men the still greater gift of being able to take their own lives away." The gospel was, and is, power, power to conquer self, power to master circumstances, power to go on living when life is unlivable, power to be a Christian when being a Christian looks impossible.

(ii) It is the gospel of *salvation*. God is the God who saves us. The gospel is rescue. It is rescue from sin; it liberates a man from the things which have him in their grip; it enables him to break with the habits which are unbreakable. The gospel is a rescuing force which can make bad men good.

(iii) It is the gospel of *consecration*. It is not simply rescue from the consequences of past sin; it is a summons to walk the way of holiness. In *The Bible in World Evangelism* A. M. Chirgwin quotes two amazing instances of the miraculous changing power of Christ.

There was a New York gangster who had recently been in prison for robbery with violence. He was on his way to join his old gang with a view to taking part in another robbery when he picked a man's pocket in Fifth Avenue. He went into Central Park to see what he had succeeded in stealing and discovered to his disgust that it was a New Testament. Since he had time to spare, he began idly to turn over the pages and to read. Soon he was deep in the book, and he read to such effect that a few hours later he went to his old comrades and broke with them for ever. For that ex-convict the gospel was the call to holiness.

There was a young Arab in Aleppo who had a bitter quarrel with a former friend. He told a Christian evangelist: "I hated him so much that I plotted revenge, even to the point of murder. Then," he went on, "one day I ran into you and you induced me to buy a copy of St. Matthew. I only bought it to please you. I never intended to read it. But as I was going to bed that night the book fell out of my pocket, and I picked it up and started to read. When I reached the place where it says: 'Ye have heard that it hath been said of old time, Thou shalt not kill. . . . But I say unto you that whosoever is angry with his brother without a cause shall be in danger of the judgment,' I remembered the hatred I was nourishing against my enemy. As I read on my uneasiness grew until I reached the words, 'Come unto me all ye who labour and are heavy laden, and I will give you rest. Take my yoke upon you, and learn of me; for I am meek and lowly in heart; and ye shall find rest unto your souls.' Then I was compelled to cry: 'God be merciful to me a sinner.' Joy and peace filled my heart and my hatred disappeared. Since then I have been a new man, and my chief delight is to read God's word."

It was the gospel which set the ex-convict in New York and the would-be murderer in Aleppo on the road to holiness. It is here that so much of our Church Christianity falls down. It does not change people; and therefore is not real. The man who has known the saving power of the gospel is a changed man, in his business, in his pleasure, in his home, in his character. There should be an essential difference between the Christian and the non-Christian, because the Christian has obeyed the summons to walk the road to holiness.

A GOSPEL WORTH SUFFERING FOR

2 *Timothy* 1: 8–11 (*continued*)

(iv) It is the gospel of *grace*. It is not something which we achieve, but something which we accept. God did not call us because we are holy; he called us to make us holy. If we had to deserve the love of God, our situation would be helpless and hopeless. The gospel is the free gift of God. He does not love us because we deserve his love; he loves us out of the sheer generosity of his heart.

(v) It is the gospel of *God's eternal purpose*. It was planned before time began. We must never think that once God was stern law and that only since the life and death of Jesus, he has been forgiving love. From the beginning of time God's love has been searching for men, and his grace and forgiveness have been offered to them. Love is the essence of the eternal nature of God.

(vi) It is the gospel of *life and immortality*. It is Paul's conviction that Christ Jesus brought life and incorruption to light. The ancient world feared death; or, if it did not fear it, regarded it as extinction. It was the message of Jesus that death was the way to life, and that so far from separating men from God, it brought men into his nearer presence.

(vii) It is the gospel of *service*. It was this gospel which made Paul a herald, an apostle and a teacher of the faith. It did not leave him comfortably feeling that now his own soul was saved and he did not need to worry any more. It laid on him the inescapable task of wearing himself out in the service of God and of his fellow-men. This gospel laid three necessities on Paul.

(*a*) It made him a herald. The word is *kērux*, which has three main lines of meaning, each with something to suggest about our Christian duty. The *kērux* was the herald who brought the announcement from the king. The *kērux* was the emissary when two armies were opposed to each other, who brought the terms of or the request for truce and peace. The *kērux* was the man whom an auctioneer or a merchantman employed to shout his wares and invite people to come and buy. So the Christian is to be the man who brings the message to his fellow-men; the man who brings men into peace with God; the man who calls on his fellow-men to accept the rich offer which God is making to them.

(*b*) It made him an *apostle*, *apostolos*, literally *one who is sent out*. The word can mean an *envoy* or an *ambassador*. The *apostolos* did not speak for himself, but for him who sent him. He did not come in his own authority, but in the authority of him who sent him. The Christian is the ambassador of

Christ, come to speak for him and to represent him to men.

(*c*) It made him a *teacher*. There is a very real sense in which the teaching task of the Christian and of the Church is the most important of all. Certainly the task of the teacher is very much harder than the task of the evangelist. The evangelist's task is to appeal to men and confront them with the love of God. In a moment of vivid emotion, a man may respond to that summons. But a long road remains. He must learn the meaning and discipline of the Christian life. The foundations have been laid but the edifice has still to be raised. The flame of evangelism has to be followed by the steady glow of Christian teaching. It may well be that people drift away from the Church, after their first decision, for the simple, yet fundamental, reason that they have not been taught into the meaning of the Christian faith.

Herald, ambassador, teacher—here is the threefold function of the Christian who would serve his Lord and his Church.

(viii) It is the gospel of *Christ Jesus*. It was full displayed through his *appearance*. The word Paul uses for *appearance* is one with a great history. It is *epiphaneia,* a word which the Jews repeatedly used of the great saving manifestations of God in the terrible days of the Maccabaean struggles, when the enemies of Israel were deliberately seeking to obliterate him.

In the days of Onias the High Priest there came a certain Heliodorus to plunder the Temple treasury at Jerusalem. Neither prayers nor entreaties would stop him carrying out this sacrilege. And, so the story runs, as Heliodorus was about to set hands on the treasury, "the Lord of Spirits and the Prince of Power caused a great *epiphaneia*. . . . For there appeared unto them an horse with a terrible rider upon him . . . and he ran fiercely and smote at Heliodorus with his forefeet. . . . And Heliodorus fell suddenly to the ground and was compassed with great darkness" (2 *Maccabees* 3: 24–30). What exactly happened we may never know; but in Israel's hour of need there came this tremendous *epiphaneia* of God. When Judas Maccabaeus and his little army were confronted with the might of Nicanor, they prayed: "O Lord, who didst send thine angel in the time of Hezekiah king of Judaea, and didst slay in the host of Sennacherib an hundred fourscore and five thousand (cp. 2 *Kings* 19: 35, 36), wherefore now also, O Lord of Heaven, send a good angel before us for a fear and a dread unto them; and through the might of thine arm let those be stricken with terror, that come against thy holy people to blaspheme." And then the story goes on: "Then Nicanor and they that were with him came forward with trumpets and with songs. But Judas and his company encountered the enemy with invocation and prayer. So that, fighting with their hands and praying unto God with their hearts, they slew no less than thirty and five thousand men; for through the *epiphaneia* of God they were greatly cheered" (2 *Maccabees* 15: 22–27). Once again we do not know exactly what happened; but God made a great and saving appearance for his people. To the Jew *epiphaneia* denoted a rescuing intervention of God.

To the Greek this was an equally great word. The accession of the Emperor to his throne was called his *epiphaneia*. It was his manifestation. Every Emperor came to the throne with high hopes; his coming was hailed as the dawn of a new and precious day, and of great blessings to come.

The gospel was full displayed with the *epiphaneia* of Jesus; the very word shows that he was God's great, rescuing intervention and manifestation into the world.

TRUST HUMAN AND DIVINE

2 *Timothy* 1: 12–14

And that is the reason why I am going through these things I am going through. But I am not ashamed, for I know him in whom my belief is fixed, and I am quite certain that he is able to keep safe what I have entrusted to him until the last day comes. Hold fast the pattern of health-giving words you have received from me, never slackening in that faith and love which are in Christ Jesus. Guard the fine trust that has been given to you through the Holy Spirit who dwells in you.

THIS passage uses a very vivid Greek word in a most suggestive double way. Paul talks of that which he has entrusted to God; and he urges Timothy to safeguard the trust God has reposed in him. In both cases the word is *parathēkē*, which means *a deposit committed to someone's trust.* A man might deposit something with a friend to be kept for his children or his loved ones; he might deposit his valuables in a temple for safe keeping, for the temples were the banks of the ancient world. In each case the thing deposited was a *parathēkē*. In the ancient world there was no more sacred duty than the safe-guarding of such a deposit and the returning of it when in due time it was claimed.

There was a famous Greek story which told just how sacred such a trust was (*Herodotus* 6: 89; Juvenal: *Satires*, 13: 199–208). The Spartans were famous for their strict honour and honesty. A certain man of Miletus came to a certain Glaucus of Sparta. He said that he had heard such great reports of the honesty of the Spartans that he had turned half his possessions into money and wished to deposit that money with Glaucus, until he or his heirs should claim it again. Certain symbols were given and received which would identify the rightful claimant when he should make his claim. The years passed on; the man of Miletus died; his sons came to Sparta to see Glaucus, produced the identifying tallies and asked for the return of the deposited money. But Glaucus claimed that he had no memory of ever receiving it. The sons from Miletus went sorrowfully away; but Glaucus went to the famous oracle at Delphi to see whether he should admit the trust or, as Greek law entitled him to do, should swear that he knew nothing about it. The oracle answered:

> "Best for the present it were, O Glaucus, to do as thou wishest,
>   Swearing an oath to prevail, and so to make prize of the money.
>   Swear then—death is the lot even of those who never swear falsely.

Yet hath the Oath-god a son who is nameless, footless and
   handless;
Mighty in strength he approaches to vengeance, and whelms in
   destruction
All who belong to the race, or the house of the man who is
   perjured.
But oath-keeping men leave behind them a flourishing off-
   spring."

Glaucus understood; the oracle was telling him that if he
wished for momentary profit, he should deny the trust, but
such a denial would inevitably bring eternal loss. He
besought the oracle to pardon his question; but the answer
was that to have tempted the god was as bad as to have done
the deed. He sent for the sons of the man of Miletus and
restored the money. Herodotus goes on: "Glaucus at this
present time has not a single descendant; nor is there any
family known as his; root and branch has he been removed
from Sparta. It is a good thing therefore, when a pledge has
been left with one, not even in thought to doubt about
restoring it." To the Greeks a *parathēkē* was completely sacred.

Paul says that he has made his deposit with God. He
means that he has entrusted both his work and his life to him.
It might seem that he had been cut off in mid-career; that
he should end as a criminal in a Roman gaol might seem the
undoing of all his work. But he had sowed his seed and
preached his gospel, and the result he left in the hands of God.
Paul had entrusted his life to God; and he was sure that in
life and in death he was safe. Why was he so sure? Because
he knew *whom* he had believed in. We must always remember
that Paul does not say that he knew *what* he had believed.
His certainty did not come from the intellectual knowledge of
a creed or a theology; it came from a personal knowledge of
God. He knew God personally and intimately; he knew what
he was like in love and in power; and to Paul it was
inconceivable that he should fail him. If we have worked
honestly and done the best that we can, we can leave the result
to God, however meagre that work may seem to us. With

him in this or any other world life is safe, for nothing can separate us from his love in Christ Jesus our Lord.

TRUST HUMAN AND DIVINE

2 Timothy 1: 12–14 (*continued*)

BUT there is another side to this matter of trust; there is another *parathēkē*. Paul urges Timothy to safeguard and keep inviolate the trust God has reposed in him. Not only do we put our trust in God; he also puts his trust in us. The idea of God's dependence on men is never far from New Testament thought. When God wants something done, he has to find a man to do it. If he wants a child taught, a message brought, a sermon preached, a wanderer found, a sorrowing one comforted, a sick one healed, he has to find some instrument to do his work.

The trust that God had particularly reposed in Timothy was the oversight and the edification of the Church. If Timothy was truly to discharge that trust, he had to do certain things.

(i) He had to hold fast to *the pattern of health-giving words*. That is to say, he had to see to it that Christian belief was maintained in all its purity and that false and misleading ideas were not allowed to enter in. That is not to say that in the Christian Church there must be no new thought and no development in doctrine and belief; but it does mean to say that there are certain great Christian verities which must always be preserved intact. And it may well be that the one Christian truth which must for ever stand is summed up in the creed of the early Church, "Jesus Christ is Lord" (*Philippians* 2: 11). Any theology which seeks to remove Christ from the topmost niche or take from him his unique place in the scheme of revelation and salvation is necessarily wrong. The Christian Church must ever be restating its faith— but the faith restated must be faith in Christ.

(ii) He must never slacken in *faith*. Faith here has two ideas at its heart. (*a*) It has the idea of *fidelity*. The Christian leader must be for ever true and loyal to Jesus Christ. He must never be ashamed to show whose he is and whom he serves. Fidelity is the oldest and the most essential virtue in the world. (*b*) But faith also has in it the idea of *hope*. The Christian must never lose his confidence in God; he must never despair. As A. H. Clough wrote:

> "Say not, 'The struggle naught availeth;
>   The labour and the wounds are vain;
> The enemy faints not, nor faileth,
>   And as things have been they remain.'
>
> For while the tired waves, vainly breaking,
>   Seem here no painful inch to gain,
> Far back, through creeks and inlets making,
>   Comes silent, flooding in, the main."

There must be no pessimism, either for himself or for the world, in the heart of the Christian.

(iii) He must never slacken in *love*. To love men is to see them as God sees them. It is to refuse ever to do anything but seek their highest good. It is to meet bitterness with forgiveness; it is to meet hatred with love; it is to meet indifference with a flaming passion which cannot be quenched. Christian love insistently seeks to love men as God loves them and as he has first loved us.

THE FAITHLESS MANY AND
THE FAITHFUL ONE

2 *Timothy* 1: 15–18

You know this, that as a whole the people who live in Asia deserted me, and among the deserters are Phygelus and Hermogenes. May the Lord give mercy to the family of Onesiphorus, because he

often refreshed me, and was not ashamed of my chain. So far
from that, when he arrived in Rome he eagerly sought me out and
found me—may the Lord grant to him mercy from the Lord on
that day—and you know better than I do the many services he
rendered in Ephesus.

HERE is a passage in which pathos and joy are combined. In
the end the same thing happened to Paul as happened to
Jesus, his Master. His friends forsook him and fled. In the
New Testament *Asia* is not the continent of Asia, but the
Roman province which consisted of the western part of Asia
Minor. Its capital was the city of Ephesus. When Paul was
imprisoned his friends abandoned him—most likely out of
fear. The Romans would never have proceeded against him on
a purely religious charge; the Jews must have persuaded them
that he was a dangerous troublemaker and disturber of the
public peace. There can be no doubt that in the end Paul
would be held on a political charge. To be a friend of a man
like that was dangerous; and in his hour of need his friends
from Asia abandoned him because they were afraid for their
own safety.

But however others might desert, one man was loyal to the
end. His name was Onesiphorus, which means *profitable*.
P. N. Harrison draws a vivid picture of Onesiphorus's search
for Paul in Rome: "We seem to catch glimpses of one
purposeful face in a drifting crowd, and follow with
quickening interest this stranger from the far coasts of the
Aegean, as he threads the maze of unfamiliar streets,
knocking at many doors, following up every clue, warned
of the risks he is taking but not to be turned from his
quest; till in some obscure prison-house a known voice
greets him, and he discovers Paul chained to a Roman
soldier. Having once found his way Onesiphorus is not content
with a single visit, but, true to his name, proves unwearied
in his ministrations. Others have flinched from the menace
and ignominy of that chain; but this visitor counts it the
supreme privilege of his life to share with such a criminal

the reproach of the Cross. One series of turnings in the vast labyrinth (of the streets of Rome) he comes to know as if it were his own Ephesus." There is no doubt that, when Onesiphorus sought out Paul and came to see him again and again, he took his life in his hands. It was dangerous to keep asking where a certain criminal could be found; it was dangerous to visit him; it was still more dangerous to keep on visiting him; but that is what Onesiphorus did.

Again and again the Bible brings us face to face with a question which is real for every one of us. Again and again it introduces and dismisses a man from the stage of history with a single sentence. Hermogenes and Phygelus—we know nothing whatever of them beyond their names and the fact that they were traitors to Paul. Onesiphorus—we know nothing of him except that in his loyalty to Paul he risked—and perhaps lost—his life. Hermogenes and Phygelus go down to history branded as deserters; Onesiphorus goes down to history as the friend who stuck closer than a brother. If we were to be described in one sentence, what would it be? Would it be the verdict on a traitor, or the verdict on a disciple who was true?

Before we leave this passage we must note that in one particular connection it is a storm centre. Each one must form his own opinion, but there are many who feel that the implication is that Onesiphorus is dead. It is for his family that Paul first prays. Now if he was dead, this passage shows us Paul praying for the dead, for it shows him praying that Onesiphorus may find mercy on the last day.

Prayers for the dead are a much-disputed problem which we do not intend to discuss here. But one thing we can say—to the Jews prayers for the dead were by no means unknown. In the days of the Maccabaean wars there was a battle between the troops of Judas Maccabaeus and the army of Gorgias, the governor of Idumaea, which ended in a victory for Judas Maccabaeus. After the battle the Jews were gathering the bodies of those who had fallen in battle. On each one of them they found "things consecrated to the idols of the

Jamnites, which is forbidden the Jews by the law." What is meant is that the dead Jewish soldiers were wearing heathen amulets in a superstitious attempt to protect their lives. The story goes on to say that every man who had been slain was wearing such an amulet and it was because of this that he was in fact slain. Seeing this, Judas and all the people prayed that the sin of these men "might be wholly put out of remembrance." Judas then collected money and made a sin-offering for those who had fallen, because they believed that, since there was a resurrection, it was not superfluous "to pray and offer sacrifices for the dead." The story ends with the saying of Judas Maccabaeus that "it was an holy and good thing to pray for the dead. Whereupon he made a reconciliation for the dead, that they might be delivered from sin" (2 *Maccabees* 12: 39–45).

It is clear that Paul was brought up in a way of belief which saw in prayers for the dead, not a hateful, but a lovely thing. This is a subject on which there has been long and bitter dispute; but this one thing we can and must say—if we love a person with all our hearts, and if the remembrance of that person is never absent from our minds and memories, then, whatever the intellect of the theologian may say about it, the instinct of the heart is to remember such a one in prayer, whether he is in this or in any other world.

THE CHAIN OF TEACHING

2 *Timothy* 2: 1, 2

> As for you, my child, find your strength in the grace which is in Christ Jesus; and entrust the things which you have heard from me, and which are confirmed by many witnesses, to faithful men who will be competent to teach others too.

HERE we have in outline two things—the reception and the transmission of the Christian faith.

(i) The reception of the faith is founded on two things. It is founded on hearing. It was from Paul that Timothy heard the truth of the Christian faith. But the words he heard were confirmed by the witness of many who were prepared to say: "These words are true—and I know it, because I have found it so in my own life." It may be that there are many of us who have not the gift of expression, and who can neither teach nor expound the Christian faith. But even he or she who has not the gift of teaching is able to witness to the living power of the gospel.

(ii) It is not only a privilege to receive the Christian faith; it is a duty to transmit it. Every Christian must look on himself as a link between two generations. E. K. Simpson writes on this passage: "The torch of heavenly light must be transmitted unquenched from one generation to another, and Timothy must count himself an intermediary between apostolic and later ages."

(iii) The faith is to be transmitted to faithful men who in their turn will teach it to others. The Christian Church is dependent on an unbroken chain of teachers. When Clement was writing to the Church at Corinth, he sketched that chain. "Our apostles appointed the aforesaid persons (that is, the elders) and afterwards they provided a continuance, that, if these should fall asleep, other approved men should succeed to their ministry." The teacher is a link in the living chain which stretches unbroken from this present moment back to Jesus Christ.

These teachers are to be *faithful* men. The Greek for faithful, *pistos*, is a word with a rich variety of closely connected meanings. A man who is a *pistos* is a man who is *believing*, a man who is *loyal,* a man who is *reliable*. All these meanings are there. Falconer said that these believing men are such "that they will yield neither to persecution nor to error." The teacher's heart must be so stayed on Christ that no threat of danger will lure him from the path of loyalty and no seduction of false teaching cause him to stray from the straight path of the truth. He must be steadfast alike in life and in thought.

THE SOLDIER OF CHRIST

2 Timothy 2: 3, 4

Accept your share in suffering like a fine soldier of Christ Jesus. No soldier who is on active service entangles himself in ordinary civilian business; he lays aside such things, so that by good service he may please the commander who has enrolled him in his army.

THE picture of man as a soldier and life as a campaign is one which the Romans and the Greeks knew well. "To live," said Seneca, "is to be a soldier" (Seneca: *Epistles* 96: 5). "The life of every man," said Epictetus, "is a kind of campaign, and a campaign which is long and varied" (Epictetus: *Discourses,* 3, 24, 34). Paul took this picture and applied it to all Christians, but specially to the leaders and outstanding servants of the Church. He urges Timothy to fight a fine campaign (1 *Timothy* 1: 18). He calls Archippus, in whose house a Church met, our fellow soldier (*Philemon* 2). He calls Epaphroditus, the messenger of the Philippian Church, "my fellow soldier", (*Philippians* 2: 25). Clearly Paul saw in the life of the soldier a picture of the life of the Christian. What then were the qualities of the soldier which Paul would have repeated in the Christian life?

(i) The soldier's service must be a *concentrated service.* Once a man has enlisted on a campaign he can no longer involve himself in the ordinary daily business of life and living; he must concentrate on his service as a soldier. The Roman code of Theodosius said: "We forbid men engaged on military service to engage in civilian occupations." A soldier is a soldier and nothing else; the Christian must concentrate on his Christianity. That does not mean that he must engage on no worldly task or business. He must still live in this world, and he must still make a living; but it does mean that he must use whatever task he is engaged upon to demonstrate his Christianity.

(ii) The soldier is conditioned to *obedience.* The early

training of a soldier is designed to make him unquestioningly obey the word of command. There may come a time when such instinctive obedience will save his life and the lives of others. There is a sense in which it is no part of the soldier's duty "to know the reason why." Involved as he is in the midst of the battle, he cannot see the over-all picture. The decisions he must leave to the commander who sees the whole field. The first Christian duty is obedience to the voice of God, and acceptance even of that which he cannot understand.

(iii) The soldier is conditioned to *sacrifice*. A. J. Gossip tells how, as a chaplain in the 1914–18 war, he was going up the line for the first time. War and blood, and wounds and death were new to him. On his way he saw by the roadside, left behind after the battle, the body of a young kilted Highlander. Oddly, perhaps, there flashed into his mind the words of Christ: "This is my body broken for you." The Christian must ever be ready to sacrifice himself, his wishes and his fortune, for God and for his fellow-men.

(iv) The soldier is conditioned to *loyalty*. When the Roman soldier joined the army he took the *sacramentum,* the oath of loyalty to his emperor. Someone records a conversation between Marshal Foch and an officer in the 1914–18 war. "You must not retire," said Foch, "you must hold on at all costs." "Then," said the officer aghast, "that means we must all die." And Foch answered: "Precisely!" The soldier's supreme virtue is that he is faithful unto death. The Christian too must be loyal to Jesus Christ, through all the chances and the changes of life, down even to the gates of death.

THE ATHLETE OF CHRIST

2 *Timothy* 2: 5

And if anyone engages in an athletic contest, he does not win the crown unless he observes the rules of the game.

PAUL has just used the picture of the soldier to represent the Christian, and now he uses two other pictures—those of the athlete and of the toiling husbandman. He uses the same three pictures close together in 1 *Corinthians* 9: 6, 7, 24–27.

Paul says that the athlete does not win the crown of victory unless he observes the rules of the contest. There is a very interesting point in the Greek here which is difficult to bring out in translation. The Authorized Version speaks of *striving lawfully*. The Greek is *athlein nomimōs*. In fact that is the Greek phrase which was used by the later writers to describe a *professional* as opposed to an *amateur* athlete. The man who strove *nomimōs* was the man who concentrated everything on his struggle. His struggle was not just a spare-time thing, as it might be for an amateur; it was a whole-time dedication of his life to excellence in the contest which he had chosen. Here then we have the same idea as in Paul's picture of the Christian as a soldier. A Christian's life must be concentrated upon his Christianity just as a professional athlete's life is concentrated upon his chosen contest. The spare-time Christian is a contradiction in terms; a man's whole life should be an endeavour to live out his Christianity. What then are the characteristics of the athlete which are in Paul's mind?

(i) The athlete is a man under *discipline* and *self-denial*. He must keep to his schedule of training and let nothing interfere with it. There will be days when he would like to drop his training and relax his discipline; but he must not do so. There will be pleasures and indulgences he would like to allow himself; but he must refuse them. The athlete who would excel knows that he must let nothing interfere with that standard of physical fitness which he has set himself. There must be discipline in the Christian life. There are times when the easy way is very attractive; there are times when the right thing is the hard thing; there are times when we are tempted to relax our standards. The Christian must train himself never to relax in the life-long attempt to make his soul pure and strong.

(ii) The athlete is a man who *observes the rules*. After the discipline and the rules of the training, there come the contest and the rules of the contest. An athlete cannot win unless he plays the game. The Christian, too, is often brought into contest with his fellow-men. He must defend his faith; he must seek to convince and to persuade; he will have to argue and to debate. He must do so by the Christian rules. No matter how hot the argument, he must never forget his courtesy. He must never be anything else but honest about his own position and fair to that of his opponent. The *odium theologicum*, the hatred of theologians, has become a byword. There is often no bitterness like religious bitterness. But the real Christian knows that the supreme rule of the Christian life is love, and he will carry that love into every debate in which he is engaged.

THE TOILER OF CHRIST

2 *Timothy* 2: 6, 7

It is the toiling husbandman who must be first to receive his share of the fruits. Think of what I am saying, for the Lord will give you understanding in all things.

To represent the Christian life Paul has used the picture of the soldier and of the athlete, and now he uses the picture of the farmer. It is not the lazy husbandman, but the husbandman who toils, who must be the first to receive the share of the fruits of the harvest. What then are the characteristics of the husbandman which Paul would wish to see in the life of the Christian?

(i) Often the husbandman must be content, first, to work, and, then, to wait. More than any other workman, he has to learn that there are no such things as quick results. The Christian too must learn to work and to wait. Often he must sow the good seed of the word into the hearts and minds of his hearers and see no immediate result. A teacher has often to teach, and see no difference in those he teaches. A parent has often to seek to train and guide, and see no difference in the child. It is only when the years go by that the result is seen; for it often happens that when that same young person has grown to manhood, he or she is faced with some overmastering temptation or some terrible decision or some intolerable effort, and back into his mind comes some word of God or some flash of remembered teaching; and the teaching, the guidance, the discipline bears fruit, and brings honour where without it there would have been dishonour, salvation where without it there would have been ruin. The farmer has learned to wait with patience, and so must the Christian teacher and the Christian parent.

(ii) One special thing characterizes the husbandman—he must be prepared to work at any hour. In harvest time we can see farmers at work in their fields so long as the last streak of light is left; they know no hours. Neither must the Christian. The trouble with so much Christianity is that it is spasmodic. But from dawn to sunset the Christian must be for ever at his task of being a Christian.

One thing remains in all three pictures. The soldier is upheld by the thought of final victory. The athlete is upheld by the vision of the crown. The husbandman is upheld by the hope of the harvest. Each submits to the discipline and the toil for the sake of the glory which shall be. It is so with the Christian. The Christian struggle is not without a goal; it is always going somewhere. The Christian can be certain that after the effort of the Christian life, there comes the joy of heaven; and the greater the struggle, the greater the joy.

THE ESSENTIAL MEMORY

2 Timothy 2: 8–10

> Remember Jesus Christ, risen from the dead, born of the seed of David, as I preached the gospel to you; that gospel for which I suffer, even to the length of fetters, on the charge of being a criminal.

But though I am fettered, the word of God is not bound. Therefore I endure everything for the sake of God's chosen ones, that they too may obtain the salvation which is in Christ Jesus, with eternal glory.

RIGHT from the beginning of this letter Paul has been trying to inspire Timothy to his task. He has reminded him of his own belief in him and of the godly parentage from which he has come; he has shown him the picture of the Christian soldier, the Christian athlete and the Christian toiler. And now he comes to the greatest appeal of all—*Remember Jesus Christ*. Falconer calls these words: "The heart of the Pauline gospel." Even if every other appeal to Timothy's gallantry should fail, surely the memory of Jesus Christ cannot. In the words which follow, Paul is really urging Timothy to remember three things.

(i) Remember Jesus Christ *risen from the dead*. The tense of the Greek does not imply one definite act in time, but a continued state which lasts for ever. Paul is not so much saying to Timothy: "Remember the actual resurrection of Jesus"; but rather: "Remember your risen and ever-present Lord." Here is the great Christian inspiration. We do not depend on a memory, however great. We enjoy the power of a presence. When a Christian is summoned to a great task that he cannot but feel is beyond him, he must go to it in the certainty that he does not go alone, but that there is with him for ever the presence and the power of his risen Lord. When fears threaten, when doubts assail, when inadequacy depresses, remember the presence of the risen Lord.

(ii) Remember Jesus Christ *born of the seed of David*. This is the other side of the question. "Remember," says Paul to Timothy, "the manhood of the Master." We do not remember one who is only a spiritual presence; we remember one who trod this road, and lived this life, and faced this struggle, and who therefore knows what we are going through. We have with us the presence not only of the glorified Christ, but also of the Christ who knew the desperate struggle of being a man and followed to the bitter end the will of God.

(iii) Remember the *gospel*, the good news. Even when the gospel demands much, even when it leads to an effort which seems to be beyond human ability and to a future which seems dark with every kind of threat, remember that it is good news, and remember that the world is waiting for it. However hard the task the gospel offers, that same gospel is the message of liberation from sin and victory over circumstances for us and for all mankind.

So Paul kindles Timothy to heroism by calling upon him to remember Jesus Christ, to remember the continual presence of the risen Lord, to remember the sympathy which comes from the manhood of the Master, to remember the glory of the gospel for himself and for the world which has never heard it and is waiting for it.

THE CRIMINAL OF CHRIST

2 Timothy 2: 8–10 (*continued*)

WHEN Paul wrote these words he was in a Roman prison, bound by a chain. This was literally true, for all the time he was in prison night and day he would be chained to the arm of a Roman soldier. Rome took no risks that her prisoners should escape.

Paul was in prison on the charge of being a criminal. It seems strange that even a hostile government should be able to regard a Christian, and especially Paul, as a criminal. There were two possible ways in which Paul might appear a criminal to the Roman government.

First, Rome had an empire which was almost co-extensive with the then known world. It was obvious that such an empire was subject to stresses and to strains. The peace had to be kept and every possible centre of disaffection had to be eliminated. One of the things about which Rome was very particular was the formation of associations. In the ancient world there were many associations. There were, for instance, dinner clubs who met at stated intervals. There were what we would call friendly societies designed for charity for the dependants of members who had died. There were burial societies to see that their members were decently buried. But so particular were the Roman authorities about associations that even these humble and harmless societies had to receive special permission from the emperor before they were allowed to meet. Now the Christians were in effect an illegal association; and that is one reason why Paul, as a leader of such an association, might well be in the very serious position of being a political criminal.

Second, the first persecution of the Christians was intimately connected with one of the greatest disasters which ever befell the city of Rome. On 19 July A.D. 64 the great fire broke out. It burned for six days and seven nights and devastated the city. The most sacred shrines and the most famous buildings perished in the flames. But worse—the homes of the common people were destroyed. By far the greater part of the population lived in great tenements built largely of wood and they went up like tinder. People were killed and injured; they lost their nearest and dearest; they were left homeless and destitute. The population of Rome was reduced to what someone has called "a vast brotherhood of hopeless wretchedness."

It was believed that Nero, the emperor, himself was responsible for the fire. It was said that he had watched the fire from the Tower of Maecenas and declared himself charmed with "the flower and loveliness of the flames." It was said that when the fire showed signs of dying down men were seen rekindling it with burning brands, and that these men were the servants of Nero. Nero had a passion for building, and it was said that he had deliberately fired the city so that from the ruins he might build a new and nobler Rome. Whether the story was true or not—the chances are that it was—one thing was certain. Nothing would kill the rumour. The destitute citizens of Rome were sure that Nero had been responsible.

There was only one thing for the Roman government to do; they must find a scapegoat. And a scapegoat was found. Let Tacitus, the Roman historian, tell how it was done: "But all human efforts, all the lavish gifts of the emperor, and the propitiations of the gods did not banish the sinister belief that the conflagration was the result of an order. Consequently, to get rid of the report, Nero fastened the guilt and inflicted the most exquisite tortures on a class hated for their abominations, called Christians by the populace" (Tacitus: *Annals*, 15: 44). Obviously slanders were already circulating regarding the Christians. No doubt the influential Jews were responsible. And the hated Christians were saddled with the blame for the disastrous fire of Rome. It was from that event that the first great persecution sprang. Paul was a Christian. More, he was the great leader of the Christians. And it may well be that part of the charge against Paul was that he was one of those responsible for the fire of Rome and the resulting misery of the populace.

So, then, Paul was in prison as a criminal, a political prisoner, member of an illegal association and leader of that hated sect of incendiaries, on whom Nero had fastened the blame for the destruction of Rome. It can easily be seen how helpless Paul was in face of charges like that.

FREE YET IN FETTERS BOUND

2 Timothy 2: 8–10 (*continued*)

EVEN though he was in prison on charges which made release impossible, Paul was not dismayed and was very far from despair. He had two great uplifting thoughts.

(i) He was certain that, though he might be bound, nothing could bind the word of God. Andrew Melville was one of the earliest heralds of the Scottish Reformation. One day the Regent Morton sent for him and denounced his writings. "There will never be quietness in this country," he said, "till half a dozen of you be hanged or banished the country." "Tush! sir," answered Melville, "threaten your courtiers in that fashion. It is the same to me whether I rot in the air or in the ground. The earth is the Lord's; my fatherland is wherever well-doing is. I have been ready to give my life when it was not half as well worn, at the pleasure of my God. I lived out of your country ten years as well as in it. Yet God be glorified, it will not lie in your power to hang nor exile his truth!"

You can exile a man, but you cannot exile the truth. You can imprison a preacher, but you cannot imprison the word he preaches. The message is always greater than the man; the truth is always mightier than the bearer. Paul was quite certain that the Roman government could never find a prison which could contain the word of God. And it is one of the facts of history that if human effort could have obliterated Christianity, it would have perished long ago; but men cannot kill that which is immortal.

(ii) Paul was certain that what he was going through would in the end be a help to other people. His suffering was not pointless and profitless. The blood of the martyrs has ever been the seed of the Church; and the lighting of the pyre where Christians were burned has always been the lighting of a fire which could never be put out. When anyone has to suffer for his Christianity, let him remember that his suffering makes the road easier for someone else who is still to come. In suffering we bear our own small portion of the weight of the Cross of Christ and do our own small part in the bringing of God's salvation to men.

THE SONG OF THE MARTYR

2 *Timothy* 2: 11–13

This is a saying which can be relied upon:

> If we die with him,
> > we shall also live with him.

> If we endure,
>> we shall also reign with him.
> If we deny him,
>> he too will deny us.
> If we are faithless,
>> he remains faithful
> For he cannot deny himself.

THIS is a peculiarly precious passage because in it is enshrined one of the first hymns of the Christian Church. In the days of persecution the Christian Church put its faith into song. It may be that this is only a fragment of a longer hymn. *Polycarp* (5: 2) seems to give us a little more of it, when he writes: "If we please Christ in the present world, we shall inherit the world to come; as he has promised to raise us from the dead, and has said:

> 'If we walk worthily of him,
>> So shall we reign with him'."

There are two possible interpretations of the first two lines— "If we die with him, we shall also live with him." There are those who wish to take these lines as a reference to baptism. In *Romans* 6 baptism is likened to dying and rising with Christ. "We were buried therefore with him by baptism into death, so that as Christ was raised from the dead by the glory of the Father, we too might walk in newness of life." "But if we have died with Christ, we believe that we shall also live with him" (*Romans* 6: 4, 8). No doubt the language is the same; but the thought of baptism is quite irrelevant here; it is the thought of martyrdom that is in Paul's mind. Luther, in a great phrase, said: "*Ecclesia haeres crucis est*," "The Church is the heir of the Cross." The Christian inherits Christ's Cross, but he also inherits Christ's Resurrection. He is partner both in the shame and in the glory of his Lord.

The hymn goes on: "If we endure, we shall also reign with him." It is he who endures to the end who will be saved. Without the Cross there cannot be the Crown.

Then comes the other side of the matter: "If we deny him, he too will deny us." That is what Jesus himself said: "So every one who acknowledges me before men, I also will acknowledge before my Father who is in heaven; but whoever denies me before men, I also will deny before my Father who is in heaven" (*Matthew* 10: 32, 33). Jesus Christ cannot vouch in eternity for a man who has refused to have anything to do with him in time; but he is for ever true to the man who, however much he has failed, has tried to be true to him.

These things are so because they are part of the very nature of God. A man may deny himself, but God cannot. "God is not man that he should lie, or a son of man that he should repent" (*Numbers* 23: 19). God will never fail the man who has tried to be true to him, but not even he can help the man who has refused to have anything to do with him.

Long ago Tertullian said: "The man who is afraid to suffer cannot belong to him who suffered" (Tertullian: *De Fuga,* 14). Jesus died to be true to the will of God; and the Christian must follow that same will, whatever light may shine or shadow fall.

THE DANGER OF WORDS

2 *Timothy* 2: 14

Remind your people of these things; and charge them before the Lord not to engage in battles of words—a thing of no use at all, and a thing which can only result in the undoing of those who listen to it.

ONCE again Paul returns to the inadequacy of words. We must remember that the Pastoral Epistles were written against a background of those Gnostics who produced their long words and their fantastic theories, and tried to make Christianity into a recondite philosophy instead of an adventure of faith.

There is both fascination and peril in words. They can become a substitute for deeds. There are people who are more concerned to talk than to act. If the world's problems could have been solved by discussion, they would have been solved long ago. But words cannot replace deeds. As Charles Kingsley wrote in *A Farewell:*

> "Be good, sweet maid, and let who will be clever;
> Do noble things, not dream them, all day long."

As Philip James Bailey wrote in *Festus:*

> "We live in deeds, not years; in thoughts, not breaths;
> In feelings, not in figures on a dial.
> We should count time by heart-throbs. He most lives
> Who thinks most—feels the noblest—acts the best."

Dr. Johnson was one of the great talkers of all time; John Wesley was one of the great men of action of all time. They knew each other, and Johnson had only one complaint about Wesley: "John Wesley's conversation is good, but he is never at leisure. He is always obliged to go at a certain hour. This is very disagreeable to a man who loves to fold his legs and have his talk out, as I do." But the fact remains that Wesley, the man of action, wrote his name across England in a way in which Johnson, the man of talk, never did.

It is not even true that talk and discussion fully solve intellectual problems. One of the most suggestive things Jesus ever said was: "If any man's will is to do his will, he shall know whether the teaching is from God" (*John* 7: 17). Often understanding comes not by talking, but by doing. In the old Latin phrase, *solvitur ambulando*, the thing will solve itself as you go on. It often happens that the best way to understand the deep things of Christianity is to embark on the unmistakable duties of the Christian life.

There remains one further thing to be said. Too much talk and too much discussion can have two dangerous effects.

First, they may give the impression that Christianity is nothing but a collection of questions for discussion and problems for solution. The discussion circle is a characteristic phenomenon of this age. As G. K. Chesterton once said: "We have asked all the questions which can be asked. It is time we stopped looking for questions, and started looking for answers." In any society the discussion circle must be balanced by the action group.

Second, discussion can be invigorating for those whose approach to the Christian faith is intellectual, for those who have a background of knowledge and of culture, for those who have a real knowledge of, or interest in, theology. But it sometimes happens that a simple-minded person finds himself in a group which is tossing heresies about and propounding unanswerable questions, and his faith, so far from being helped, is upset. It may well be that that is what Paul means when he says that wordy battles can undo those who listen to them. The normal word used for building a person up in the Christian faith, for *edification*, is the same as is used for literally *building a house;* the word which Paul uses here for ruin *(katastrophē)* is what might well be used for the *demolition* of a house. And it may well happen that clever, subtle, speculative, intellectually reckless discussion may have the effect of demolishing, and not building up, the faith of some simple person who happens to become involved in it. As in all things, there is a time to discuss and a time to be silent.

THE WAY OF TRUTH AND THE WAY OF ERROR

2 *Timothy* 2: 15–18

> Put out every effort to present yourself to God as one who has stood the test, as a workman who has no need to be ashamed, as one who rightly handles the word of truth.
>
> Avoid these godless chatterings, for the people who engage in them only progress further and further into ungodliness, and their talk eats its way into the Church like an ulcerous gangrene.
>
> Amongst such people are Hymenaeus and Philetus, who, as far as the truth is concerned, have lost the way, when they say that the resurrection has already happened, and who by such statements are upsetting the faith of some.

PAUL urges Timothy to present himself, amidst the false teachers, as a real teacher of the truth. The word he uses for *to present* is *parastēsai,* which characteristically means *to present oneself for service.* The following words and phrases all develop this idea of usefulness for service.

The Greek for *one who has stood the test* is *dokimos,* which describes anything which has been tested and is fit for service. For instance, it describes gold or silver which has been purified of all alloy in the fire. It is therefore the word for money which is genuine, or, as we would say, *sterling.* It is the word used for a stone which is fit to be fitted into its place in a building. A stone with a flaw in it was marked with a capital A, standing for *adokimastos,* which means *tested and found wanting.* Timothy was to be tested that he might be a fit weapon for the work of Christ, and therefore a workman who had no need to be ashamed.

Further, Timothy is urged in a famous phrase *rightly to divide* the word of truth. The Greek word translated *to divide rightly* is interesting. It is *orthotomein,* which literally means *to cut rightly.* It has many pictures in it. Calvin connected it with a father dividing out the food at a meal and cutting it up so that each member of the family received the right portion. Beza connected it with the cutting up of sacrificial victims so that each part was correctly apportioned to the altar or to the priest. The Greeks themselves used the word in three different connections. They used it for driving a straight road across country, for ploughing a straight furrow across a field, and for the work of a mason in cutting and squaring a stone so that it fitted into its correct place in the structure of the building. So the man who rightly divides the word of truth, drives a straight road through the truth and refuses to be lured down pleasant but irrelevant bypaths; he ploughs a straight furrow across the field of truth; he takes each section of the truth, and fits it into its correct position, as a mason does a stone, allowing no part to usurp an undue place and so knock the whole structure out of balance.

On the other hand, the false teacher engages on what

Paul would call "godless chatterings." Then Paul uses a vivid phrase. The Greeks had a favourite word for making progress *(prokoptein)*. It literally means *to cut down in front;* to remove the obstacles from a road so that straight and uninterrupted progress is possible. Paul says of these senseless talkers that they progress further and further into ungodliness. They progress in reverse. The more they talk, the farther they get from God. Here then is the test. If at the end of our talk, we are closer to one another and to God, then all is well; but if we have erected barriers between one another and have left God more distant, then all is not well. The aim of all Christian discussion and of all Christian action is to bring a man nearer to his fellows and to God.

THE LOST RESURRECTION

2 *Timothy* 2: 15–18 *(continued)*

AMONGST the false teachers Paul numbers especially Hymenaeus and Philetus. Who these men were we do not know. But we get a brief glimpse of their teaching in at least one of its aspects. They said that the resurrection had already happened. This of course does not refer to the Resurrection of Jesus; it refers to the resurrection of the Christian after death. We do know two false views of the resurrection of the Christian which had some influence in the early Church.

(i) It was claimed that the real resurrection of the Christian took place at baptism. It is true that in *Romans* 6 Paul had written vividly about how the Christian dies in the moment of baptism and rises to life anew. There were those who taught that the resurrection happened in that moment of baptism and that it was resurrection to new life in Christ here and now, not after death.

(ii) There were those who taught that the meaning of individual resurrection was nothing more than that a man lived on in his children.

The trouble was that this kind of teaching found an echo in both the Jewish and the Greek side of the Church. On the Jewish side, the Pharisees believed in the resurrection of the body but the Sadducees did not. Any teaching which did away with the conception of life after death would appeal to the Sadducees; the trouble with the Pharisees was that they were wealthy materialists, who had so big a stake in this world that they were not interested in any world to come.

On the Greek side, the trouble was much greater. In the early days of Christianity, the Greeks, generally speaking, believed in immortality but not in the resurrection of the body. The highest belief was that of the Stoics. They believed that God was what might be called fiery spirit. The life in man was a spark of that spirit, a spark of God himself, a *scintilla* of deity. But they believed that when a man died that spark went back to God and was reabsorbed in him. That is a noble belief but it clearly abolishes *personal* survival after death. Further, the Greeks believed that the body was entirely evil. They had their play on words as a watchword: "*Sōma Sēma*," "The body is a tomb." The last thing they desired or believed in was the resurrection of the body; and therefore they, too, were open to receive any teaching about the resurrection which fitted their beliefs.

It is obvious that the Christian does not believe in the resurrection of *this* body. No one could conceive of someone smashed in an accident or dying of cancer reawakening in heaven with the same body. But the Christian does believe in the survival of personal identity; he believes most strenuously that after death you will still be you and I will still be I. Any teaching which removes that certainty of the personal survival of each individual man strikes at the very root of Christian belief.

When Hymenaeus and Philetus and their like taught that the resurrection had already happened, either at the moment of baptism or in a man's children, they were teaching something which Sadducean Jews and philosophic Greeks would be by no means averse to accepting; but they were also teaching something which undermined one of the central beliefs of the Christian faith.

THE FIRM FOUNDATION

2 *Timothy* 2: 19

But the firm foundation of God stands fast with this inscription: "The Lord knows those who are his," and, "Let every one who names the name of the Lord depart from unrighteousness."

IN English we use *foundation* in a double sense. We use it to mean the basis on which a building is erected; and also in the sense of an association, a college, a city which has been *founded* by someone. For instance, we talk about the *foundation* of a house; and we also say that King's College, Cambridge, is a *foundation* of Henry the Sixth. Greek used the word *themelios* in the same two ways; and the *foundation* of God here means the *Church*, the association which he has founded.

Paul goes on to say that the Church has a certain *inscription* on it. The word he uses is *sphragis* whose usual meaning is *seal*. The *sphragis* is the seal which proves genuineness or ownership. The seal on a sack of goods proved that the contents were genuine and had not been interfered with; and it also indicated the ownership and the source of the goods. But *sphragis* had other uses. It was used to denote the *brandmark*, what we would call the *trademark*. Galen, the Greek doctor, speaks of the *sphragis* on a certain phial of eyesalve, meaning the mark which showed what brand of eyesalve the phial contained. Still further, the *sphragis* was the *architect's mark*. Always on a monument or a statue or a building the architect put his mark, to show that he was responsible for its design. The *sphragis* can also be the inscription which indicates the purpose for which a building has been built.

The Church has a *sphragis* which shows at once what it is

designed to be. The sign on the Church Paul gives in two
quotations. But the way in which these two quotations are
made is very illuminating in regard to the manner in which
Paul and the early Church used scripture. The two quotations
are: "The Lord knows those who are his," and "Let every
one who names the name of the Lord depart from unrighteousness." The interesting thing is that neither is a literal
quotation from any part of scripture.

The first is a reminiscence of a saying of Moses to the
rebellious friends and associates of Korah in the wilderness
days. When they gathered themselves together against him,
Moses said: "The Lord will show who is his" (*Numbers* 16: 5).
But that Old Testament text was read in the light of the
saying of Jesus in *Matthew* 7: 22: "Many will say to me in
that day, 'Lord, Lord did we not prophesy in your name,
and cast out demons in your name, and do many mighty
works in your name?' And then will I declare to them, I
never knew you: depart from me you evil-doers." The Old
Testament text is, as it were, retranslated into the words of
Jesus.

The second is another reminiscence of the Korah story.
It was Moses' command to the people: "Depart, I pray you,
from the tents of these wicked men, and touch nothing of
theirs" (*Numbers* 16: 26). But that, too, is read in the light of
the words of Jesus in *Luke* 13: 27, where he says to those who
falsely claim to be his followers: "Depart from me, all you
workers of iniquity."

Two things emerge. The early Christians always read the
Old Testament in the light of the words of Jesus; and they
were not interested in verbal niceties, but to any problem they
brought the general sense of the whole range of scripture. These
are still excellent principles by which to read and use
scripture.

The two texts give us two broad principles about the
Church.

The first tells us that the Church consists of those who
belong to God, who have given themselves to him in such a

way that they no longer possess themselves and the world no longer possesses them, but God possesses them.

The second tells us that the Church consists of those who have departed from unrighteousness. That is not to say that it consists of perfect people. If that were so, there would be no Church. It has been said that the great interest of God is not so much in where a man has reached, as in the direction in which he is facing. And the Church consists of those whose faces are turned to righteousness. They may often fall and the goal may sometimes seem distressingly far away, but their faces are ever set in the right direction.

The Church consists of those who belong to God and have dedicated themselves to the struggle for righteousness.

VESSELS OF HONOUR AND OF DISHONOUR

2 Timothy 2: 20, 21

> In any great house there are not only gold and silver vessels; there are also vessels of wood and earthenware. And some are put to a noble use and some to an ignoble use. If anyone purifies himself from these things, he will be a vessel fit to be put to a noble use, ready for any good work.

THE connection between this passage and the one which immediately precedes it is very practical. Paul had just given a great and high definition of the Church as consisting of those who belong to God and are on the way to righteousness. The obvious rejoinder is: How do you explain the existence of the chattering heretics in the Church? How do you explain the existence of Hymenaeus and Philetus? Paul's reply is that in any great house there are all kinds of utensils; there are things of precious metal and things of base metal; there are things which have a dishonourable use and things which have an honourable use. It must be so in the Church. So long as it is an earthly institution it must be a mixture. So long as it consists of men and women, it must remain a cross-section of humanity. Just as it takes all kinds of people to make a world, so it takes all kinds of people to make the Church.

That is a practical truth which Jesus had stated long before, in the Parable of the Wheat and the Tares (*Matthew* 13: 24–30, 36–43). The point of that parable is that the wheat and the tares grow together, and, in the early stages, are so like each other that it is impossible to separate them. He stated it again in the Parable of the Drag-net (*Matthew* 13: 47, 48). The drag-net gathered *of every kind*. In both parables Jesus teaches that the Church is necessarily a mixture and that human judgment must be suspended, but that God's judgment will in the end make the necessary separations.

Those who criticize the Church because there are imperfect people in it are criticizing it because it is composed of men and women. It is not given to us to judge; judgment belongs to God.

But it is the duty of a Christian to keep himself free from polluting influences. And if he does, his reward is not special honour and special privilege but special service.

Here is the very essence of the Christian faith. A really good man does not regard his goodness as entitling him to special honour; his one desire will be to have more and more work to do, for his work will be his greatest privilege. If he is good, the last thing he will do will be to seek to stand aloof from his fellow-men. He will rather seek to be among them, at their worst, serving God by serving them. His glory will not be in exemption from service; it will be in still more demanding service. No Christian should ever think of fitting himself for honour but always as fitting himself for service.

ADVICE TO A CHRISTIAN LEADER

2 *Timothy* 2: 22–26

Flee from youthful passions; run in pursuit of righteousness in the company of those who call on the Lord from a clean conscience.

Have nothing to do with foolish and stupid arguments, for you know that they only breed quarrels. The servant of the Lord must not fight, rather he must be kindly to all, apt to teach, forbearing, disciplining his opponents by gentleness. It may be that God will enable them to repent, so that they will come to know the truth, and so that they will escape from the snare of the devil, when they are captured alive by God's servant that they may do God's will.

HERE is a passage of most practical advice for the Christian leader and teacher.

He must flee from youthful lusts. Many commentators have made suggestions as to what these youthful lusts are. They are far more than the passions of the flesh. They include that *impatience*, which has never learned to hasten slowly and has still to discover that too much hurry can do far more harm than good; that *self-assertion,* which is intolerant in its opinions and arrogant in its expression of them, and which has not yet learned to see the good in points of view other than its own; that *love of disputation*, which tends to argue long and act little, and which will talk the night away and be left with nothing but a litter of unsolved problems; that *love of novelty*, which tends to condemn a thing simply because it is old and to desire a thing simply because it is new, underrating the value of experience. One thing is to be noted—the faults of youth are the faults of idealism. It is simply the freshness and intensity of the vision which makes youth run into these mistakes. Such faults are matters not for austere condemnation but for sympathetic correction, for every one has a virtue hidden beneath it.

The Christian teacher and leader is to aim at *righteousness,* which means giving both to men and to God their due; at *faith,* which means loyalty and reliability which both come from trust in God; at *love*, which is the utter determination never to seek anything but the highest good of our fellow-men, no matter what they do to us, and which has for ever put away all bitterness and all desire for vengeance; at *peace*, which is the right relationship of loving fellowship with God and with men.

And all these things are to be sought *in the company of those who call upon the Lord*. The Christian must never seek to live detached and aloof from his fellow-men. He must find his strength and his joy in the Christian fellowship. As John Wesley said: "A man must have friends or make friends; for no one ever went to heaven alone."

The Christian leader must not get involved in senseless controversies which are the curse of the Church. In the modern Church Christian arguments are usually doubly senseless, for they are seldom about great matters of life and doctrine and faith, but almost always about unimportant things like teacups and the like. Once a leader is involved in senseless and unchristian controversy, he has forfeited all right to lead.

The Christian leader must be *kindly* to all; even when he has to criticize and point out a fault, it must be done with the gentleness which never seeks to hurt. He must be *apt to teach;* he must not only know the truth, but also be able to communicate it, and he will do that, not so much by talking about it, as by living in such a way that he shows men Christ. He must be *forbearing;* like his Master, if he is reviled, he must not revile again; he must be able to accept insult and injury, slights and humiliations, as Jesus accepted them. There may be greater sins than touchiness, but there is none which does greater damage in the Christian Church. He must discipline his opponents in *gentleness;* his hand like the hand of a surgeon, unerring to find the diseased spot, yet never for a moment causing unnecessary pain. He must love men, not batter them, into submission to the truth.

The last sentence of this passage is in very involved Greek, but it seems to be a hope that God will awaken repentance and the desire for the truth in the hearts of men, so that those who are caught in the snare of the devil may be rescued while their souls are still alive and brought into obedience to the will of God by the work of his servant. It is God who awakes the repentance; it is the Christian leader who opens the door of the Church to the penitent heart.

TIMES OF TERROR

2 *Timothy* 3: 1

> You must realize this—that in the last days difficult times will
> set in.

THE early Church lived in an age when the time was waxing
late; they expected the Second Coming at any moment.
Christianity was cradled in Judaism and very naturally thought
largely in Jewish terms and pictures. Jewish thought had one
basic conception. The Jews divided all time into *this present
age* and *the age to come*. This present age was altogether
evil; and the age to come would be the golden age of God.
In between there was *The Day of the Lord,* a day when God
would personally intervene and shatter the world in order to
remake it. That Day of the Lord was to be preceded by a time
of terror, when evil would gather itself for its final assault and
the world would be shaken to its moral and physical
foundations. It is in terms of these last days that Paul is
thinking in this passage.

He says that in them *difficult* times would set in. *Difficult*
is the Greek word *chalepos*. It is the normal Greek word for
difficult, but it has certain usages which explain its meaning
here. It is used in *Matthew* 8: 28 to describe the two
Gergesene demoniacs who met Jesus among the tombs. They
were violent and dangerous. It is used in Plutarch to describe
what we would call an *ugly* wound. It is used by ancient
writers on astrology to describe what we would call a
threatening conjunction of the heavenly bodies. There is the
idea of menace and of danger in this word. In the last days
there would come times which would menace the very
existence of the Christian Church and of goodness itself, a kind
of last tremendous assault of evil before its final defeat.

In the Jewish pictures of these last terrible times we get
exactly the same kind of picture as we get here. There would
come a kind of terrible flowering of evil, when the moral
foundations seemed to be shaken. In the *Testament of Issachar,*

one of the books written between the Old and the New
Testaments, we get a picture like this:

> "Know ye, therefore, my children, that in the last times
> Your sons will forsake singleness
> And will cleave unto insatiable desire;
> And leaving guilelessness, will draw near to malice;
> And forsaking the commandments of the Lord,
> They will cleave unto Beliar.
> And leaving husbandry,
> They will follow after their own wicked devices,
> And they shall be dispersed among the Gentiles,
> And shall serve their enemies."
>
>   *(Testament of Issachar,* 6: 1, 2).

In 2 *Baruch* we get an even more vivid picture of the
moral chaos of these last times:

> "And honour shall be turned into shame,
> And strength humiliated into contempt,
> And probity destroyed,
> And beauty shall become ugliness . . .
> And envy shall rise in those who had not thought aught of
>   themselves,
> And passion shall seize him that is peaceful,
> And many shall be stirred up in anger to injure many;
> And they shall rouse up armies in order to shed blood,
> And in the end they shall perish together with them."
>
>   (2 *Baruch* 27).

In this picture which Paul draws he is thinking in terms
familiar to the Jews. There was to be a final show-down
with the forces of evil.

Nowadays we have to restate these old pictures in modern
terms. They were never meant to be anything else but
visions; we do violence to Jewish and to early Christian
thought if we take them with a crude literalness. But they do
enshrine the permanent truth that some time there must come
the consummation when evil meets God in head-on collision
and there comes the final triumph of God.

THE QUALITIES OF GODLESSNESS

2 *Timothy* 3 : 2–5

> For men will live a life that is centred in self; they will be lovers
> of money, braggarts, arrogant, lovers of insult, disobedient to their
> parents, thankless, regardless even of the ultimate decencies of life,
> without human affection, implacable in hatred, revelling in slander,
> ungovernable in their passions, savage, not knowing what the love
> of good is, treacherous, headlong in word and action, inflated with
> pride, lovers of pleasure rather than lovers of God. They will
> maintain the outward form of religion, but they will deny its power.
> Avoid such people.

HERE is one of the most terrible pictures in the New
Testament of what a godless world would be like, with the
terrible qualities of godlessness set out in a ghastly series. Let
us look at them one by one.

It is no accident that the first of these qualities will be *a
life that is centred in self*. The adjective used is *philautos*, which
means *self-loving*. Love of self is the basic sin, from which all
others flow. The moment a man makes his own will the centre
of life, divine and human relationships are destroyed,
obedience to God and charity to men both become impossible.
The essence of Christianity is not the enthronement but the
obliteration of self.

Men would become *lovers of money (philarguros)*. We must
remember that Timothy's work lay in Ephesus, perhaps the
greatest market in the ancient world. In those days trade tended
to flow down river valleys; Ephesus was at the mouth of the
River Cayster, and commanded the trade of one of the richest
hinterlands in all Asia Minor. At Ephesus some of the greatest
roads in the world met. There was the great trade route from
the Euphrates valley which came by way of Colosse and
Laodicaea and poured the wealth of the east into the lap of
Ephesus. There was the road from north Asia Minor and from
Galatia which came in via Sardis. There was the road from the
south which centred the trade of the Maeander valley in
Ephesus. Ephesus was called "The Treasure-house of the

ancient world," "The Vanity Fair of Asia Minor." It has been pointed out that the writer of *Revelation* may well have been thinking of Ephesus when he wrote that haunting passage which describes the merchandise of men: "The cargo of gold, silver, jewels and pearls, fine linen, purple, silk and scarlet, all kinds of scented wood, all articles of ivory, all articles of costly wood, bronze, iron and marble, cinnamon, spice, incense, myrrh, frankincense, wine, oil, fine flour and wheat, cattle and sheep, horses and chariots, and slaves, that is, human souls" (*Revelation* 18: 12, 13). Ephesus was the town of a prosperous, materialistic civilization; it was the kind of town where a man could so easily lose his soul.

There is peril when men assess prosperity by material things. It is to be remembered that a man may lose his soul far more easily in prosperity than in adversity; and he is on the way to losing his soul when he assesses the value of life by the number of things which he possesses.

THE QUALITIES OF GODLESSNESS

2 *Timothy* 3: 2–5 (*continued*)

IN these terrible days men would be *braggarts* and *arrogant*. In Greek writings these two words often went together; and they are both picturesque.

Braggart has an interesting derivation. It is the word *alazōn* and was derived from the *alē*, which means *a wandering about*. Originally the *alazōn* was a wandering quack. Plutarch uses the word to describe a quack doctor. The *alazōn* was a mountebank who wandered the country with medicines and spells and methods of exorcism which, he claimed, were panaceas for all diseases. We can still see this kind of man in fairs and market-places shouting the virtues of a patent medicine which will act like magic. Then the word went on to widen its meaning until it meant any *braggart*.

The Greek moralists wrote much about this word. The

Platonic Definitions defined the corresponding noun *(alazoneia)* as: "The claim to good things which a man does not really possess." Aristotle *(Nicomachean Ethics,* 7: 2) defined the *alazōn* as "the man who pretends to creditable qualities that he does not possess, or possesses in a lesser degree than he makes out." Xenophon tells us how Cyrus, the Persian king, defined the *alazōn:* "The name *alazōn* seems to apply to those who pretend that they are richer than they are or braver than they are, and to those who promise to do what they cannot do, and that, too, when it is evident that they do this only for the sake of getting something or making some gain" (Xenophon: *Cyropoedia,* 2, 2, 12). Xenophon in the *Memorabilia* tells how Socrates utterly condemned such imposters. Socrates said that they were to be found in every walk of life but were worst of all in politics. "Much the greatest rogue of all is the man who has gulled his city into the belief that he is fit to direct it."

The world is full of these braggarts to this day; the clever know-alls who deceive people into thinking that they are wise, the politicians who claim that their parties have a programme which will bring in the Utopia and that they alone are born to be leaders of men, the people who crowd the advertisement columns with claims to give beauty, knowledge or health by their system, the people in the Church who have a kind of ostentatious goodness.

Closely allied with the *braggart,* but—as we shall see—even worse, is the man who is *arrogant.* The word is *huperēphanos.* It is derived from two Greek words which mean *to show oneself above.* The man who is *huperēphanos,* said Theophrastus, has a kind of contempt for everyone except himself. He is the man who is guilty of the "sin of the high heart." He is the man whom God resists, for it is repeatedly said in scripture, that God receives the humble but resists the man who is proud, *huperēphanos (James* 4: 6; 1 *Peter* 5: 5; *Proverbs* 3: 24). Theophylact called this kind of pride *akropolis kakōn,* the citadel of evils.

The difference between the braggart and the man who is

arrogant is this. The braggart is a swaggering creature, who tries to bluster his way into power and eminence. No one can possibly mistake him. But the sin of the man who is *arrogant* is in his heart. He might even seem to be humble; but in his secret heart there is contempt for everyone else. He nourishes an all-consuming, all-pervading pride; and in his heart there is a little altar where he bows down before himself.

THE QUALITIES OF GODLESSNESS

2 Timothy 3: 2–5 *(continued)*

THESE twin qualities of the braggart and the arrogant man inevitably result in *love of insult (blasphēmia)*. *Blasphēmia* is the word which is transliterated into English as *blasphemy*. In English we usually associate it with insult against God, but in Greek it means insult against man and God alike. Pride always begets insult. It begets disregard of God, thinking that it does not need him and that it knows better than he. It begets a contempt of men which can issue in hurting actions and in wounding words. The Jewish Rabbis ranked high in the list of sins what they called *the sin of insult*. The insult which comes from anger is bad but it is forgivable, for it is launched in the heat of the moment; but the cold insult which comes from arrogant pride is an ugly and an unforgivable thing.

Men will be *disobedient to their parents*. The ancient world set duty to parents very high. The oldest Greek laws disfranchised the man who struck his parents; to strike a father was in Roman law as bad as murder; in the Jewish law honour for father and mother comes high in the list of the Ten Commandments. It is the sign of a supremely decadent civilization when youth loses all respect for age and fails to recognize the unpayable debt and the basic duty it owes to those who gave it life.

Men will be *thankless (acharistos)*. They will refuse to recognize the debt they owe both to God and to men. The

strange characteristic of ingratitude is that it is the most
hurting of all sins because it is the blindest. Lear's words
remain true:

> "How sharper than a serpent's tooth it is
> To have a thankless child!"

It is the sign of a man of honour that he pays his debts; and
for every man there is a debt to God and there are debts to
his fellow-men, which he must remember and repay.

Men will *refuse to recognize even the ultimate decencies of
life*. The Greek word is that men will become *anosios*.
Anosios does not so much mean that men will break the
written laws; it means that they will offend against the un-
written laws which are part and parcel of the essence of life.
To the Greek it was *anosios* to refuse burial to the dead;
it was *anosios* for a brother to marry a sister, or a son a
mother. The man who is *anosios* offends against the fundamental decencies of life. Such offence can and does happen
yet. The man who is mastered by his lower passions will
gratify them in the most shameless way, as the streets of any
great city will show when the night is late. The man who has
exhausted the normal pleasures of life and still unsated, will
seek his thrill in pleasures which are abnormal.

Men will be *without human affection (astorgos)*. *Storgē* is the
word used especially of *family love*, the love of child for
parent and parent for child. If there is no human affection,
the family cannot exist. In the terrible times men will be so set
on self that even the closest ties will be nothing to them.

Men will be *implacable in their hatreds (aspondos)*. *Spondē*
is the word for a truce or an agreement. *Aspondos* can mean
two things. It can mean that a man is so bitter in his hatred
that he will never come to terms with the man with whom he
has quarrelled. Or it can mean that a man is so dishonourable that he breaks the terms of the agreement he has made.
In either case the word describes a certain harshness of mind
which separates a man from his fellow-men in unrelenting
bitterness. It may be that, since we are only human, we cannot

live entirely without differences with our fellow-men, but to perpetuate these differences is one of the worst—and also one of the commonest—of all sins. When we are tempted to do so, we should hear again the voice of our blessed Lord saying on the Cross: "Father, forgive them."

THE QUALITIES OF GODLESSNESS

2 *Timothy* 3: 2–5 (*continued*)

IN these terrible days men will be *slanderers*. The Greek for *slanderer* is *diabolos* which is precisely the English word *devil*. The devil is the patron saint of all slanderers and of all slanderers he is chief. There is a sense in which slander is the most cruel of all sins. If a man's goods are stolen, he can set to and build up his fortunes again; but if his good name is taken away, irreparable damage has been done. It is one thing to start an evil and untrue report on its malicious way; it is entirely another thing to stop it. As Shakespeare had it:

"Good name in man and woman, dear my lord,
  Is the immediate jewel of their souls:
  Who steals my purse steals trash; 'tis something, nothing;
  'Twas mine, 'tis his, and has been slave to thousands:
  But he that filches from me my good name
  Robs me of that which not enriches him
  And makes me poor indeed."

Many men and women, who would never dream of stealing, think nothing—even find pleasure—in passing on a story which ruins someone else's good name, without even trying to find out whether or not it is true. There is slander enough in many a church to make the recording angel weep as he records it.

Men will be *ungovernable in their desires (akratēs)*. The Greek verb *kratein* means *to control*. A man can reach a stage when, so far from controlling it, he can become a slave to some habit or desire. That is the inevitable way to ruin, for no man can master anything unless he first masters himself.

Men will be *savage*. The word is *anēmeros* and would be more fittingly applied to a wild beast than to a human being. It denotes a savagery which has neither sensitiveness nor sympathy. Men can be savage in rebuke and savage in pitiless action. Even a dog may be sorry when he has hurt his master, but there are people who, in their treatment of others, can be lost to human sympathy and feeling.

THE QUALITIES OF GODLESSNESS

2 *Timothy* 3: 2–5 (*continued*)

IN these last terrible days men will come *to have no love for good things or good persons (aphilagathos)*. There can come a time in a man's life when the company of good people and the presence of good things is simply an embarrassment. He who feeds his mind on cheap literature can in the end find nothing in the great masterpieces. His mental palate loses its taste. A man has sunk far when he finds even the presence of good people something which he would only wish to avoid.

Men will be *treacherous*. The Greek word *(prodotēs)* means nothing less than a *traitor*. We must remember that this was written just at the beginning of the years of persecution, when it was becoming a crime to be a Christian. At this particular time in the ordinary matters of politics one of the curses of Rome was the existence of *informers (delatores)*. Things were so bad that Tacitus could say: "He who had no foe was betrayed by his friend." There were those who would revenge themselves on an enemy by informing against him. What Paul is thinking of here is more than faithlessness in friendship—although that in all truth is wounding enough—he is thinking of those who to pay back an old score would inform against the Christians to the Roman government.

Men would be *headlong* in words and action. The word is *propetēs*, precipitate. It describes the man who is swept on by passion and impulse to such an extent that he is totally unable to think sensibly. Far more harm is done from want of thought than almost anything else. Many and many a time we would be saved from hurting ourselves and from wounding other people, if we would only stop to think.

Men will be *inflated with conceit (tetuphōmenos)*. The word is almost exactly the English *swelled-headed*. They will be inflated with a sense of their own importance. There are still Church dignitaries whose main thought is their own dignity; but the Christian is the follower of him who was meek and lowly in heart.

They will be *lovers of pleasure rather than lovers of God.* Here we come back to where we started; such men place their own wishes in the centre of life. They worship self instead of God.

The final condemnation of these people is that they retain the outward form of religion but deny its power. That is to say, they go through all the correct movements and maintain all the external forms of religion; but they know nothing of Christianity as a dynamic power which changes the lives of men. It is said that, after hearing an evangelical sermon, Lord Melbourne once remarked: "Things have come to a pretty pass when religion is allowed to invade the sphere of private life." It may well be that the greatest handicap to Christianity is not the scarlet sinner but the sleek devotee of an unimpeachable orthodoxy and a dignified convention, who is horrified when it is suggested that real religion is a dynamic power which changes a man's personal life.

SEDUCTION IN THE NAME OF RELIGION

2 Timothy 3: 6, 7

For from among these there come those who enter into houses, and take captive foolish women, laden with sins and driven by varied

desires, ready to listen to any teacher but never able to come
to a knowledge of the truth.

THE Christian emancipation of women inevitably brought its
problems. We have already seen how secluded the life of the
respectable Greek woman was, how she was brought up under
the strictest supervision, how she was not allowed "to see
anything, to hear anything, or to ask any questions," how
she never appeared, even on a shopping expedition, alone on
the streets, how she was never allowed even to appear at a
public meeting. Christianity changed all that and a new set of
problems arose. It was only to be expected that certain
women would not know how to use their new liberty. There
were false teachers who were quick to take advantage of that.

Irenaeus draws a vivid picture of the methods of just such
a teacher in his day. True, he is telling of something
which happened later than this, but the wretched story would
be the same (Irenaeus: *Against Heresies,* 1, 13, 3). There was
a certain heretic called Marcus who dealt in magic. "He
devotes himself specially to women, and those such as are well-
bred, and elegantly attired, and of great wealth." He tells such
women that by his spells and incantations he can enable them
to prophesy. The woman protests that she has never done so
and cannot do so. He says: "Open thy mouth, speak
whatsoever occurs to thee, and thou shalt prophesy." The
woman, thrilled to the heart, does so and is deluded into
thinking that she can prophesy. "She then makes the effort
to reward Marcus, not only by the gift of her possessions (in
which way he has collected a very large fortune), but also by
yielding up to him her person, desiring in every way to be
united to him, that she may become altogether one with him."
The technique would be the same in the days of Timothy
as it was in the later days of Irenaeus.

There would be two ways in which these heretics in the
days of Timothy could exert an evil influence. We must
remember that they were Gnostics and that the basic
principle of Gnosticism was that spirit was altogether good
and matter altogether evil. We have already seen that that

teaching issued in one of two things. The Gnostic heretics taught, either that, since matter is altogether evil, a rigid asceticism must be practised and all the things of the body as far as possible eliminated, or that it does not matter what we do with the body and its desires can be indulged in to the limit because they do not matter. The Gnostic insinuators would teach these doctrines to impressionable women. The result would often be either that the woman broke off married relationships with her husband in order to live the ascetic life, or that she gave the lower instincts full play and abandoned herself to promiscuous relationships. In either case home and family life were destroyed.

It is still possible for a teacher to gain an undue and unhealthy influence over others, especially when they are impressionable.

It is Paul's charge that such people are "willing to learn from anyone, and yet never able to come to a knowledge of the truth." E. F. Brown has pointed out the danger of what he calls "intellectual curiosity without moral earnestness." There is a type of person who is eager to discuss every new theory, who is always to be found deeply involved in the latest fashionable religious movement, but who is quite unwilling to accept the day-to-day discipline—even drudgery—of living the Christian life. No amount of intellectual curiosity can ever take the place of moral earnestness. We are not meant to titillate our minds with the latest intellectual crazes; we are meant to purify and strengthen ourselves in the moral battle to live the Christian life.

THE OPPONENTS OF GOD

2 Timothy 3: 8, 9

In the same way as Jannes and Jambres opposed Moses, so these also oppose the truth, men whose minds are corrupt, and whose faith is counterfeit. But they will not get much further, for their folly will be as clear to all as that of those ancient impostors.

IN the days between the Old and the New Testaments many Jewish books were written which expanded the Old Testament stories. In certain of these books Jannes and Jambres figured largely. These were the names given to the court magicians of Pharaoh who opposed Moses and Aaron, when Moses was leading the children of Israel out of their slavery in Egypt. At first these magicians were able to match the wonders which Moses and Aaron did, but in the end they were defeated and discredited. In the Old Testament they are not named, but they are referred to in *Exodus* 7: 11; 8: 7; 9: 11.

A whole collection of stories gathered round their names. They were said to be the two servants who accompanied Balaam when he was disobedient to God (*Numbers* 22: 22); they were said to have been part of the great mixed multitude who accompanied the children of Israel out of Egypt (*Exodus* 12: 38); some said that they perished at the crossing of the Red Sea; other stories said that it was Jannes and Jambres who were behind the making of the golden calf and that they perished among those who were killed for that sin (*Exodus* 32: 28); still other stories said that in the end they became proselytes to Judaism. Amidst all the stories one fact stands out—Jannes and Jambres became legendary figures typifying all those who opposed the purposes of God and the work of his true leaders.

The Christian leader will never lack his opponents. There will always be those who have their own twisted ideas of the Christian faith, and who wish to win others to their mistaken beliefs. But of one thing Paul was sure—the days of the deceivers were numbered. Their falsity would be demonstrated and they would receive their appropriate reward.

The history of the Christian Church teaches us that falsity cannot live. It may flourish for a time, but when it is exposed to the light of truth it is bound to shrivel and die. There is only one test for falsity—"You will know them by their fruits." The best way to overcome and to banish the false is to live in such a way that the loveliness and the graciousness of the truth is plain for all to see. The defeat of error depends not on skill in controversy but in the demonstration in life of the more excellent way.

THE DUTIES AND THE QUALITIES
OF AN APOSTLE

2 Timothy 3: 10–13

> But you have been my disciple in my teaching, my training, my aim in life, my faith, my patience, my love, my endurance, my persecutions, my sufferings, in what happened to me at Antioch, at Iconium, at Lystra, in the persecutions which I underwent; and the Lord rescued me from them all. And those who wish to live a godly life in Christ Jesus will be persecuted; while evil men and impostors will go from bad to worse, deceived themselves and deceiving others.

PAUL contrasts the conduct of Timothy, his loyal disciple, with the conduct of the heretics who were doing their utmost to wreck the Church. The word we have translated *to be a disciple* includes so much that is beyond translation in any single English word. It is the Greek *parakolouthein* and literally means *to follow alongside;* but it is used with a magnificent width of meaning. It means to follow a person *physically*, to stick by him through thick and thin. It means to follow a person *mentally*, to attend diligently to his teaching and fully to understand the meaning of what he says. It means to follow a person *spiritually*, not only to understand what he says, but also to carry out his ideas and be the kind of person he wishes us to be. *Parakolouthein* is indeed the word for the disciple, for it includes the unwavering loyalty of the true comrade, the full understanding of the true scholar and the complete obedience of the dedicated servant.

Paul goes on to list the things in which Timothy has been his disciple; and the interest of that list is that it consists of the strands out of which the life and work of an apostle are woven. In it we find the *duties*, the *qualities* and the *experiences* of an apostle.

First, there are the *duties* of an apostle. There is *teaching*. No man can teach what he does not know, and therefore before a man can teach Christ to others he must know him himself. When Carlyle's father was discussing the kind of minister his parish needed, he said: "What this parish needs is a man who knows Christ other than at secondhand." Real teaching is always born of real experience. There is *training*. The Christian life does not consist only in knowing something; it consists even more in being something. The task of the apostle is not only to tell men the truth; it is also to help them do it. The true leader gives training in living.

Second, there are the *qualities* of the apostle. First and foremost he has an *aim in life*. Two men were talking of a great satirist who had been filled with moral earnestness. "He kicked the world about," said one, "as if it had been a football." "True," said the other, "but he kicked it to a goal." As individuals, we should sometimes ask ourselves: what is our aim in life? As teachers we should sometimes ask ourselves: what am I trying to do with these people whom I teach? Once Agesilaus, the Sparta king, was asked, "What shall we teach our boys?" His answer was: "That which will be most useful to them when they are men." Is it knowledge, or is it life, that we are trying to transmit?

As members of the Church, we should sometimes ask ourselves, what are we trying to do in it? It is not enough to be satisfied when a church is humming like a dynamo and every night in the week has its own crowded organization. We should be asking: what, if any, is the unifying purpose which binds all this activity together? In all life there is nothing so creative of really productive effort as a clear consciousness of a purpose.

Paul goes on to other qualities of an apostle. There is *faith*, complete belief that God's commands are binding and that his promises are true. There is *patience*. The word here is *makrothumia;* and *makrothumia,* as the Greeks used it, usually meant *patience with people*. It is the ability not to lose patience when people are foolish, not to grow irritable when they seem unteachable. It is the ability to accept the folly, the perversity, the blindness, the ingratitude of men and still to remain gracious, and still to toil on. There is *love*. This is God's attitude to men. It is the attitude which bears with everything men can do and refuses to be either angry or embittered, and which will never seek anything but their highest good. To love men is to forgive them and care for them as God forgave and cares—and it is only he who can enable us to do that.

THE EXPERIENCES OF AN APOSTLE

2 *Timothy* 3: 10–13 (*continued*)

PAUL completes the story of the things in which Timothy has shared, and must share, with him, by speaking of the *experiences* of an apostle; and he prefaces that list of experiences by setting down the quality of *endurance*. The Greek is *hupomonē,* which means not a passive sitting down and bearing things but a triumphant facing of them so that even out of evil there can come good. It describes, not the spirit which *accepts* life, but the spirit which *masters* it.

And that quality of conquering endurance is necessary, because persecution is an essential part of the experience of an apostle. Paul cites three instances when he had to suffer for Christ. He was driven from Antioch in Pisidia (*Acts* 13: 50); he had to flee from Iconium to avoid lynching (*Acts* 14: 5, 6); in Lystra he was stoned and left for dead (*Acts* 14: 19). It is true that these things happened before the young Timothy had definitely entered on the Christian way, but they all happened in the district of which he was a native; and he may well have been an eyewitness of them. It may well be a proof of Timothy's courage and consecration that he had seen very clearly what could happen to an apostle and had yet not hesitated to cast in his lot with Paul.

It is Paul's conviction that the real follower of Christ cannot escape persecution. When trouble fell on the Thessalonians, Paul wrote to them: "When we were with you, we told you beforehand that we were to suffer affliction; just as it has come to pass, and as you know" (1 *Thessalonians* 3: 4). It is as if he said to them: "You have been well warned." He returned after the first missionary journey to visit the Churches he had founded, "strengthening the souls of the disciples, exhorting them to continue in the faith, and saying that through many tribulations we must enter the kingdom of God" (*Acts* 14: 22). The Kingdom had its price. And Jesus himself had said: "Blessed are those who are persecuted for righteousness' sake" (*Matthew* 5: 10). If anyone proposes to accept a set of standards quite different from the world's, he is bound to encounter trouble. If anyone proposes to introduce into his life a loyalty which surpasses all earthly loyalties, there are bound to be clashes. And that is precisely what Christianity demands that a man should do.

Persecution and hardships will come, but of two things Paul is sure.

He is sure that God will rescue the man who puts his faith in him. He is sure that in the long run it is better to suffer with God and the right than to prosper with men and the wrong. Certain of the temporary persecution, he is equally certain of the ultimate glory.

He is sure that the ungodly man will go from bad to worse and that there is literally no future for the man who refuses to accept the way of God.

THE VALUE OF SCRIPTURE

2 *Timothy* 3: 14–17

But as for you, remain loyal to the things which you have learned, and in which your belief has been confirmed, for you know from whom you learned them, and you know that from childhood you have known the sacred writings which are able to give you the wisdom that will bring you salvation through the faith which is in

Christ Jesus. All God-inspired scripture is useful for teaching, for the conviction of error, for correction, and for training in righteousness, that the man of God may be complete, fully equipped for every good work.

PAUL concludes this section with an appeal to Timothy to remain loyal to all the teaching he had received. On his mother's side Timothy was a Jew, although his father had been a Greek (*Acts* 16: 1); and it is clear that it was his mother who had brought him up. It was the glory of the Jews that their children from their earliest days were trained in the law. They claimed that their children learned the law even from their swaddling clothes and drank it in with their mother's milk. They claimed that the law was so imprinted on the heart and mind of a Jewish child that he would sooner forget his own name than he would forget it. So from his earliest childhood Timothy had known the sacred writings. We must remember that the scripture of which Paul is writing is the Old Testament; as yet the New Testament had not come into being. If what he claims for scripture is true of the Old Testament, how much truer it is of the still more precious words of the New.

We must note that Paul here makes a distinction. He speaks of "all God-inspired scripture." The Gnostics had their own fanciful books; the heretics all produced their own literature to support their claims. Paul regarded these as man-made things; but the great books for a man's soul were the God-inspired ones which tradition and the experience of men had sanctified.

Let us then see what Paul says of the usefulness of scripture.

(i) He says that the Scriptures give *the wisdom which will bring salvation*. A. M. Chirgwin in *The Bible in World Evangelism* tells the story of a ward sister in a children's hospital in England. She had been finding life, as she herself said, futile and meaningless. She had waded through book after book and laboured with philosophy after philosophy in an attempt to find satisfaction. She had never tried the Bible, for a friend had convinced her by subtle arguments that it could not be true. One day a visitor came to the ward and left a supply of gospels. The sister was persuaded to read a copy of *St. John.* "It shone and glowed with truth," she said, "and my whole being responded to it. The words that finally decided me were those in *John* 18: 37: 'For this I was born, and for this I have come into the world, to bear witness to the truth. Every one who is of the truth hears my voice.' So I listened to that voice, and heard the truth, and found my Saviour."

Again and again Scripture has opened for men and women the way to God. In simple fairness, no man seeking for the truth has any right to neglect the reading of the Bible. A book with a record such as it has cannot be disregarded. Even an unbeliever is acting unfairly unless he tries to read it. The most amazing things may happen if he does, for there is a saving wisdom here that is in no other book.

(ii) The Scriptures are of use in *teaching.* Only in the New Testament have we any picture of Jesus, any account of his life and any record of his teaching. For that very reason it is unanswerable that, whatever a man might argue about the rest of the Bible, it is impossible for the Church ever to do without the Gospels. It is perfectly true—as we have so often said—that Christianity is not founded on a printed book but on a living person. The fact remains that the only place in all the world where we get a first-hand account of that person and of his teaching is in the New Testament. That is why the church which has no Bible Class is a church in whose work an essential element is missing.

(iii) The Scriptures are valuable for *reproof.* It is not meant that the Scriptures are valuable for *finding fault;* what is meant is that they are valuable for convincing a man of the error of his ways and for pointing him on the right path. A. M. Chirgwin has story after story of how the Scriptures came by chance into the hands of men and changed their lives.

In Brazil Signor Antonio of Minas bought a New Testament which he took home to burn. He went home and found the fire was out. Deliberately he lit it. He flung the New Testament on it. It would not burn. He opened out the pages to make it burn more easily. It opened at the Sermon on the Mount. He glanced at it as he consigned it to the flames. His mind was caught; he took it back. "He read on, forgetful of time, through the hours of the night, and just as the dawn was breaking, he stood up and declared, 'I believe'."

Vincente Quiroga of Chile found a few pages of a book washed up on the seashore by a tidal wave following an earthquake. He read them and never rested until he obtained the rest of the Bible. Not only did he become a Christian; he devoted the rest of his life to the distribution of the Scriptures in the forgotten villages of northern Chile.

One dark night in a forest in Sicily a brigand held up a colporteur at the point of a revolver. He was ordered to light a bonfire and burn his books. He lit the fire, and then he asked if he might read a little from each book before he dropped it in the flames. He read the twenty-third psalm from one; the story of the Good Samaritan from another; from another the Sermon on the Mount; from another 1 *Corinthians* 13. At the end of each reading, the brigand said: "That's a good book; we won't burn that one; give it to me." In the end not a book was burned; the brigand left the colporteur and went off into the darkness with the books. Years later that same brigand turned up again. *This time he was a Christian minister,* and it was to the reading of the books that he attributed his change.

It is beyond argument that the Scriptures can convict a man of his error and convince him of the power of Christ.

(iv) The Scriptures are of use for *correction.* The real meaning of this is that all theories, all theologies, all ethics, are to be tested against the Bible. If they contradict the teaching of the Bible, they are to be refused. It is our duty to use our minds and set them adventuring; but the test must ever be agreement with the teaching of Jesus Christ as the Scriptures present it to us.

(v) Paul makes a final point. The study of the Scriptures trains a man in righteousness until he is equipped for every

good work. Here is the essential conclusion. The study of the
Scriptures must never be selfish, never simply for the good of a
man's own soul. Any conversion which makes a man think
of nothing but the fact that *he* has been saved is no true
conversion. He must study the Scriptures to make himself
useful to God and to his fellow-men. No man is saved unless
he is on fire to save his fellow-men.

PAUL'S GROUNDS OF APPEAL

2 Timothy 4: 1-5

> I charge you before God and Christ Jesus, who is going to judge
> the living and the dead—I charge you by his appearing and by his
> Kingdom—herald forth the word; be urgent in season and out of
> season; convict, rebuke, exhort, and do it all with a patience and
> a teaching which never fail. For there will come a time when men
> will refuse to listen to sound teaching, but, because they have ears
> which have to be continually titillated with novelties, they will bury
> themselves under a mound of teachers, whose teaching suits their
> own lusts after forbidden things. They will avert their ears from the
> truth, and they will turn to extravagant tales. As for you, be
> steady in all things; accept the suffering which will come upon you;
> do the work of an evangelist; leave no act of your service
> unfulfilled.

As Paul comes to the end of his letter, he wishes to nerve and
to challenge Timothy to his task. To do so he reminds him of
three things concerning Jesus.

(i) Jesus is the judge of the living and the dead. Some
day Timothy's work will be tested, and that by none other
than Jesus himself. A Christian must do every task in such a
way that he can offer it to Christ. He is not concerned with
either the criticism or the verdict of men. The one thing he
covets is the "Well done!" of Jesus Christ. If we all did our
work in that spirit, the difference would be incalculable. It
would save us from the touchy spirit which is offended by
criticism; it would save us from the self-important spirit

which is concerned with personal rights and personal prestige;
it would save us from the self-centred spirit which demands
thanks and praise for its every act; it would even save us from
being hurt by men's ingratitude.

(ii) Jesus is the returning conqueror. "I charge you," says
Paul, "by his *appearing*." The word is *epiphaneia*. *Epiphaneia*
was used in two special ways. It was used for the manifest
intervention of some god; and it was specially used in
connection with the Roman Emperor. His accession to the
throne was his *epiphaneia;* and in particular—and this is the
background of Paul's thought here—it was used of his visit
to any province or town. Obviously when the Emperor was
due to visit any place, everything was put in perfect order.
The streets were swept and garnished and all work was brought
up-to-date so that the town might be fit for *epiphaneia*. So
Paul says to Timothy: "You know what happens when any
town is expecting the *epiphaneia* of the Emperor; *you* are
expecting the *epiphaneia* of Jesus Christ. Do your work in
such a way that all things will be ready whenever he
appears." The Christian should so order life that at any
moment he is ready for the coming of Christ.

(iii) Jesus is King. Paul urges Timothy to action by the
remembrance of the Kingdom of Jesus Christ. The day comes
when the kingdoms of the world will be the Kingdom of the
Lord; and so Paul says to Timothy: "So live and work that
you will rank high in the roll of its citizens when the
Kingdom comes."

Our work must be such that it will stand the scrutiny of
Christ. Our lives must be such that they will welcome the
appearance of the King. Our service must be such that it will
demonstrate the reality of our citizenship of the Kingdom of
God.

THE CHRISTIAN'S DUTY

2 *Timothy* 4: 1–5 (*continued*)

THERE can be few New Testament passages where the duties

of the Christian teacher are more clearly set out than here.

The Christian teacher is to be *urgent*. The message he brings is literally a matter of life and death. The teachers who really get their message across are those who have the note of earnestness in their voice. Spurgeon had a real admiration for Martineau, who was a Unitarian and therefore denied the divinity of Jesus Christ which Spurgeon believed in with passionate intensity. Someone once said to Spurgeon: "How can you possibly admire Martineau? You don't believe what he preaches." "No," said Spurgeon, "*but he does.*" Any man with the note of urgency in his voice demands, and will receive, a hearing from other men.

The Christian teacher is to be *persistent*. He is to urge the claims of Christ "in season and out of season." As someone has put it: "Take or make your opportunity." As Theodore of Mospeuestia put it: "The Christian must count every time an opportunity to speak for Christ." It was said of George Morrison of Wellington Church in Glasgow that with him wherever the conversation started, it went straight across country to Christ. This does not mean that we will not choose our time to speak, for there should be courtesy in evangelism as in every other human contact; but it does mean that perhaps we are far too shy in speaking to others about Jesus Christ.

Paul goes on to speak of the effect the Christian witness must produce.

He must *convict*. He must make the sinner aware of his sin. Walter Bagehot once said: "The road to perfection lies through a series of disgusts." Somehow or other the sinner must be made to feel disgusted with his sin. Epictetus draws a contrast between the false philosopher, who is out for popularity, and the real philosopher, whose one aim is the good of his hearers. The false philosopher deals in flattery and panders to self-esteem. The real philosopher says: "Come and be told that you are in a bad way." "The philosopher's lecture," he said, "is a surgery; when you go away you ought to have felt not pleasure, but pain." It was Alcibiades, the brilliant but spoiled darling of Athens, who used to say to Socrates: "Socrates, I hate you, because every time I meet you, you make me see what I am." The first essential is to compel a man to see himself as he is.

He must *rebuke*. In the great days of the Church there was an utter fearlessness in its voice; and because of that things happened. E. F. Brown tells of an incident from India. A certain young nobleman in the Viceroy's suite in Calcutta became notorious for his profligacy. Bishop Wilson one day put on his robes, drove to Government House, and said to the Viceroy: "Your excellency, if Lord —— does not leave Calcutta before next Sunday, I shall denounce him from the pulpit in the Cathedral." Before Sunday came that young man was gone.

Ambrose of Milan was one of the great figures of the early Church. He was an intimate friend of Theodosius, the Emperor, who was a Christian, but a man of violent temper. Ambrose never hesitated to tell the Emperor the truth. "Who," he demanded, "will dare to tell you the truth if a priest does not dare?" Theodosius had appointed one of his close friends, Botherich, as governor of Thessalonica. Botherich, a good governor, had occasion to imprison a famous charioteer for infamous conduct. The popularity of these charioteers was incredible and the populace rose in a riot and murdered Botherich. Theodosius was mad with anger. Ambrose pled with him for discrimination in punishment, but Rufinus, his minister of state, deliberately inflamed his anger and Theodosius sent out orders for a massacre of vengeance. Later he countermanded the order, but too late for the new order to reach Thessalonica in time. The theatre was crammed to capacity with the doors shut, and the soldiers of Theodosius went to and fro slaughtering men, women and children for three hours. More than seven thousand people were killed. News of the massacre came back to Milan and when Theodosius presented himself at the Church service the next Sunday, Ambrose refused him admission. The Emperor pled for pardon. Eight months passed and again he came to Church. Again Ambrose refused him entry. In the end the Emperor of Rome had to lie prostrate on the ground with the penitents before he was allowed to worship with the Church again. In its great days the Church was fearless in rebuke.

In our personal relationships a word of warning and rebuke would often save a brother from sin and shipwreck. But, as someone has said, that word must always be spoken as "brother setting brother right." It must be spoken with a consciousness of our common guilt. It is not our place to set ourselves up as moral judges of anyone; nonetheless it is our duty to speak that warning word when it needs to be spoken.

He must *exhort*. Here is the other side of the matter. No rebuke should ever be such that it drives a man to despair and takes the heart and the hope out of him. Not only must men be rebuked, they must also be encouraged.

Further, the Christian duty of conviction, of rebuke and of encouragement, must be carried out with unwearied *patience*. The word is *makrothumia*, and it describes the spirit which never grows irritated, never despairs and never regards any man as beyond salvation. The Christian patiently believes in men because he unconquerably believes in the changing power of Christ.

FOOLISH LISTENERS

2 *Timothy* 4: 1–5 (*continued*)

PAUL goes on to describe the foolish listeners. He warns Timothy that the day is coming when men will refuse to listen to sound teaching and will collect teachers who will titillate their ears with precisely the easy-going, comfortable things they want to hear.

In Timothy's day it was tragically easy to find such

teachers. They were called *sophists* and wandered from city to city, offering to teach anything for pay. Isocrates said of them: "They try to attract pupils by low fees and big promises." They were prepared to teach the whole of virtue for £15 or £20. They would teach a man to argue subtly and to use words cleverly until he could make the worse appear the better reason. Plato described them savagely: "Hunters after young men of wealth and position, with sham education as their bait, and a fee for their object, making money by a scientific use of quibbles in private conversation, while quite aware that what they are teaching is wrong."

They competed for customers. Dio Chrysostom wrote of them: "You might hear many poor wretches of sophists shouting and abusing one another, and their disciples, as they call them, squabbling, and many writers of books reading their stupid compositions, and many poets singing their poems, and many jugglers exhibiting their marvels, and many sooth-sayers giving the meaning of prodigies, and ten thousand rhetoricians twisting lawsuits, and no small number of traders driving their several trades."

Men in the days of Timothy were beset by false teachers hawking round sham knowledge. Their deliberate policy was to find arguments whereby a man could justify himself for doing what he wanted to do. Any teacher, to this day, whose teaching tends to make men think less of sin is a menace to Christianity and to mankind.

In contradistinction to that, certain duties are to be laid on Timothy.

He is to be *steady in all things*. The word *(nēphein)* means that he is to be sober and self-contained, like an athlete who has his passions and his appetites and his nerves well under control. Hort says that the word describes "a mental state free from all perturbations or stupefactions . . . every faculty at full command, to look all facts and all considerations deliberately in the face." The Christian is not to be the victim of crazes; stability is his badge in an unbalanced and often insane world.

C8

He is to *accept whatever suffering comes upon him.* Christianity will cost something, and the Christian is to pay the price of it without grumbling and without regret.

He is to do *the work of an evangelist.* In spite of the conviction and the rebuke the Christian is essentially *the bringer of good news.* If he insists on discipline and self-denial, it is that an even greater happiness may be attained than ever cheap pleasures can bring.

He is to leave *no act of service unfulfilled.* The Christian should have only one ambition—to be of use to the Church of which he is a part and the society in which he lives. The chance he dare not miss is not that of a cheap profit but that of being of service to his God, his Church and his fellow-men.

PAUL COMES TO THE END

2 Timothy 4: 6–8

> For my life has reached the point when it must be sacrificed, and the time of my departure has come. I have fought the good fight: I have completed the course: I have kept the faith. As for what remains, there is laid up for me the crown of righteousness which on that day the Lord, the righteous judge, will give to me—and not only to me, but also to all who have loved his appearing.

FOR Paul the end is very near and he knows it. When Erasmus was growing old, he said: "I am a veteran, and have earned my discharge, and must leave the fighting to younger men." Paul, the aged warrior, is laying down his arms that Timothy may take them up.

No passage in the New Testament is more full of vivid pictures than this.

"My life," says Paul, "has reached the point where it must be sacrificed." The word he uses for *sacrifice* is the verb *spendesthai* which literally means *to pour out as a libation to the gods*. Every Roman meal ended with a kind of sacrifice. A cup of wine was taken and was poured out *(spendesthai)* to the gods. It is as if Paul were saying: "The day is ended; it is time to rise and go; and my life must be poured out as a sacrifice to God." He did not think of himself as going to be executed; he thought of himself as going to offer his life to God. Ever since his conversion, he had offered everything to God—his money, his scholarship, his time, the vigour of his body, the acuteness of his mind, the devotion of his heart. Only life itself was left to offer, and gladly he was going to lay it down.

He goes on to say: "The time of my departure is at hand." The word *(analusis)* he uses for departure is a vivid one. It has many a picture in it and each tells us something about leaving this life. (*a*) It is the word for unyoking an animal from the shafts of the cart or the plough. Death to Paul was rest from toil. As Spenser had it, ease after toil, port after stormy seas, death after life, are lovely things. (*b*) It is the word for loosening bonds or fetters. Death for Paul was a release. He was to exchange the confines of a Roman prison for the glorious liberty of the courts of heaven. (*c*) It is the word for loosening the ropes of a tent. For Paul it was time to strike camp again. Many a journey he had made across the roads of Asia Minor and of Europe. Now he was setting out on his last and greatest journey; he was taking the road that led to God. (*d*) It is the word for loosening the mooring-ropes of a ship. Many a time Paul had felt his ship leave the harbour for the deep waters. Now he is to launch out into the greatest deep of all, setting sail to cross the waters of death to arrive in the haven of eternity.

So then, for the Christian, death is laying down the burden in order to rest; it is laying aside the shackles in order to be free; it is striking camp in order to take up residence in the heavenly places; it is casting off the ropes which bind us to this world in order to set sail on the voyage which ends in the presence of God. Who then shall fear it?

THE JOY OF THE WELL-FOUGHT CONTEST

2 Timothy 4: 6–8 (*continued*)

PAUL goes on, still speaking in these vivid pictures of which he was such a master: "I have fought the good fight: I have completed the race: I have kept the faith." It is likely that he is not using different pictures from three different spheres of life, but one picture from the games.

(i) "I have fought the good fight." The word he uses for fight is *agōn*, which is the word for a contest in the arena. When an athlete can really say that he has done his best, then, win or lose, there is a deep satisfaction in his heart. Paul has come to the end, and he knows that he has put up a good show. When his mother died, Barrie made a great claim. "I can look back," he said, "and I cannot see the smallest thing undone." There is no satisfaction in all the world like knowing that we have done our best.

(ii) "I have finished the race." It is easy to begin but hard to finish. The one thing necessary for life is staying-power, and that is what so many people lack. It was suggested to a certain very famous man that his biography should be written while he was still alive. He absolutely refused to give permission, and his reason was: "I have seen so many men fall out on the last lap." It is easy to wreck a noble life or a fine record by some closing folly. But it was Paul's claim that he had finished the race. There is a deep satisfaction in reaching the goal.

Perhaps the world's most famous race is the marathon. The Battle of Marathon was one of the decisive battles of the world. In it the Greeks met the Persians, and, if the Persians had conquered, the glory that was Greece would never have flowered upon the world. Against fearful odds the Greeks won the victory, and, after the battle, a Greek soldier ran all the way, day and night, to Athens with the news. Straight to the magistrates he ran. "Rejoice," he gasped, "we have conquered," and even as he delivered his message he fell dead. He had

completed his course and done his work, and there is no finer
way for any man to die.

(iii) "I have kept the faith." This phrase can have more
than one meaning. If we are to keep the background of the
games, it is this. The great games in Greece were the
Olympics. To these came all the greatest athletes in the world.
On the day before the games all the competitors met and took
a solemn oath before the gods that they had done not less
than ten months training and that they would not resort to any
trickery to win. So Paul may be saying: "I have kept the rules:
I have played the game." It would be a great thing to die
knowing that we had never transgressed the rules of honour
in the race of life.

But this phrase may have other meanings. It is also a
business phrase. It was the regular Greek for: "I have kept
the conditions of the contract; I have been true to my
engagement." If Paul used it in that way, he meant that he had
engaged himself to serve Christ and had stood by that
engagement and never let his Master down. Further, it could
mean: "I have kept my faith: I have never lost my
confidence and my hope." If Paul used it in that way, he
meant that (through thick and thin, in freedom and in
imprisonment, in all his perils by land and sea, and now in
the very face of death, he had never lost his trust in Jesus
Christ.)

Paul goes on to say there is laid up for him the crown.
In the games the greatest prize was the laurel wreath. With it
the victor was crowned; and to wear it was the greatest
honour which could come to any athlete. But this crown in a
few short days would wither. Paul knew that there awaited
him a crown which would never fade.

In this moment Paul is turning from the verdict of men to
the verdict of God. He knew that in a very short time he
would stand before the Roman judgment seat and that his
trial could have only one end. He knew what Nero's verdict
would be, but he also knew what God's verdict would be.
The man whose life is dedicated to Christ is indifferent to the

verdict of men. He cares not if they condemn him so long
as he hears his Master's "Well done!")

Paul sounds still another note—this crown awaits not only
him but all who wait with expectation for the coming of the
King. It is as if he said to the young Timothy: "Timothy,
my end is near: and I know that I go to my reward. (If you
follow in my steps, you will feel the same confidence and the
same joy when the end comes to you." The joy of Paul is open
to every man who also fights that fight and finishes the race
and keeps the faith.)

A ROLL OF HONOUR AND DISHONOUR

2 *Timothy* 4: 9-15

> Do your best to come and see me soon. Demas has deserted me,
> because he loved this present world, and has gone to Thessalonica.
> Crescens has gone to Galatia, Titus to Dalmatia. Luke alone is with
> me. Take Mark and bring him with you, for he is very useful in
> service. I have sent Tychicus to Ephesus.
>
> When you come bring with you the cloak which I left behind
> at Troas at Carpus's house, and bring the books, especially the
> parchments.
>
> Alexander, the coppersmith, did me a great deal of harm. The
> Lord will reward him according to his deeds. You yourself must
> be on your guard against him, for he hotly opposed our words.

PAUL draws up a roll of honour and of dishonour of his
friends. Some are only names to us; of some, as we read the
Acts and the *Epistles*, we get little revealing glimpses. Some
of the stories, if we are allowed to use our imagination, we
can reconstruct.

THE SPIRITUAL PILGRIMAGE OF DEMAS

First on the list comes Demas. There are three mentions of
him in Paul's letters; and it may well be that they have in

them the story of a tragedy. (i) In *Philemon* 24 he is listed amongst a group of men whom Paul calls his *fellow-labourers*. (ii) In *Colossians* 4: 14 he is mentioned without any comment at all. (iii) Here he has forsaken Paul because he loved this present world. First, Demas the fellow-labourer, then, just Demas, and, finally, Demas the deserter who loved the world. Here is the history of a spiritual degeneration. Bit by bit the fellow-labourer has become the deserter; the title of honour has become the name of shame.

What happened to Demas? That we cannot tell for sure, but we can guess.

(i) It may be that he had begun to follow Christ without first counting the cost; and it may be that he was not altogether to blame. There is a kind of evangelism which proclaims: "Accept Christ and you will have rest and peace and joy." There is a sense, the deepest of all senses, in which that is profoundly and blessedly true. But it is also true that when we accept Christ our troubles begin. Up to this time we have lived in conformity with the world and its standards. Because of that life was easy, because we followed the line of least resistance and went with the crowd. But once a man accepts Christ, he accepts an entirely new set of standards and is committed to an entirely new kind of life at his work, in his personal relationships, in his pleasures, and there are bound to be collisions. It may be that Demas was swept into the Church in a moment of emotion without ever thinking things out; and then when unpopularity, persecution, the necessity of sacrifice, loneliness, imprisonment came, he quit because he had never bargained for anything like that. When a man undertakes to follow Christ, the first essential is that he should know what he is doing.

(ii) It may be that there came to Demas the inevitable weariness of the years. They have a way of taking our ideals away, of lowering our standards, of accustoming us to defeat.

Halliday Sutherland tells how he felt when he first qualified as a doctor. If on the street or in any company there came the call: "Is there a doctor here?" he thrilled to it, proud and eager to step forward and help. But as the years went on, a request like that became a nuisance. The thrill was gone.

W. H. Davies, the tramp who was also one of the greatest poets, has a revealing passage about himself. He had walked to see Tintern Abbey which he had last seen twenty-seven years ago. He says: "As I stood there now, twenty-seven years after, and compared that young boy's enthusiasm with my present lukewarm feelings, I was not very well pleased with myself. For instance, at that time I would sacrifice both food and sleep to see anything wonderful; but now in my prime I did not go seeking things of beauty, and only sang of things that came my way by chance."

Dean Inge had a sermon on *Psalm* 91: 6—"the destruction that wastes at noonday." Which he called "The Peril of Middle Age." There is no threat so dangerous as the threat of the years to a man's ideals; and it can be kept at bay only by living constantly in the presence of Jesus Christ.

(iii) Paul said of Demas that "he loved this present world." His trouble may have been quite simple, and yet very terrible. It may simply be that he loved comfort more than he loved Christ, that he loved the easy way more than he loved the way which led first to a cross and then to the stars.

We think of Demas, not to condemn, but to sympathize, for so many of us are like him.

It is just possible that this is neither the beginning nor the end of the story of Demas. The name *Demas* is a shortened and familiar form of Demetrius and twice we come upon a Demetrius in the New Testament story. There was a Demetrius who led the riot of the silversmiths at Ephesus and wished to lynch Paul because he had taken their temple trade away (*Acts* 19:25). There was a Demetrius of whom John wrote that he had a good report of all and of the truth itself, a fact to which John bore willing and decisive witness (3 *John* 12). May this be the beginning and the end of the story? Did Demetrius the silversmith find something about Paul and Christ which twined itself round his heart? Did the hostile leader of the riot become the convert to Christ? Did he for a time fall away from the Christian way and become Demas, the deserter, who loved this present world? And did the grace of God lay hands on him again, and bring him back, and make him the Demetrius of Ephesus of whom John wrote that he was a servant of the truth of whom all spoke well? That we will never know, but it is a lovely thing to think that the charge of being a deserter may not have been the final verdict on the life of Demas.

A ROLL OF HONOUR AND DISHONOUR

2 *Timothy* 4: 9–15 (*continued*)

THE GENTILE OF WHOM ALL SPOKE WELL

After Paul has spoken of the man who was the deserter, he goes on to speak of the man who was faithful unto death. "Luke alone is with me," he says. We know very little about Luke, and yet even from that little he emerges as one of the loveliest characters in the New Testament.

(i) One thing we know by implication—Luke accompanied Paul on his last journey to Rome and to prison. He was the writer of the *Book of Acts*. Now there are certain passages of *Acts* which are written in the first person plural and we can be quite sure that Luke is here describing occasions on which he himself was actually present. *Acts* 27 describes Paul setting out under arrest for Rome and the story is told in the first person. Therefore we can be sure that Luke was there. From that we deduce something else. It is thought that when an arrested prisoner was on his way to trial at Rome, he was allowed to be accompanied by only two slaves, and it is therefore probable that Luke enrolled himself as Paul's slave in order to be allowed to accompany him to Rome and to prison. Little wonder that Paul speaks of him with love in his voice. Surely devotion could go no farther.

(ii) There are only two other definite references to Luke in the New Testament. In *Colossians* 4: 14 he is described as *the beloved physician*. Paul owed much to Luke. All his life he had the torturing thorn in his flesh; and Luke must have been the man who used his skill to ease his pain and enable him to go on. Luke was essentially a man who was kind. He does not seem to have been a great evangelist; he was the man who made his contribution in terms of personal service. God had given him healing skill in his hands, and Luke gave back that skill to God. Kindness is the quality which lifts a man out of the ruck of ordinary men. Eloquence will be forgotten; mental cleverness may live on the printed page; but kindness lives on enthroned in the hearts of men.

Dr. Johnson had certain contacts with a young man called Harry Hervey. Hervey was rich and more than something of a rake. But he had a London house where Johnson was always welcome. Years later Harry Hervey was being unkindly discussed. Johnson said seriously: "He was a vicious man, but very kind to me. If you call a dog Hervey, I shall love him." Kindness covered a multitude of sins.

Luke was loyal and Luke was kind.

(iii) The other definite reference to Luke is in *Philemon* 24; where Paul calls him his *fellow-labourer*. Luke was not content only to write nor to confine himself to his job as a doctor; he set his hand to the work. The Church is full of talkers and of people who are there more for what they can get than for what they can give; Luke was one of these priceless people—the workers of the Church.

(iv) There is one other possible reference to Luke in the New Testament. 2 *Corinthians* 8: 18 speaks of "the brother who is famous among all the Churches." From the earliest times that brother has been identified with Luke. He was the man of whom all men spoke well. He was the man who was loyal unto death; he was the man who was essentially kind; he was the man who was dedicated to the work. Such a man will always be one of whom all speak well.

A ROLL OF HONOUR AND DISHONOUR

2 *Timothy* 4: 9–15 (*continued*)

THERE is still another name with an untold, yet thrilling, story behind it in this roll.

THE MAN WHO REDEEMED HIMSELF

Paul urges Timothy to bring Mark with him "for he is profitable to me for the ministry." The word *ministry* is not used in its narrower sense of the ministry of the Church but in its wider sense of *service*. "Bring Mark," says Paul, "for he is very useful in service." As E. F. Scott puts it; "Bring Mark, for he can turn his hand to anything." Or, as we might put it in our own everyday language: "Bring Mark, for he is a useful man to have about the place."

Mark had a curiously chequered career. He was very young when the Church began, but he lived at the very centre of its life. It was to the house of Mary, Mark's mother, that Peter turned his steps when he escaped from prison, and we may take it that this house was the central meeting place of the Jerusalem Church (*Acts* 12: 12).

When Paul and Barnabas set out on their first missionary journey they took Mark with them—John Mark was his full name—to be their assistant (*Acts* 13: 5). It looked as if he was earmarked for a great career in the company of Paul and in the service of the Church. Then something happened. When Paul and Barnabas left Pamphylia and struck inland on the hard and dangerous road that led to the central plateau of Asia Minor, Mark left them and went home (*Acts* 13: 13). His nerve failed him, and he turned back.

Paul took that defection very hard. When he set out with Barnabas on their second missionary journey, Barnabas—he was related to Mark (*Colossians* 4: 10)—planned to take Mark with them again. But Paul absolutely refused to have the quitter a second time, and so fierce was the argument and so acute the difference that Paul and Barnabas split company and never, so far as we know, worked together again (*Acts* 15: 36–40). So then, there was a time when Paul had no use for Mark, when he looked on him as a spineless deserter and completely refused to have him on his staff.

What happened to Mark after that we do not know. Tradition has it that he went to Egypt and that he was the founder of the Christian Church in that country. But, whatever he did, he certainly redeemed himself. When Paul comes to write *Colossians* from his Roman prison, Mark is with him, and Paul commends him to the Colossian Church and charges them to receive him. And now, when the end is near, the one man Paul wants, besides his beloved Timothy, is Mark, for he is a useful man to have about. The quitter has become the man who can turn his hand to anything in the service of Paul and of the gospel.

Fosdick has a sermon with the great and uplifting title, "No man need stay the way he is." Mark is proof of that. He is our encouragement and our inspiration, for he was the man who failed and yet made good. Still to this day Jesus Christ can make the coward spirit brave and nerve the feeble arm for fight. He can release the sleeping hero in the soul of every man. He can turn the shame of failure into the joy of triumphant service.

A ROLL OF HONOUR AND DISHONOUR

2 *Timothy* 4: 9–15 (*continued*)

HELPERS AND A HINDERER
AND A LAST REQUEST

So the list of names goes on. Of Crescens we know nothing at all. Titus was another of Paul's most faithful lieutenants. "My true child," Paul calls him (*Titus* 1: 4). When the trouble with the Church at Corinth had been worrying him, Titus had been one of Paul's emissaries in the struggle to mend things (2 *Corinthians* 2: 13; 7: 6, 13; 12: 18). Tychicus had been entrusted with the delivery of the letter to the Colossians (*Colossians* 4: 7), and of the letter to the Ephesians (*Ephesians* 6: 21). The little group of helpers was being dispersed throughout the Church, for even if Paul was in prison the work had still to go on, and Paul must go lonely that his scattered people might be strengthened and guided and comforted.

Then comes the mention of a man who had hindered instead of helping: "Alexander the coppersmith did me a great deal of harm." We do not know what Alexander had done; but perhaps we can deduce it. The word that Paul uses for *did me much evil* is the Greek *endeiknumi*. That verb literally means *to display*, and was in fact often used for *the laying of information* against a man. Informers were one of the great curses of Rome at this time. And it may well be that Alexander was a renegade Christian, who went to the magistrates with false information against Paul, seeking to ruin him in the most dishonourable way.

Paul has certain personal requests to make. He wants the cloak he had left behind at the house of Carpus in Troas. The cloak *(phainolē)* was a great circular rug-like garment. It had a hole for the head in the middle and it covered a man like a little tent, reaching right down to the ground. It was a garment for the winter time and no doubt Paul was feeling his Roman prison cold.

He wants the *books;* the word is *biblia*, which literally means papyrus rolls; and it may well be that these rolls contained the earliest forms of the gospels. He wanted the *parchments*. They could be one of two things. They might be Paul's necessary legal documents, especially his certificate of Roman citizenship; but more likely they were copies of the Hebrew Scriptures, for the Hebrews wrote their sacred books on parchment made from the skins of animals. It was the word of Jesus and the word of God that Paul wanted most of all, when he lay in prison awaiting death.

Sometimes history has a strange way of repeating itself.

Fifteen hundred years later William Tyndale was lying in prison in Vilvorde, waiting for death because he had dared to give the people the Bible in their own language. It is a cold damp winter, and he writes to a friend: "Send me, for Jesus's sake, a warmer cap, something to patch my leggings, a woollen shirt, and *above all my Hebrew Bible*." When they were up against it and the chill breath of death was on them, the great ones wanted more than anything else the word of God to put strength and courage into their souls.

LAST WORDS AND GREETINGS

2 *Timothy* 4: 16–22

> At my first defence no one was there to stand by me, but all forsook me. May it not be reckoned against them! But the Lord stood beside me, and he strengthened me, so that through me the proclamation of the gospel was fully made so that the Gentiles might hear it. So I was rescued from the mouth of the lion. The Lord will rescue me from every evil, and will save me for his heavenly kingdom. Glory be to him for ever and ever. Amen.
>
> Greet Prisca and Aquila, and the family of Onesiphorus. Erastus stayed in Corinth. I left Trophimus at Miletus. Eubulus sends greetings to you, as do Pudens, Linus and Claudia, and all the brothers.
>
> The Lord be with your spirit.
> Grace be with you.

A ROMAN trial began with a preliminary examination to formulate the precise charge against the prisoner. When Paul was brought to that preliminary examination, not one of his friends stood by him. It was too dangerous to proclaim oneself the friend of a man on trial for his life.

One of the curious things about this passage is the number of reminiscences of Psalm 22. "Why hast thou forsaken me?—all forsook me." "There is none to help—no one was there to stand by me." "Save me from the mouth of the lion—I was rescued from the mouth of the lion." "All the ends of the earth shall turn to the Lord—that the Gentiles might hear it." "Dominion belongs to the Lord—The Lord will save me for his heavenly kingdom." It seems certain that the words of this psalm were running in Paul's mind. And the lovely thing is that this was the psalm which was in the mind of Jesus when he hung upon his Cross. As Paul faced death, he encouraged his heart with the same psalm as his Lord used in the same circumstances.

Three things brought Paul courage in that lonely hour.

(i) All men had forsaken him but the Lord was with him. Jesus had said that he would never leave his own or forsake them and that he would be with them to the end of the world. Paul is a witness that Jesus kept his promise. If to do the right means to be alone, as Joan of Arc said, "It is better to be alone with God."

(ii) Paul would use even a Roman court to proclaim the message of Christ. He obeyed his own commandment; in season and out of season he pressed the claims of Christ on men. He was so busy thinking of the task of preaching that he forgot the danger. A man who is immersed in his task has conquered fear.

(iii) He was quite certain of the ultimate rescue. In time he might seem to be the victim of circumstances and a criminal condemned at the bar of Roman justice; but Paul saw beyond time and knew that his eternal safety was assured. It is always better to be in danger for a moment and safe for eternity, than to be safe for a moment and jeopardize eternity.

A HIDDEN ROMANCE?

2 Timothy 4: 16–22 (*continued*)

FINALLY there come greetings sent and given. There is a greeting to Priscilla and Aquila, that husband and wife whose home was ever a church, wherever it might be, and who had at some time risked their lives for Paul's sake (*Acts* 18: 2; *Romans* 16: 3; 1 *Corinthians* 16: 19). There is a greeting to the gallant Onesiphorus, who had sought out Paul in prison in Rome (2 *Timothy* 1: 16) and who, it may be, had paid for his loyalty with his life. There is a greeting to Erastus, whom once Paul sent as his emissary to Macedonia (*Acts* 19: 22), and who, it may be, was afterwards within the Church at Rome (*Romans* 16: 23). There is a greeting to Trophimus, whom Paul had been accused of bringing into the Temple precincts in Jerusalem, although a Gentile, an incident for which Paul's last imprisonment began (*Acts* 20: 4; 21: 29). Finally there are greetings from Linus, Pudens and Claudia. In the later lists Linus stands as the first bishop of Rome.

Around the names of Pudens and Claudia a romance has been woven. The story may be impossible, or at least improbable, but it is too interesting not to quote. Martial was a famous Roman poet, a writer of epigrams, who flourished from A.D. 66 to A.D. 100. Two of his epigrams celebrate the marriage of a highborn and distinguished Roman called Pudens to a lady called Claudia. In the second of them Claudia is called a stranger in Rome, and it is said that she came from Britain. Now Tacitus tells us that in A.D. 52, in the reign of the Emperor Claudius, certain territories in south-east Britain were given to a British king called Cogidubnus, for his loyalty to Rome; and in 1723 a marble tablet was dug up in Chichester which commemorates the erection of a heathen temple by Cogidubnus, the king, and by Pudens, his son. In the inscription the full name of the king is given and, no doubt in honour of the Roman Emperor, we find that the British king had taken the name of Tiberius Claudius Cogidubnus. If that king had a daughter her name must have been Claudia, for that is the name that she would take from her father. We can carry the story further. It may be that Cogidubnus would send his daughter Claudia to stay in Rome. That he should do so would be almost certain, for when a foreign king entered into an alliance with Rome, as Cogidubnus had done, some members of his family were always sent to Rome as pledges of keeping the agreement. If Claudia went to Rome, she would certainly stay in the house of a Roman called Aulus Plautius, who had been the governor in Britain from A.D. 43–52, and to whom Cogidubnus had rendered his faithful service. The wife of Aulus Plautius was a lady called Pomponia, and we learn from Tacitus that she had been arraigned before the Roman courts in A.D. 57 because she was "tainted with a foreign superstition." That "foreign superstition" may well have been Christianity. Pomponia may have been a Christian, and from her Claudia, the British princess, may have learned of Jesus also.

We cannot say whether the guesses in that story are true. But it would be wonderful to think that this Claudia was actually a British princess who had come to stay in Rome and become a Christian, and that Pudens was her husband.

Paul comes to the end by commending his friends to the presence and the Spirit of his Lord and theirs, and, as always, his last word is grace.

THE LETTER TO TITUS

TITUS

THE MAINSPRINGS OF APOSTLESHIP

Titus 1: 1-4

This is a letter from Paul, the slave of God and the envoy of Jesus Christ, whose task it is to awaken faith in God's chosen ones, and to equip them with a fuller knowledge of that truth, which enables a man to live a really religious life, and whose whole work is founded on the hope of eternal life, which God, who cannot lie, promised before time began. In his own good time God set forth his message plain for all to see in the proclamation with which I have been entrusted by the royal command of God our Saviour. This letter is to Titus, his true son in the faith they both share. Grace be to you and peace from God the Father and from Christ Jesus our Saviour.

WHEN Paul summoned one of his henchmen to a task, he always began by setting forth his own right to speak and, as it were, laying again the foundations of the gospel. So he begins here by saying certain things about his apostleship.

(i) It set him in *a great succession*. Right at the beginning Paul calls himself "the slave *(doulos)* of God." That was a title of mingled humility and legitimate pride. It meant that his life was totally submitted to God; at the same time—and here was where the pride came in—it was the title that was given to the prophets and the great ones of the past. Moses was the slave of God *(Joshua* 1: 2); and Joshua, his successor, would have claimed no higher title *(Joshua* 24: 29). It was to the prophets, his slaves, that God revealed all his intentions *(Amos* 3: 7); it was his slaves the prophets whom God had repeatedly sent to Israel throughout the history of the nation *(Jeremiah* 7: 25). The title *slave of God* was one which gave Paul the right to walk in a great succession.

When anyone enters the Church, he does not enter an institution which began yesterday. The Church has centuries of human history behind it and goes back before the eternities in

the mind and intention of God. When anyone takes upon
himself anything of the preaching, or the teaching, or the
serving work of the Church, he does not enter on a service
which is without traditions; he walks where the saints have
trod.

(ii) It gave him *a great authority*. He was the envoy of
Jesus Christ. Paul never thought of his authority as coming
from his own mental excellence, still less from his own moral
goodness. It was in the authority of Christ that he spoke.
The man who preaches the gospel of Christ or teaches his
truth, if he is truly dedicated, does not talk about his own
opinions or offer his own conclusions; he comes with
Christ's message and with God's word. The true envoy of
Christ has reached past the stage of *perhapses* and *maybes* and
possiblys, and speaks with the certainty of one who knows.

AN APOSTLE'S GOSPEL

Titus 1 : 1–4 (*continued*)

FURTHER, in this passage we can see the essence of an
apostle's gospel and the central things in his task.

(i) The whole message of the apostle is founded on *the hope
of eternal life*. Again and again the phrase *eternal life* recurs
in the pages of the New Testament. The word for *eternal* is
aiōnios; and properly the only one person in the whole
universe to whom that word may correctly be applied is God.
The Christian offer is nothing less than the offer of a share
in the life of God. It is the offer of God's power for our
frustration, of God's serenity for our dispeace, of God's truth
for our guessing, of God's goodness for our moral failure, of
God's joy for our sorrow. The Christian gospel does not in
the first place offer men an intellectual creed or a moral code;
it offers them life, the very life of God.

(ii) To enable a man to enter into that life, two things
are necessary. It is the apostle's duty to awaken *faith* in men.

With Paul, faith always means one thing—absolute trust in God. The first step in the Christian life is to realize that we can do nothing except receive. In every sphere of life, no matter how precious an offer may be, it remains inoperative until it is received. The first duty of the Christian is to persuade others to accept the offer of God. In the last analysis, we can never argue a man into Christianity. All we can say is, "Try it, and see!"

(iii) It is the apostle's duty also to equip others with *knowledge*. Christian evangelism and Christian education must go hand in hand. Faith may begin by being a response of the heart, but it must go on to be the possession of the mind. The Christian gospel must be thought out in order to be tried out. No man can live for ever on the crest of a wave of emotion. The Christian life must be a daily loving Christ more and understanding him better.

(iv) The result of faith and knowledge must be *a truly religious life*. Faith must always issue in life and Christian knowledge is not merely intellectual knowledge but knowledge *how to live*. Many people have been great scholars and yet completely inefficient in the ordinary things of life and total failures in their personal relationships. A truly religious life is one in which a man is on the right terms with God, with himself and with his fellow-men. It is a life in which a man can cope alike with the great moments and the everyday duties. It is a life in which Jesus Christ lives again.

It is the duty of the Christian to offer to men the very life of God; to awaken faith in their hearts and to deepen knowledge in their minds; to enable them to live in such a way that others will see the reflection of the Master in them.

GOD'S PURPOSE AND GOD'S GOOD TIME

Titus 1: 1–4 (*continued*)

This passage tells us of God's purpose and of his way of working that purpose out.

(i) God's purpose for man was always one of salvation. His promise of eternal life was there before the world began. It is important to note that here Paul applies the word *Saviour* both to God and to Jesus. We sometimes hear the gospel presented in a way that seems to draw a distinction between a gentle, loving, and gracious Jesus, and a hard, stern, and severe God. Sometimes it sounds as if Jesus had done something to change God's attitude to men and had persuaded him to lay aside his wrath and not to punish them. There is no justification for that in the New Testament. But at the back of the whole process of salvation is the eternal and unchanging love of God, and it was of that love Jesus came to tell men. God is characteristically the Saviour God, whose last desire is to condemn men and whose first desire is to save them. He is the Father who desires only that his children should come home so that he may gather them to his breast.

(ii) But this passage does more than speak of God's eternal purpose; it also speaks of his method. It tells us that he sent his message in *his own good time*. That means to say that all history was a preparation for the coming of Jesus. We cannot teach any kind of knowledge to a man until he is fit to receive it. In all human knowledge we have to start at the beginning; so men had to be prepared for the coming of Jesus. All the history of the Old Testament and all the searchings of the Greek philosophers were preparations for that event. God's Spirit was moving both amongst the Jews and amongst all other peoples so that they should be ready to receive his Son when he came. We must look on all history as God's education of men.

(iii) Further, Christianity came into this world at a time when it was uniquely possible for its message to spread. There were five elements in the world situation which facilitated its spread.

(*a*) Practically all the world spoke Greek. That is not to say that the nations had forgotten their own language; but nearly all men spoke Greek in addition. It was the language of trade, of commerce, of literature. If a man was going to take any part in public life and activity he had to know Greek. People were bilingual and the first age of Christianity was one of the very few when the missionary had no language problem to solve.

(*b*) There were to all intents and purposes no frontiers. The Roman Empire was co-extensive with the known world. Wherever the traveller might go, he was within that Empire. Nowadays, if a man intended to cross Europe, he would need a passport; he would be held up at frontiers; he would find iron curtains. In the first age of Christianity a missionary could move without hindrance from one end of the known world to the other.

(*c*) Travel was comparatively easy. True, it was slow, because there was no mechanized travel, and most journeys had to be done on foot, with the baggage carried by slow-moving animals. But the Romans had built their great roads from country to country and had, for the most part, cleared the land of brigands and the sea of pirates. Travel was easier than it had ever been before.

(*d*) The first age of Christianity was one of the few when the world was very largely at peace. If wars had been raging all over Europe, the progress of the missionary would have been rendered impossible. But the *pax Romana,* the Roman peace, held sway; and the traveller could move within the Roman Empire in safety.

(*e*) It was a world which was conscious of its needs. The old faiths had broken down and the new philosophies were beyond the mind of simple people. Men were looking, as Seneca said, *ad salutem*, towards salvation. They were increasingly conscious of "their weakness in necessary things." They were searching for "a hand let down to lift them up." They were looking for "a peace, not of Caesar's proclamation, but of God's." There never was a time when the hearts of men were more open to receive the message of salvation which the Christian missionaries brought.

It was no accident that Christianity came when it did. It came in God's own time; all history had been a preparation for

it; and the circumstances were such that the way was open
for the tide to spread.

A FAITHFUL HENCHMAN

Titus 1: 1–4 (*continued*)

WE do not know a great deal about Titus, to whom this
letter was written, but from the scattered references to him,
there emerges a picture of a man who was one of Paul's
most trusted and most valuable helpers. Paul calls him "my
true son," so it is most likely that he himself converted him,
perhaps at Iconium.

Titus was the companion for an awkward and a difficult
time. When Paul paid his visit to Jerusalem, to a Church which
suspected him and was prepared to mistrust and dislike him,
it was Titus whom he took with him along with Barnabas
(*Galatians* 2: 1). It was said of Dundas, the famous Scotsman,
by one of his friends, "Dundas is no orator; but he will go
out with you in any kind of weather." Titus was like that.
When Paul was up against it, Titus was by his side.

Titus was the man for a tough assignment. When the
trouble at Corinth was at its peak, it was he who was
sent with one of the severest letters Paul ever wrote
(2 *Corinthians* 8: 16). Titus clearly had the strength of mind
and the toughness of fibre which enabled him to face and to
handle a difficult situation. There are two kinds of people.
There are the people who can make a bad situation worse,
and there are the people who can bring order out of chaos
and peace out of strife. Titus was the man to send to the
place where there was trouble. He had a gift for practical
administration. It was Titus whom Paul chose to organize the
collection for the poor members of the Church at Jerusalem
(2 *Corinthians* 8: 6, 10). It is clear that he had no great gifts
of speech, but he was the man for practical administration.

The Church ought to thank God for the people to whom we turn whenever we want a practical job well done.

Paul has certain great titles for Titus.

He calls him his *true child.* That must mean that he was Paul's convert and child in the faith (*Titus* 1: 4). Nothing in this world gives a preacher and teacher more joy than to see someone whom he has taught rise to usefulness within the Church. Titus was the son who brought joy to the heart of Paul, his father in the faith.

He calls him his *brother* (2 *Corinthians* 2: 13) and his *sharer in work and toil* (2 *Corinthians* 8: 23). The great day for a preacher or a teacher is the day when his child in the faith becomes his brother in the faith, when the one whom he has taught is able to take his place in the work of the Church, no longer as a junior, but as an equal.

He says that *Titus walked in the same spirit* (2 *Corinthians* 12: 18). He knew that Titus would deal with things as he would have dealt with them himself. Happy is the man who has a lieutenant to whom he can commit his work, certain that it will be done in the way in which he himself would have wished to do it.

He gives to Titus a great task. He sends him to Crete to be a *pattern* to the Christians who are there (*Titus* 2: 7). The greatest compliment Paul paid Titus was that he sent him to Crete, not to *talk* to them about what a Christian should be, but to *show* them what he should be. There could be no greater responsibility and no higher compliment than that.

One very interesting suggestion has been made. 2 *Corinthians* 8: 18 and 2 *Corinthians* 12: 18 both say that when Titus was sent to Corinth another brother was sent with him, described in the former passage as "the brother who is famous among all the churches," and commonly identified with Luke. It has been suggested that Titus was Luke's brother. It is rather an odd fact that Titus is never mentioned in *Acts;* but we know that Luke wrote *Acts* and often tells the story in the first person plural, saying: "We did this," or, "We did that," and it has been suggested that in such passages he includes Titus with himself. Whether or not that suggestion is true we cannot tell, but certainly Titus and Luke have a family resemblance in that they were both men of practical service.

In the Western Church Titus is commemorated on 4th January, and in the Eastern Church on 25th August.

THE ELDER OF THE CHURCH

Titus 1: 5–7a

The reason why I left you in Crete was that any deficiencies in the organization of the Church should be rectified, and that you might appoint elders in each city as I instructed you. An elder is a man whose conduct must be beyond reproach, the husband of one wife, with children who are also believers, who cannot be accused of profligacy, and who are not undisciplined. For he who oversees the Church of God must be beyond reproach, as befits a steward of God.

WE have already studied in detail the qualifications of the elder as set out by Paul in 1 *Timothy* 3: 1–7. It is therefore not necessary to examine them in detail again.

It was always Paul's custom to ordain elders as soon as a Church had been founded (*Acts* 14: 23). Crete was an island of many cities. "Crete of the hundred cities," Homer called it. It was Paul's principle that his little Churches should be encouraged to stand on their own feet as soon as possible.

In this repeated list of the qualifications of the elder, one thing is specially stressed. He must be a man who has taught his own family in the faith. The Council of Carthage later laid it down: "Bishops, elders and deacons shall not be ordained to office before they have made all in their own households members of the Catholic Church." Christianity begins at home. It is no virtue for any man to be so engaged in public work that he neglects his own home. All the Church service in the world will not atone for neglect of a man's own family.

Paul uses one very vivid word. The family of the elder must be such that they cannot be accused of *profligacy*. The Greek word is *asōtia*. It is the word used in *Luke* 15: 13 for the *riotous* living of the prodigal son. The man who is *asōtos* is incapable of saving; he is wasteful and extravagant and pours out his substance on personal pleasure; he destroys his substance and in the end ruins himself. One who is *asōtos* is the old English *scatterling*, the Scots *ne'er-do-well*, the modern *waster*. Aristotle who always described a virtue as the mean between two extremes, declares that on the one hand there is stinginess, on the other there is *asōtia,* reckless and selfish extravagance, and the relevant virtue is liberality. The household of the elder must never be guilty of the bad example of reckless spending on personal pleasure.

Further, the family of the elder must not be *undisciplined.* Nothing can make up for the lack of parental control. Falconer quotes a saying about the household of Sir Thomas More: "He controls his family with the same easy hand: no tragedies, no quarrels. If a dispute begins, it is promptly settled. His whole house breathes happiness, and no one enters it who is not the better for the visit." The true training ground for the eldership is at least as much in the home as it is in the Church.

WHAT THE ELDER MUST NOT BE

Titus 1: 7b

> He must not be obstinately self-willed; he must not be an angry man; he must not be given to drunken and outrageous conduct; he must not be a man ready to come to blows; he must not be a seeker of gain in disgraceful ways.

HERE is a summary of the qualities from which the elder of the Church must be free; and every one is described in a vivid word.

(i) He must not be *obstinately self-willed*. The Greek is *authadēs*, which literally means *pleasing himself*. The man who is *authadēs* has been described as the man who is so pleased with himself that nothing else pleases him and he cares to please nobody. R. C. Trench said of such a man that, "he obstinately maintains his own opinion, or asserts his own rights, while he is reckless of the rights, opinions and interests of others."

The Greek ethical writers had much to say about this fault of *authadeia*. Aristotle set on the one extreme the man who pleases everybody *(areskos)*, and on the other extreme the man who pleases nobody *(authadēs)*, and between them the man who had in his life a proper dignity *(semnos)*. He said of the *authadēs* that he was the man who would not converse or associate with any man. Eudemus said that the *authadēs* was the man who "regulates his life with no respect to others, but who is contemptuous." Euripides said of him that he was "harsh to his fellow citizens through want of culture." Philodemus said that his character was compounded in equal parts of conceit, arrogance and contemptuousness. His conceit made him think too highly of himself; his contemptuousness made him think too meanly of others; and his arrogance made him act on his estimate of himself and others.

Clearly the man who is *authadēs* is an unpleasant character. He is intolerant, condemning everything that he cannot understand and thinking that there is no way of doing anything except his. Such a quality, as Lock said, "is fatal to the rule of free men." No man of contemptuous and arrogant intolerance is fit to be an office-bearer of the Church.

(ii) He must not be *an angry man*. The Greek is *orgilos*. There are two Greek words for anger. There is *thumos*, which is the anger that quickly blazes up and just as quickly subsides, like a fire in straw. There is *orgē*, the noun connected with *orgilos*, and it means inveterate anger. It is not the anger of the sudden blaze, but the wrath which a man nurses to keep it warm. A blaze of anger is an unhappy thing; but this long-lived, purposely maintained anger is still worse. The man who nourishes his anger against any man is not fit to be an office-bearer of the Church.

(iii) He must not be *given to drunken and outrageous conduct*. The word is *paroinos,* which literally means *given to over-indulgence in wine*. But the word widened its meaning until it came to describe all conduct which is outrageous. The Jews, for instance, used it of the conduct of Jews who married Midianite women; the Christians used it of the conduct of those who crucified Christ. It describes the character of the man who, even in his sober moments, acts with the outrageousness of a drunken man.

(iv) He must not be a man *ready to come to blows*. The word is *plēktēs*, which literally means *a striker*. It would seem that in the early Church there were over-zealous bishops who chastised erring members of their flock with physical violence, for the *Apostolic Canons* lay it down: "We order that the bishop who strikes an erring believer should be deposed." Pelagius says: "He cannot strike anyone who is the disciple of that Christ who, being struck, returned no answering blow." The Greeks themselves widened the meaning of this word to include, not only violence in action, but also violence in speech. The word came to mean one who *browbeats* his fellow-men, and it may well be that it should be so translated here. The man who abandons love and resorts to violence of action or of speech is not fit to be an office-bearer of the Christian Church.

(v) He must not be *a seeker of gain in disgraceful ways*. The word is *aischrokerdēs*, and it describes a man who does not care how he makes money so long as he makes it. It so happens that this was a fault for which the Cretans were notorious. Polybius said: "They are so given to making gain in disgraceful and acquisitive ways that among the Cretans alone of all men no gain is counted disgraceful." Plutarch said that they stuck to money like bees to honey. The Cretans counted material gain far above honesty and honour. They did not care how much their money cost them; but the Christian knows that there are some things which cost too much. The man whose only aim in life is to amass material things, irrespective of how he does so, is not fit to be an office-bearer of the Christian Church.

WHAT THE ELDER MUST BE

Titus 1: 8, 9

Rather he must be hospitable, a lover of all good things and all good people, prudent, just, pious, self-controlled, with a strong grip on the truly reliable message which Christian teaching gave to him, that he may be well able to encourage the members of the Church with health-giving teaching, and to convict the opponents of the faith.

THE previous passage set out the things which the elder of the Church must not be; this one sets out what he must be. These necessary qualities group themselves into three sections.

(i) First, there are the qualities which the elder of the Church must display *to other people*.

He must be *hospitable*. The Greek is *philoxenos*, which literally means *a lover of strangers*. In the ancient world there were always many who were on the move. Inns were notoriously expensive, dirty and immoral; and it was essential that the wayfaring Christian should find an open door within the Christian community. To this day no one needs Christian fellowship more than the stranger in a strange place.

He must also be *philagathos,* a word which means either a lover of good things, or a lover of good people, and which Aristotle uses in the sense of *unselfish*, that is, a lover of good actions. We do not have to choose between these three meanings; they are all included. The Christian office-bearer must be a man whose heart answers to the good in whatever person, in whatever place and in whatever action he finds it.

(ii) Second, there comes a group of terms which tell us the qualities which the Christian office-bearer must have *within himself*.

He must be *prudent (sōphrōn)*. Euripides called this prudence "the fairest gift the gods have given to men." Socrates called it "the foundation stone of virtue." Xenophon said that it was that spirit which shunned evil, not only when evil could be seen but even when no one would ever see it. Trench defined it as "entire command over the passions and desires, so that they receive no further allowance than that which the law and right reason admit and approve." *Sōphrōn* is the adjective to be applied to the man, as the Greeks said themselves, "whose thoughts are saving thoughts." The Christian office-bearer must be a man who wisely controls every instinct.

He must be *just (dikaios)*. The Greeks defined the just man as he who gives both to men and to the gods what is due to them. The Christian office-bearer must be such that he gives to man the respect and to God the reverence, which are their due.

He must be *pious (hosios)*. The Greek word is hard to translate, for it describes the man who reverences the fundamental decencies of life, the things which go back beyond any man-made law.

He must be *self-controlled (egkratēs)*. The Greek word describes the man who has achieved complete self-mastery. Any man who would serve others must first be master of himself.

(iii) Finally, there comes a description of the qualities of the Christian office-bearer *within the Church*.

He must be able *to encourage* the members of the Church. The navy has a rule which says that no officer shall speak discouragingly to any other officer in the performance of his duties. There is always something wrong with preaching or teaching whose effect is to discourage others. The function of the true Christian preacher and teacher is not to drive a man to despair, but to lift him up to hope.

He must be able *to convict* the opponents of the faith. The Greek is *elegchein* and is a most meaningful word. It means to rebuke a man in such a way that he is compelled to

C9

admit the error of his ways. Trench says that it means "to rebuke another, with such an effectual wielding of the victorious arms of the truth, as to bring him, if not always to a confession, yet at least to a conviction, of his sin." Demosthenes said that it describes the situation in which a man unanswerably demonstrates the truth of the things that he has said. Aristotle said that it means to prove that things cannot be otherwise than as we have stated them. Christian rebuke means far more than flinging angry and condemning words at a man. It means speaking in such a way that he sees the error of his ways and accepts the truth.

THE FALSE TEACHERS OF CRETE

Titus 1: 10, 11

> For there are many who are undisciplined, empty talkers, deceivers. Those of the circumcision are especially so. They must be muzzled. They are the kind of people who upset whole households, by teaching things which should not be taught in order to acquire a shameful gain.

HERE we have a picture of the false teachers who were troubling Crete. The worst were apparently Jews. They tried to persuade the Cretan converts of two things. They tried to persuade them that the simple story of Jesus and the Cross was not sufficient, but that, to be really wise, they needed all the subtle stories and the long genealogies and the elaborate allegories of the Rabbis. Further, they tried to teach them that grace was not enough, but that, to be really good, they needed to take upon themselves all the rules and regulations about foods and washings which were so characteristic of Judaism. The false teachers were seeking to persuade men that they needed more than Christ and more than grace in order to be saved. They were intellectualists for whom the truth of God was too simple and too good to be true.

One by one the characteristics of these false teachers pass before us.

They were *undisciplined;* they were like disloyal soldiers who refused to obey the word of command. They refused to accept the creed or the control of the Church. It is perfectly true that the Church does not seek to impose upon men a flat uniformity of belief; but there are certain things which a man must believe to be a Christian, the greatest of which is the all-sufficiency of Christ. Even in the Protestant Church discipline is not eliminated.

They were *empty talkers;* the word is *mataiologoi,* and the adjective *mataios, vain, empty, profitless,* was the adjective applied to heathen worship. The main idea was of a worship which produced no goodness of life. These people in Crete could talk glibly but all their talk was ineffective in bringing anyone one step nearer goodness. The Cynics used to say that all knowledge which is not profitable for virtue is vain. The teacher who simply provides his pupils with a forum for pleasant intellectual and speculative discussion teaches in vain.

They were *deceivers.* Instead of leading men to the truth they led them away from it.

Their teaching *upset whole households.* There are two things to notice there. First, their teaching was fundamentally upsetting. It is true that truth must often make a man rethink his ideas and that Christianity does not run away from doubts and questions, but faces them fairly and squarely. But it is also true that teaching which ends in nothing but doubts and questionings is bad teaching. In true teaching, out of the mental disturbance should come in the end a new and greater certainty. Second, they upset households. That is to say, they had an ill effect on family life. Any teaching which tends to disrupt the family is false for the Christian Church is built on the basis of the Christian family.

Their teaching was designed for *gain.* They were more concerned with what they could get out of the people they were teaching than with what they could put into them. Parry has said that this is indeed the besetting temptation of the professional teacher. When he looks on his teaching simply as a career designed for personal advancement and profit, he is in a perilous condition.

These men are to be *muzzled*. That does not imply that they are to be silenced by violence or by persecution. The Greek *(epistomizein)* does mean *to muzzle,* but it became the normal word for *to silence a person by reason.* The way to combat false teaching is to offer true teaching, and the only truly unanswerable teaching is the teaching of a Christian life.

A BAD REPUTATION

Titus 1 : 12

> One of themselves, a prophet of their own, has said:
>> "The Cretans are always liars, wild and evil beasts, lazy gluttons."
> His testimony is true!

No people ever had a worse reputation than the Cretans. The ancient world spoke of the three most evil C's—the Cretans, the Cilicians, and the Cappadocians. The Cretans were famed as a drunken, insolent, untrustworthy, lying, gluttonous people.

Their avarice was proverbial. "The Cretans," said Polybius, "on account of their innate avarice, live in a perpetual state of private quarrel and public feud and civil strife . . . and you will hardly find anywhere characters more tricky and deceitful than those of Crete." He writes of them: "Money is so highly valued among them, that its possession is not only thought to be necessary, but highly creditable; and in fact greed and avarice are so native to the soil in Crete, that they are the only people in the world among whom no stigma attaches to any sort of gain whatever."

Polybius tells of a certain compact that a traitor called Bolis made with a leader called Cambylus, also a Cretan. Bolis approached Cambylus "with all the subtlety of a Cretan." "This was now made the subject of discussion between them in a truly Cretan spirit. They never took into consideration the saving of the person in danger, or their obligations of honour to those who had entrusted them with the undertaking, but confined the discussion entirely to questions of their own safety and their own advantage. As they were both Cretans they were not long in coming to a unanimous agreement."

So notorious were the Cretans that the Greeks actually formed a verb *krētizein, to cretize,* which meant *to lie and to cheat;* and they had a proverbial phrase, *krētizein pros Krēta,* to cretize against a Cretan, which meant *to match lies with lies,* as diamond cuts diamond.

The quotation which Paul makes is actually from a Greek poet called Epimenides. He lived about 600 B.C. and was ranked as one of the seven wise men of Greece. The first phrase, "The Cretans are chronic liars," had been made famous by a later and equally well-known poet called Callimachus. In Crete there was a monument called *The Tomb of Zeus.* Obviously the greatest of the gods cannot die and be buried in a tomb, and Callimachus quoted this as a perfect example of Cretan lying. In his *Hymn to Zeus* he writes:

> "Cretans are chronic liars,
> For they built a tomb, O King,
> And called it thine; but you die not;
> Your life is everlasting."

The Cretans were notorious liars and cheats and gluttons and traitors but here is the wonderful thing. Knowing that, and actually experiencing it, Paul does not say to Timothy: "Leave them alone. They are hopeless and all men know it." He says: "They are bad and all men know it. *Go and convert them.*" Few passages so demonstrate the divine optimism of the Christian evangelist, who refuses to regard any man as hopeless. The greater the evil, the greater the challenge. It is the Christian conviction that there is no sin too great for the grace of Jesus Christ to conquer.

THE PURE IN HEART

Titus 1: 13–16

> For that very reason correct them with severity, that they may grow healthy in the faith and not pay attention to Jewish fables and to rules and regulations made by men who persist in turning their backs on the truth.
>
> "To the pure all things are pure."
>
> But to those who are defiled and who do not believe, nothing is pure, because their mind and conscience are defiled. They profess to know God, but they deny their profession by their deeds, because they are repulsive and disobedient and useless for any good work.

THE great characteristic of the Jewish faith was its thousands of rules and regulations. This, that and the next thing were branded as unclean; this, that and the next food were held to be tabu. When Judaism and Gnosticism joined hands even the body became unclean and the natural instincts of the body were held to be evil. The inevitable result was that long lists of sins were constantly being created. It became a sin to touch this or that; it became a sin to eat this or that food; it even became a sin to marry and to beget children. Things which were either good in themselves or quite natural became defiled.

So Paul strikes out the great principle—To the pure all things are pure. He had already said that even more definitely in *Romans* 14: 20 when, to those who were constantly involved in questions about clean and unclean foods, he said: "All things are pure." It may well be that this phrase is not only a proverb but an actual saying of Jesus. When Jesus was speaking about these countless Jewish rules and regulations, he said: "There is nothing outside a man which by going into him can defile him; but the things which come out of a man are what defile him" (*Mark* 7: 15).

It is a man's heart which makes all the difference. If he is pure in heart, all things are pure to him. If he is unclean in heart, then he makes unclean everything he thinks about or speaks about or touches. This was a principle which the great classical writers had often stated. "Unless the vessel is pure," said Horace, "everything you pour into it grows bitter." Seneca said: "Just as a diseased stomach alters the food which it receives, so the darkened mind turns everything you commit to it to its own burden and ruin. Nothing can come to evil men which is of any good to them, nay nothing can come to them which does not actually harm them. They change whatever touches them into their own nature. And even things which would be of profit to others become pernicious to them." The man with a dirty mind makes all things dirty. He can take the loveliest things and cover them with smut. But the man whose mind is pure finds all things pure.

It is said of these men that both their *mind* and *conscience* are defiled. A man comes to his decisions and forms his conclusions by using two faculties. He uses *intellect* to think things out; he uses *conscience* to listen to the voice of God. But if his intellect is warped in such a way that it can see the unclean thing anywhere, and if his conscience is darkened and numbed by his continual consent to evil, he can take no good decision at all.

A man must keep the white shield of his innocence un-stained. If he lets impurity infect his mind, he sees all things through a mist of uncleanness. His mind soils every thought that enters into it; his imagination turns to lust every picture which it forms; he misinterprets every motive; he gives a double meaning to every statement. To escape that uncleanness we must walk in the cleansing presence of Jesus Christ.

THE UGLY AND THE USELESS LIFE

Titus 1: 13–16 (*continued*)

WHEN a man gets into this state of impurity, he may know God intellectually but his life is a denial of that knowledge Three things are singled out here about such a man.

(i) He is *repulsive*. The word *(bdeluktos)* is the word particularly used of heathen idols and images. It is the word from which the noun *bdelugma*, an *abomination*, comes. There is something repulsive about a man with an obscene mind, who makes sniggering jests and is a master of the unclean innuendo.

(ii) He is *disobedient*. Such a man cannot obey the will of God. His conscience is darkened. He has made himself such that he can hardly hear the voice of God, let alone obey it. A man like that cannot be anything else but an evil influence and is therefore unfit to be an instrument in the hand of God.

(iii) That is just another way of saying that he has become *useless* to God and to his fellow-men. The word used for *useless* *(adokimos)* is interesting. It is used to describe a counterfeit coin which is below standard weight. It is used to describe a cowardly soldier who fails in the testing hour of battle. It is used of a rejected candidate for office, a man whom the citizens regarded as useless. It is used of a stone which the builders rejected. (If a stone had a flaw in it, it was marked with a capital A, for *adokimos,* and left aside, as being unfit to have any place in the building.) The ultimate test of life is usefulness, and the man whose influence is ever towards that which is unclean is of no use to God or to his fellow-men. Instead of helping God's work in the world, he hinders it; and uselessness always invites disaster.

THE CHRISTIAN CHARACTER
(i) The Senior Men

Titus 2: 1, 2

> You must speak what befits sound teaching. You must charge the senior men to be sober, serious, prudent, healthy in Christian faith and love and fortitude.

THIS whole chapter deals with what might be called *The Christian Character in Action*. It takes people by their various ages and stations and lays down what they ought to be within the world. It begins with the *senior men*.

They must be *sober*. The word is *nēphalios,* and it literally means *sober* in contradistinction to *given to over-indulgence in wine*. The point is that when a man has reached years of seniority, he ought to have learned what are, and what are not, true pleasures. The senior men should have learned that the pleasures of self-indulgence cost far more than they are worth.

They must be *serious*. The word is *semnos,* and it describes the behaviour which is serious in the right way. It does not describe the demeanour of a person who is a gloomy killjoy, but the conduct of the man who knows that he lives in the light of eternity, and that before so very long he will leave the society of men for the society of God.

They must be *prudent*. The word is *sōphrōn,* and it describes the man with the mind which has everything under control. Over the years the senior men must have acquired that cleansing, saving strength of mind which has learned to govern every instinct and passion until each has its proper place and no more.

The three words taken together mean that the senior man must have learned what can only be called *the gravity of life*. A certain amount of recklessness and of unthinkingness may be pardonable in youth, but the years should bring their wisdom. One of the most tragic sights in life is a man who has learned nothing from them.

Further, there are three great qualities in which the senior man must be healthy.

He must be healthy in *faith*. If a man lives really close to Christ, the passing of the years and the experiences of life far from taking his faith away will make his faith even stronger. The years must teach us, not to trust God less but to trust him more.

He must be healthy in *love*. It may well be that the greatest danger of age is that it should drift into censoriousness and fault-finding. Sometimes the years take kindly sympathy away. It is fatally possible for a man to become so settled in his ways that he comes unconsciously to resent all new thoughts and ways. But the years ought to bring, not increasing intolerance but increasing sympathy with the views and mistakes of others.

He must be healthy in *fortitude*. The years should temper a man like steel, so that he can bear more and more, and emerge more and more the conqueror over life's troubles.

THE CHRISTIAN CHARACTER

(ii) The Older Women

Titus 2: 3–5

> In the same way you must charge the older women to be in demeanour such as befits those who are engaged in sacred things. You must charge them not to spread slanderous stories, not to be enslaved by over indulgence in wine, to be teachers of fine things, in order that they may train the young women to be devoted to their husbands and their children, to be prudent, to be chaste, to be home-keepers and home-minders, to be kindly, to be obedient to their own husbands, so that no one will have any opportunity to speak evil of the word of God.

IT is clear that in the early Church a most honoured and responsible position was given to the older women. E. F. Brown, who was himself a missionary in India and knew much about Anglo-Indian society in the old days, relates a most interesting thing. A friend of his on furlough in England was asked: "What is it you most want in India?" And his surprising answer was: "Grandmothers." In the old days there were few older women in Anglo-Indian society, because those engaged in the administration of the country almost invariably came to the end of their service and returned to Britain while still fairly young; and the lack of older women was a serious want. E. F. Brown goes on to say: "Old women play a very important part in society—how large a part one does not realize, till one witnesses a social life from which they are almost absent. Kindly grandmothers and sweet charitable old maids are the natural advisers of the

young of both sexes." The older women to whom the years
have brought serenity and sympathy and understanding have
a part to play in the life of the Church and of the
community which is peculiarly their own.

Here the qualities which characterize them are laid down.
Their demeanour must be such as befits those who are
engaged in sacred things. As has been said: "They must
carry into daily life the demeanour of priestesses in a temple."
As Clement of Alexandria had it: "The Christian must live
as if all life was a sacred assembly." It is easy to see what
a difference it would make to the peace and fellowship of the
Church, if it was always remembered that we are engaged in
sacred things. Much of the embittered argument and the
touchiness and the intolerance which all too frequently
characterize church activities would vanish overnight.

They must not spread slanderous stories. It is a curious trait
of human nature that most people would rather repeat and
hear a malicious tale than one to someone's credit. It is no
bad resolution to make up our minds to say nothing at all
about people if we cannot find anything good to say.

The older women must teach and train the younger.
Sometimes it would seem that the only gift experience gives
to some is that of pouring cold water on the plans and
dreams of others. It is a Christian duty ever to use experience
to guide and encourage, and not to daunt and discourage.

THE CHRISTIAN CHARACTER

(iii) The Younger Women

Titus 2: 3–5 (*continued*)

THE younger women are bidden to be devoted to their
husbands and their children, to be prudent and chaste, to
manage their households well, to be kindly to their servants
and to be obedient to their husbands; and the object of such
conduct is that no one will be able to speak evil of the
word of God.

In this passage there is both something that is temporary and something that is permanent.

In the ancient Greek world the respectable woman lived a completely secluded life. In the house she had her own quarters and seldom left them, not even to sit at meals with the menfolk of the family; and into them came no man except her husband. She never attended any public assemblies or meetings; she seldom appeared on the streets, and, when she did, she never did so alone. In fact it has been said that there was no honourable way in which a Greek woman could make a living. No trade or profession was open to her; and if she tried to earn a living, she was driven to prostitution. If the women of the ancient Church had suddenly burst every limitation which the centuries had imposed upon them, the only result would have been to bring discredit on the Church and cause people to say that Christianity corrupted womanhood. The life laid down here seems narrow and circumscribed, but it is to be read against its background. In that sense this passage is temporary.

But there is also a sense in which it is permanent. It is the simple fact that there is no greater task, responsibility and privilege in this world than to make a home. It may well be that when women are involved in the hundred and one wearing duties which children and a home bring with them, they may say: "If only I could be done with all this, so that I could live a truly religious life." There is in fact nowhere where a truly religious life can better be lived than within the home. As John Keble had it:

> "We need not bid, for cloistered cell,
>   Our neighbour and our work farewell,
>   Nor strive to wind ourselves too high
>   For sinful man beneath the sky;
>   The trivial round, the common task,
>   Will furnish all we need to ask—
>   Room to deny ourselves, a road
>   To bring us daily nearer God."

In the last analysis there can be no greater career than that of homemaking. Many a man, who has set his mark upon the world, has been enabled to do so simply because someone at home loved him and tended him. It is infinitely more important that a mother should be at home to put her children to bed and hear them say their prayers than that she should attend all the public and Church meetings in the world.

THE CHRISTIAN CHARACTER
(iv) The Younger Men

Titus 2: 6

In the same way urge on the younger men the duty of prudence.

THE duty of the younger men is summed up in one sentence, but it is a pregnant one. They are bidden remember the duty of prudence. As we have already seen, the man who is *prudent, sōphrōn,* has that quality of mind which keeps life safe. He has the security which comes from having all things under control.

The time of youth is necessarily a time of danger.

(i) In youth the blood runs hotter and the passions speak more commandingly. The tide of life runs strongest in youth and it sometimes threatens to sweep a young person away.

(ii) In youth there are more opportunities for going wrong. Young people are thrown into company where temptation can speak with a most compelling voice. Often they have to study or to work away from home and from the influences which would keep them right. He has not yet taken upon himself the responsibility of a home and a family; he has not yet given hostages to fortune; and he does not yet possess the anchors which hold an older person in the right way through a sheer sense of obligation. In youth there are far more opportunities to make shipwreck of life.

(iii) In youth there is often that confidence which comes from lack of experience. In almost every sphere of life a younger person will be more reckless than his elders, for the simple reason that he has not yet discovered all the things which can go wrong. To take a simple example, he will often drive a motor car much faster simply because he has not yet discovered how easily an accident can take place or on how slender a piece of metal the safety of a car depends. He will often shoulder a responsibility in a much more carefree spirit than an older person, because he has not known the difficulties and has not experienced how easily shipwreck may be made. No one can buy experience; that is something for which only the years can pay. There is a risk, as there is a glory, in being young.

For that very reason, the first thing at which any young person must aim is self-mastery. No one can ever serve others until he has mastered himself. "He who rules his spirit is greater than he who takes a city" (*Proverbs* 16: 32).

Self-discipline is not among the more glamorous of the virtues, but it is the very stuff of life. When the eagerness of youth is buttressed by the solidity of self-mastery, something really great comes into life.

THE CHRISTIAN CHARACTER

(v) The Christian Teacher

Titus 2: 7, 8

> And all the time you are doing this you must offer yourself as a pattern of fine conduct; and in your teaching you must display absolute purity of motive, dignity, a sound message which no one could condemn, so that your opponent may be turned to shame, because he can find nothing bad to say about us.

If Titus's teaching is to be effective, it must be backed by the witness of his own life. He is himself to be the demonstration of all that he teaches.

(i) It must be clear that his motives are absolutely pure. The Christian teacher and preacher is always faced with certain temptations. There is always the danger of self-display, the temptation to demonstrate one's own cleverness and to seek to attract notice to oneself rather than to God's message. There is always the temptation to power. The teacher, the preacher, the pastor is always confronted with the temptation to be a dictator. Leader he must be, but dictator never. He will find that men can be led, but that they will never be driven. If there is one danger which confronts the Christian teacher and preacher more than another, it is to set before himself the wrong standards of success. It can often happen that the man who has never been heard of outside his own sphere of work is in God's eyes a far greater success than the man whose name is on every lip.

(ii) He must have dignity. Dignity is not aloofness, or arrogance, or pride; it is the consciousness of having the terrible responsibility of being the ambassador of Christ. Other men may stoop to pettiness; he must be above it. Other men may bear their grudges; he must have no bitterness. Other men may be touchy about their place; he must have a humility which has forgotten that it has a place. Other men may grow irritable or blaze into anger in an argument; he must have a serenity which cannot be provoked. Nothing so injures the cause of Christ as for the leaders of the Church and the pastors of the people to descend to conduct and to words unbefitting an envoy of Christ.

(iii) He must have a sound message. The Christian teacher and preacher must be certain to propagate the truths of the gospel and not his own ideas. There is nothing easier for him than to spend his time on side-issues; he might well have one prayer: "God, give me a sense of proportion." The central things of the faith will last him a lifetime. As soon as he becomes a propagandist either for his own ideas or for some sectional interest, he ceases to be an effective preacher or teacher of the word of God.

The duty laid on Titus is the tremendous task, not of talking to men about Christ, but of showing him to them. It must be true of him as it was of Chaucer's saintly parson:

"But Cristes love, and his apostles twelve
He taught, but first he folwed it him-selve."

The greatest compliment that can be paid a teacher is to say of him: "First he wrought, and then he taught."

THE CHRISTIAN CHARACTER

(vi) The Christian Workman

Titus 2: 9, 10

Impress upon slaves the duty of obeying their own masters. Urge them to seek to give satisfaction in every task, not to answer back, not to pilfer, but to display all fidelity with hearty good-will, that they may in all things adorn the teaching which God our Saviour gave to them.

IN the early Church the problem of the Christian workman was acute. It was one which could operate in two directions.

If the master was a heathen, the responsibility laid upon the servant was heavy indeed, for it was perhaps only through his conduct that the master could ever come to see what Christianity was. It was the task of the workman to show the master what a Christian could be; and that responsibility still lies upon the Christian workman. A large number of people never willingly darken a Church door; a minister of the Church seldom gets a chance to speak to them. How then is Christianity ever to make contact with them? The only possible way is for a fellow workman to *show* them what Christianity is. There is a famous story of St. Francis. One day he said to one of his young friars: "Let us go down to the village and preach to the people." So they went. They stopped to talk to this man and to that. They begged a crust at this door and that. Francis stopped to play with the children, and exchanged a greeting with the passers-by. Then they turned to go home. "But father," said the novice, "when do we preach?" "Preach?" smiled Francis. "Every step we took, every word we spoke, every action we did, has been a sermon."

There was another side to the problem. If the master was a Christian, a new temptation came into the life of the Christian workman. He might attempt to trade on his Christianity. He might think that, because he was a Christian, special allowances would be made for him. He might expect to "get away" with things because both he and the master were members of the same Church. It is perfectly possible for a man to trade on his Christianity—and there is no worse advertisement for it than a man who does that.

Paul lists the qualities of the Christian workman.

He is *obedient*. The Christian is never a man who is above taking orders. His Christianity teaches him how to serve. He is *efficient*. He is determined to give satisfaction. The Christian workman can never put less than his best into any task that is given him to do. He is *respectful*. He does not think that his Christianity gives him a special right to be undisciplined. Christianity does not obliterate the necessary lines of authority in the world of industry and of commerce. He is *honest*. Others may stoop to the petty dishonesties of which the world is full. His hands are clean. He is *faithful*. His master can rely upon his loyalty.

It may well be that the man who takes his Christianity to his work will run into trouble; but, if he sticks to it, he will end by winning the respect of all men.

E. F. Brown tells of a thing which happened in India. "A Christian servant in India was once sent by his master with a verbal message which he knew to be untrue. He refused to deliver it. Though his master was very angry at the time, he respected the servant all the more afterwards and knew that he could always trust him in his own matters."

The truth is that in the end the world comes to see that the Christian workman is the one most worth having. In one sense, it is hard to be a Christian at our work; in another sense, it is easier than we think, for there is not a

master under the sun who is not desperately looking for
workmen on whose loyalty and efficiency he can rely.

THE MORAL POWER OF THE INCARNATION

Titus 2: 11–14

> For the grace of God, which brings salvation to all men, has
> appeared, schooling us to renounce godlessness and worldly desires
> for forbidden things, and to live in this world prudently, justly and
> reverently, because we expectantly await the realization of our
> blessed hope—I mean the glorious appearing of our great God
> and Saviour Jesus Christ, who gave himself for us to redeem us
> from the power of all lawlessness, and to purify us as a special
> people for himself, a people eager for all fine works.

THERE are few passages in the New Testament which so
vividly set out the moral power of the Incarnation as this
does. Its whole stress is the miracle of moral change which
Jesus Christ can work.

This miracle is repeatedly here expressed in the most
interesting and significant way. Isaiah once exhorted his
people: "Cease to do evil; learn to do good" (*Isaiah* 1: 16, 17).
First, there is the negative side of goodness, the giving up of
that which is evil and the liberation from that which is low;
second, there is its positive side, the acquisition of the shining
virtues which mark the Christian life.

First, there is the renunciation of all godlessness and worldly
desires. What did Paul mean by worldly desires? Chrysostom
said that worldly things are things which do not pass over
with us into heaven but are dissolved together with this present
world. A man is very short-sighted if he sets all his heart and
expends all his labour on things which he must leave behind
when he quits this world. But an even simpler interpretation
of *worldly desires* is that they are for things we could not show
to God. It is only Christ who can make not only our
outward life but also our inward heart fit for God to see.

That was the negative side of the moral power of the

Incarnation; now comes the positive side. Jesus Christ makes us able to live with the *prudence* which has everything under perfect control, and which allows no passion or desire more than its proper place; with the *justice* which enables us to give both to God and to men that which is their due; with the *reverence* which makes us live in the awareness that this world is nothing other than the temple of God.

The dynamic of this new life is the expectation of the coming of Jesus Christ. When a royal visit is expected, everything is cleansed and decorated, and made fit for the royal eye to see. The Christian is the man who is always prepared for the coming of the King of kings.

Finally Paul goes on to sum up what Jesus Christ has done, and once again he does it first negatively and then positively.

Jesus has redeemed us from the power of lawlessness, that power which makes us sin.

Jesus can purify us until we are fit to be the special people of God. The word we have translated *special (periousios)* is interesting. It means *reserved for;* and it was specially used for that part of the spoils of a battle or a campaign which the king who had conquered set apart specially for himself. Through the work of Jesus Christ, the Christian becomes fit to be the special possession of God.

The moral power of the Incarnation is a tremendous thought. Christ not only liberated us from the penalty of past sin; he can enable us to live the perfect life within this world of space and time; and he can so cleanse us that we become fit in the life to come to be the special possession of God.

THE THREEFOLD TASK

Titus 2: 15

Let these things be the substance of your message. Deal out encouragement and rebuke with all the authority which your royal commission confers upon you. Let no one regard your authority as cheap.

HERE Paul succinctly lays before Titus the threefold task of the Christian preacher, teacher and leader.

It is a task of *proclamation*. There is a message to be proclaimed. There are some things about which argument is not possible and on which discussion is not relevant. There are times when he must say: "Thus saith the Lord."

It is a task of *encouragement*. Any preacher who reduces his audience to bleak despair has failed in his task. Men must be convicted of their sin, not that they may feel that their case is hopeless, but that they may be led to the grace which is greater than all their sin.

It is a task of *conviction*. The eyes of the sinner must be opened to his sin; the mind of the misguided must be led to realize its mistake; the heart of the heedless must be stabbed awake. The Christian message is no opiate to send men to sleep; it is rather the blinding light which shows men themselves as they are and God as he is.

THE CHRISTIAN CITIZEN

Titus 3: 1, 2

Remind them to be duly subject to those who are in power and authority, to obey each several command, to be ready for every work so long as it is good, to slander no one, not to be aggressive, to be kindly, to show all gentleness to all men.

HERE is laid down the public duty of the Christian; and it is advice which was particularly relevant to the people of Crete. The Cretans were notoriously turbulent and quarrelsome and impatient of all authority. Polybius, the Greek historian, said of them that they were constantly involved in "insurrections, murders and internecine wars." This passage lays down six qualifications for the good citizen.

The good citizen is *law-abiding*. He recognizes that, unless the laws are kept, life becomes chaos. He gives a proper respect to those who are set in authority and carries out whatever command is given to him. Christianity does not insist that a man should cease to be an individual, but it does insist that he remember that he is also a member of a group. "Man," said Aristotle, "is a political animal." That means that a man best expresses his personality not in isolated individualism but within the framework of the group.

The good citizen is *active in service*. He is ready for every work, so long as it ,is good. The characteristic modern disease is boredom; and boredom is the direct result of selfishness. So long as a man lives on the principle of, "Why should I do it? Let someone else do it," he is bound to be bored. The interest of life lies in service.

The good citizen is *careful in speech*. He must slander no one. No man should say about other people what he would not like them to say about him. The good citizen will be as careful of the words he speaks as of the deeds he does.

The good citizen is *tolerant*. He is not aggressive. The Greek word is *amachos*, which means *not a fighter*. This does not mean that the good citizen will not stand for the principles which he believes to be right, but that he will never be so opinionated as to believe that no other way than his own is right. He will allow to others the same right to have their convictions as he claims for himself to have his own.

The good citizen is *kind*. The word is *epieikēs*, which describes the man who does not stand upon the letter of the law. Aristotle said of this word that it denotes "indulgent consideration of human infirmities" and the ability "to consider not only the letter of the law, but also the mind and intention of the legislator." The man who is *epieikēs* is ever ready to avoid the injustice which often lies in being strictly just.

The good citizen is *gentle*. The word is *praus,* which describes the man whose temper is always under complete control. He knows when to be angry and when not to be angry. He patiently bears wrongs done to himself but is ever chivalrously ready to spring to the help of others who are wronged.

Qualities like these are possible only for the man in whose heart Christ reigns supreme. The welfare of any community depends on the acceptance by the Christians within it of the duty of demonstrating to the world the nobility of Christian citizenship

THE DOUBLE DYNAMIC

Titus 3: 3–7

> For we too were once senseless, disobedient, misguided, slaves to all kinds of desires and pleasures, living in maliciousness and envy, detestable ourselves, and hating each other. But when the goodness and the love to men of God our Saviour appeared, it was not by works wrought in righteousness, which we ourselves had done, but by his own mercy that he saved us. That saving act was made effective to us through that washing, through which there comes to us the rebirth and the renewal which are the work of the Holy Spirit, whom he richly poured out upon us, through Jesus Christ our Saviour. And the aim of all this was that we might be put into a right relationship with God through his grace, and so enter into possession of eternal life, for which we have been taught to hope.

THE dynamic of the Christian life is twofold.

It comes first from the realization that converts to Christianity were once no better than their heathen neighbours. Christian goodness does not make a man proud; it makes him supremely grateful. When he looks at others, living the pagan life, he does not regard them with contempt; he says, as Whitefield said when he saw the criminal on the way to the gallows: "There but for the grace of God go I."

It comes from the realization of what God has done for men in Jesus Christ. Perhaps no passage in the New Testament more summarily, and yet more fully, sets out the work of Christ for men than this. There are seven outstanding facts about that work here.

(i) Jesus put us into a new relationship with God. Till he

came, God was the King before whom men stood in awe, the Judge before whom men cringed in terror, the Potentate whom they could regard only with fear. Jesus came to tell men of the Father whose heart was open and whose hands were stretched out in love. He came to tell them not of the justice which would pursue them for ever but of the love which would never let them go.

(ii) The love and grace of God are gifts which no man could ever earn; they can only be accepted in perfect trust and in awakened love. God offers his love to men simply out of the great goodness of his heart and the Christian thinks never of what he has earned but only of what God has given. The keynote of the Christian life must always be wondering and humble gratitude, never proud self-satisfaction. The whole process is due to two great qualities of God.

It is due to his *goodness*. The word is *chrēstotēs* and means *benignity*. It means that spirit which is so kind that it is always eager to give whatever gift may be necessary. *Chrēstotēs* is an all-embracing kindliness, which issues not only in warm feeling but also in generous action at all times.

It is due to God's *love to men*. The word is *philanthrōpia,* and it is defined as *love of man as man*. The Greeks thought much of this beautiful word. They used it for the good man's kindliness to his equals, for a good king's graciousness to his subjects, for a generous man's active pity for those in any kind of distress, and specially for the compassion which made a man ransom a fellow-man when he had fallen into captivity.

At the back of all this is no merit of man but only the benign kindliness and the universal love which are in the heart of God.

(iii) This love and grace of God are mediated to men through the Church. They come through the sacrament of baptism. That is not to say that they can come in no other way, for God is not confined within his sacraments; but the door to them is ever open through the Church. When we think of baptism in the earliest days of the Church, we must remember that it was the baptism of grown men and women coming directly out of paganism. It was the deliberate leaving of one way of life to enter upon another. When Paul writes to the people of Corinth, he says: "You were washed, you were sanctified, you were justified" (1 *Corinthians* 6: 11). In the letter to the Ephesians he says that Jesus Christ took the Church that "he might sanctify her, having cleansed her by the washing of water with the word" (*Ephesians* 5: 26). In baptism there came to men the cleansing, re-creating power of God.

In this connection Paul uses two words.

He speaks of *rebirth (paliggenesia)*. Here is a word which had many associations. When a proselyte was received into the Jewish faith, after he had been baptized he was treated as if he were a little child. It was as if he had been reborn and life had begun all over again. The Pythagoreans used the word frequently. They believed in reincarnation and that men returned to life in many forms until they were fit to be released from it. Each return was a rebirth. The Stoics used the word. They believed that every three thousand years the world went up in a great conflagration, and that then there was a rebirth of a new world. When people entered the Mystery Religions they were said to be "reborn for eternity." The point is that when a man accepts Christ as Saviour and Lord, life begins all over again. There is a newness about life which can be likened only to a new birth.

He speaks of a *renewing*. It is as if life were worn out and when a man discovers Christ there is an act of renewal, which is not over and done with in one moment of time but repeats itself every day.

CAUSE AND EFFECT

Titus 3: 3–7 (*continued*)

(iv) The grace and love of God are mediated to men within the Church, but behind it all is the power of the Holy Spirit.

All the work of the Church, all the words of the Church, all the sacraments of the Church are inoperative unless the power of the Holy Spirit is there. However highly a Church be organized, however splendid its ceremonies may be, however beautiful its buildings, all is ineffective without that power. The lesson is clear. Revival in the Church comes not from increased efficiency in organization but from waiting upon God. Not that efficiency is not necessary, but no amount of efficiency can breathe life into a body from which the Spirit has departed.

(v) The effect of all this is threefold. It brings forgiveness for past sins. In his mercy God does not hold our sins against us. Once a man was mourning gloomily to Augustine about his sins. "Man," said Augustine, "look away from your sins and look to God." It is not that a man must not be all his life repentant for his sins; but the very memory of his sins should move him to wonder at the forgiving mercy of God.

(vi) The effect is also present life. Christianity does not confine its offer to blessings which shall be. It offers a man here and now life of a quality which he has never known before. When Christ enters into a man's life, for the first time he really begins to live.

(vii) Lastly, there is the hope of even greater things. The Christian is a man for whom the best is always still to be; he knows that, however wonderful is life on earth with Christ, the life to come will be greater yet. The Christian is the man who knows the wonder of past sin forgiven, the thrill of present life with Christ, and the hope of the greater life which is yet to be.

THE NECESSITY OF ACTION AND THE DANGER OF DISCUSSION

Titus 3: 8–11

This is a saying which we are bound to believe—and I want you to keep on affirming these things—that those who have put their

faith in God must think and plan how to practise fine deeds.
These are fine things and useful to men. But have nothing to do
with foolish speculations and genealogies and contentious and
legalistic battles, for they are no good to anyone and serve no useful
purpose. Avoid a contentious and opinionative man, after giving
him a first and a second warning, for you must be well aware that
such a man is perverted and stands a self-condemned sinner.

THIS passage stresses the need for Christian action and the
danger of a certain kind of discussion.

The word we have translated to *practise* fine deeds is
proistasthai, which literally means *to stand in front of* and was
the word used for a shopkeeper standing in front of his shop
crying his wares. The phrase may mean either of two things.
It might be a command to Christians to engage only in
respectable and useful trades. There were certain professions
which the early Church insisted that a man should quit before
he was allowed even to ask for membership. More probably
the phrase has the wider meaning that a Christian must
practise good deeds which are helpful to men.

The second part of the passage warns against useless
discussions. The Greek philosophers spent their time on their
fine-spun problems. The Jewish Rabbis spent their time
building up imaginary genealogies for the characters of the
Old Testament. The Jewish scribes spent endless hours
discussing what could and could not be done on the Sabbath,
and what was and was not unclean. It has been said that there
is a danger that a man may think himself religious because
he discusses religious questions. It is much easier to discuss
theological questions than to be kind and considerate and
helpful at home, or efficient and diligent and honest at work.
There is no virtue in sitting discussing deep theological
questions when the simple tasks of the Christian life are
waiting to be done. Such discussion can be nothing other than
an evasion of Christian duties.

Paul was certain that the real task of the Christian lay in
Christian action. That is not to say that there is no place for

Christian discussion; but the discussion which does not end in action is very largely wasted time.

It is Paul's advice that the contentious and opinionative man should be avoided. The Authorized Version calls him the *heretic*. The Greek is *hairetikos*. The verb *hairein* means *to choose;* and *hairesis* means a party, or a school or a sect. Originally the word carries no bad meaning. This creeps in when a man erects his private opinion against all the teaching, the agreement and the tradition of the Church. A heretic is simply a man who has decided that he is right and everybody else is wrong. Paul's warning is against the man who has made his own ideas the test of all truth. A man should always be very careful of any opinion which separates him from the fellowship of his fellow believers. True faith does not divide men; it unites them.

FINAL GREETINGS

Titus 3: 12–15

> When I send Artemas or Tychicus to you, do your best to come to me at Nicopolis, for I have decided to spend the winter there.
>
> Do your best to help Zenas the lawyer and Apollos on their way. See to it that nothing is lacking to them.
>
> And let our people too learn to practise fine deeds, that they may be able to supply all necessary needs, and that they may not live useless lives.
>
> All who are with me send you their greetings. Greet those who love us in the faith.
>
> Grace be with you all. Amen.

As usual Paul ends his letter with personal messages and greetings. Of Artemas we know nothing at all. Tychicus was one of Paul's most trusted messengers. He was the bearer of the letters to the Colossian and the Ephesian Churches (*Colossians* 4: 7; *Ephesians* 6: 21). Nicopolis was in Epirus and was the best centre for work in the Roman province of Dalmatia. It is interesting to remember that it was there that Epictetus, the great Stoic philosopher, later had his school.

Apollos was the well-known teacher (*Acts* 18:24). Of Zenas we know nothing at all. He is here called a *nomikos*. That could mean one of two things. *Nomikos* is the regular word for *a scribe* and Zenas may have been a converted Jewish Rabbi. It is also the normal Greek for a *lawyer;* and, if that is its meaning, Zenas has the distinction of being the only lawyer mentioned in the New Testament.

Paul's last piece of advice is that the Christian people should practise good deeds, so that they themselves should be independent and also able to help others who are in need. The Christian workman works not only to have enough for himself but also to have something to give away.

Next come the final greetings; and then, as in every letter, Paul's last word is grace.

THE LETTER TO PHILEMON

INTRODUCTION TO THE LETTER TO
PHILEMON

THE UNIQUE LETTER

In one thing this little letter to Philemon is unique. It is the only *private letter* of Paul which we possess. Doubtless Paul must have written many private letters but of them all only *Philemon* has survived. Apart altogether from the grace and the charm which pervade it, this fact gives it a special significance.

ONESIMUS, THE RUNAWAY SLAVE

There are two possible reconstructions of what happened. One is quite straightforward; the other, connected with the name of E. J. Goodspeed, is rather more complicated and certainly more dramatic. Let us take the simple view first.

Onesimus was a runaway slave and very probably a thief into the bargain. "If he has done you any damage," Paul writes, "or, if he owes you anything, put it down to my account—I will repay it" (verses 18 and 19). Somehow the runaway had found his way to Rome, to lose himself in the thronging streets of that great city, somehow he had come into contact with Paul, and somehow he had become a Christian, the child whom Paul had begotten in his bonds (verse 10).

Then something happened. It was obviously impossible for Paul to go on harbouring a runaway slave and something brought the problem to a head. Perhaps it was the coming of Epaphras. It may be that Epaphras recognized Onesimus as a slave he had seen at Colosse, and that thereupon the whole wretched story came out; or, it may be that, with the coming of Epaphras, the conscience of Onesimus moved him to make a clean breast of all his discreditable past.

PAUL SENDS ONESIMUS BACK

In the time that he had been with him, Onesimus had made himself very nearly indispensable to Paul, and Paul would have liked to keep him beside him. "I would have been glad to keep him with me," he writes (verse 13). But he will do nothing without the consent of Philemon, Onesimus's master (verse 14). So he sends Onesimus back. No one knew better than Paul how great a risk he was taking. A slave was not a person; he was a living tool. A master had absolute power over his slaves. "He can box their ears or condemn them to hard labour—making them, for instance, work in chains upon his lands in the country, or in a sort of prison-factory. Or, he may punish them with blows of the rod, the lash or the knot; he can brand them upon the forehead, if they are thieves or runaways, or, in the end, if they prove irreclaimable, he can crucify them." Pliny tells how Vedius Pollio treated a slave. The slave was carrying a tray of crystal goblets into the courtyard; he dropped and broke one; on the instant Pollio ordered him to be thrown into the fishpond in the middle of the court, where the savage lampreys tore him to pieces. Juvenal draws the picture of the mistress who will beat her maidservant at her caprice and the master who "delights in the sound of a cruel flogging, deeming it sweeter than any siren's song," who is never happy "until he has summoned a torturer and he can brand someone with a hot iron for stealing a couple of towels," "who revels in clanking chains." The slave was continually at the mercy of the caprice of a master or a mistress.

What made it worse was that the slaves were deliberately held down. There were in the Roman Empire 60,000,000 of them and the danger of revolt was constantly to be guarded against. A rebellious slave was promptly eliminated. And, if a slave ran away, at best he would be branded with a red-hot iron on the forehead, with the letter F—standing for *fugitivus, runaway*—and at the worst he would be crucified to death. Paul well knew all this and that slavery was so ingrained into the ancient world that even to send Onesimus back to the Christian Philemon was a considerable risk.

PAUL'S APPEAL

So Paul gave Onesimus this letter. He puns on Onesimus's

name. *Onesimus* in Greek literally means *profitable*. Once Onesimus was a useless fellow, but he is useful now (verse 11). Now, as we might say, he is not only Onesimus by name, he is also Onesimus by nature. Maybe Philemon lost him for a time in order to have him for ever (verse 15). He must take him back, not as a slave but as a Christian brother (verse 16). He is now Paul's son in the faith, and Philemon must receive him as he would receive Paul himself.

EMANCIPATION

Such, then, was Paul's appeal. Many people have wondered why Paul says nothing in this letter about the whole matter of slavery. He does not condemn it; he does not even tell Philemon to set Onesimus free; it is still as a slave that he would have him taken back. There are those who have criticized Paul for not seizing the opportunity to condemn the slavery on which the ancient world was built. Lightfoot says, "The word *emancipation* seems to tremble on his lips, but he never utters it." But there are reasons for his silence.

Slavery was an integral part of the ancient world; the whole of society was built on it. Aristotle held that it was in the nature of things that certain men should be slaves, hewers of wood and drawers of water, to serve the higher classes of men. It may well be that Paul accepted the institution of slavery because it was almost impossible to imagine society without it. Further, if Christianity had, in fact, given the slaves any encouragement to revolt or to leave their masters, nothing but tragedy could have followed. Any such revolt would have been savagely crushed; any slave who took his freedom would have been mercilessly punished; and Christianity would itself have been branded as revolutionary and subversionary. Given the Christian faith, emancipation was bound to come—but the time was not ripe; and to have encouraged slaves to hope for it, and to seize it, would have done infinitely more harm than good. There are some things which cannot be suddenly achieved, and for which the world must wait, until the leaven works.

THE NEW RELATIONSHIP

What Christianity did was to introduce a new relationship between man and man, in which all external differences were abolished. Christians are one body whether Jews or Gentiles, slaves or free men (1 *Corinthians* 12: 13). In Christ there is neither Jew nor Greek, slave nor free man, male nor female (*Galatians* 3: 28). In Christ there is neither Greek nor Jew, circumcision nor uncircumcision, barbarian, Scythian, slave or free man (*Colossians* 3: 11). It was as a slave that Onesimus ran away and it was as a slave that he was coming back, but now he was not only a slave, he was a beloved brother in the Lord. When a relationship like that enters into life, social grades and castes cease to matter. The very names, master and slave, become irrelevant. If the master treats the slave as Christ would have treated him, and if the slave serves the master as he would serve Christ, then it does not matter if you call the one *master* and the other *slave;* their relationship does not depend on any human classification, for they are both in Christ.

Christianity in the early days did not attack slavery; to have done so would have been disastrous. But it introduced a new relationship in which the human grades of society ceased to matter. It is to be noted that this new relationship never gave the slave the right to take advantage of it; it made him rather a better slave and a more efficient servant, for now he must do things in such a way that he could offer them to Christ. Nor did it mean that the master must be soft and easy-going, willing to accept bad workmanship and inferior service; but it did mean that he no longer treated any servant as a thing, but as a person and a brother in Christ.

There are two passages in which Paul sets out the duties of slaves and masters—*Ephesians* 6: 5–9 and *Colossians* 3: 22–4: 1. Both were written when Paul was in prison in Rome, and most likely when Onesimus was with him; and it is difficult not to think that they owe much to long talks that Paul had with the runaway slave who had become a Christian.

On this view *Philemon* is a private letter, sent by Paul to Philemon, when he sent back his runaway slave; and it was written to urge Philemon to receive back Onesimus, not as a pagan master would, but as a Christian receives a brother.

ARCHIPPUS

Let us now turn to the other view of this letter.

We may begin with a consideration of the place of Archippus. He appears in both *Colossians* and *Philemon*. In *Philemon* greetings are sent to Archippus, *our fellow-soldier* (verse 2); and such a description might well mean that Archippus is the minister of the Christian community in question. He is also mentioned in *Colossians* 4: 17: "Say to Archippus, 'See that you fulfil the ministry which you have received in the Lord'." Now that injunction comes after a whole series of very definite references, not to Colosse, but to *Laodicaea* (*Colossians* 4: 13, 15, 16). May the fact that he appears among the messages sent to Laodicaea not imply that Archippus must be at Laodicaea, too? Why in any event should he get this personal message? If he was at Colosse, he would hear the letter read, as everyone else would. Why has this verbal order to be sent to him? It is surely possible that the answer is that he is not in Colosse at all, but in Laodicaea.

If that is so, it means that Philemon's house is in *Laodicaea* and that Onesimus was a runaway *Laodicaean* slave. This must mean that the letter to Philemon was, in fact, written to *Laodicaea*. And, if so, the missing letter to Laodicaea, mentioned in *Colossians* 4: 16, is none other than the letter to Philemon. This indeed solves problems.

Let us remember that in ancient society, with its view of slavery, Paul took a considerable risk in sending Onesimus back at all. So, it can be argued that *Philemon* is not really only a personal letter. It is indeed written to Philemon *and to the Church in his house*. And further it has also to be read at Colosse. What, then, is Paul doing? Knowing the risk that he takes in sending Onesimus back, he is mobilizing Church opinion both in Laodicaea and in Colosse in his favour. The decision about Onesimus is not to be left to Philemon; it is to be the decision of the whole Christian community. It so happens that there is one little, but important, linguistic point, which is very much in favour of this view. In verse 12 the Revised Standard Version makes Paul write that he has *sent back* Onesimus to Philemon. The verb is *anapempein;* this is the regular verb—it is commoner in this sense that in any other—for officially referring a case to someone for decision. And verse 12 should most probably be translated: "I am referring his case to you," that is, not only to Philemon, but also the Church in his house.

There is much to be said for this view. There is only one difficulty. In *Colossians* 4: 9 Onesimus is referred to as *one of you*, which certainly looks as if he is a Colossian. But E. J. Goodspeed, who states this view with such scholarship and persuasiveness, argues that Hierapolis, Laodicaea and Colosse were so close together, and so much a single Church, that they could well be regarded as one community, and that, therefore, *one of you* need not mean that Onesimus came from Colosse, but simply that he came from that closely connected group. If we are prepared to accept this, the last obstacle to the theory is removed.

THE CONTINUATION OF THE STORY

Goodspeed does not stop there. He goes on to reconstruct the history of Onesimus in a most moving way.

In verses 13 and 14 Paul makes it quite clear that he would much have liked to keep Onesimus with him. "I would have been glad to keep him with me, in order that he might serve me on your behalf during my imprisonment for the gospel; but I preferred to do nothing without your consent in order that your goodness might not be by compulsion but of your own free will." He reminds Philemon that he owes him his very soul (verse 19). He says, with charming wit, "Let me make some Christian profit out of you!" (verse 20). He says,

"Confident of your obedience, I write to you, knowing that you will do even more than I say" (verse 21). Is it possible that Philemon could have resisted this appeal? In face of language like that could he do anything other than send Onesimus back to Paul with his blessing? Goodspeed regards it as certain that Paul got Onesimus back and that he became Paul's helper in the work of the gospel.

THE BISHOP OF EPHESUS

Let us move on about fifty years. Ignatius, one of the great Christian martyrs, is being taken to execution from Antioch to Rome. As he goes, he writes letters—which still survive—to the Churches of Asia Minor. He stops at Smyrna and writes to the Church at Ephesus, and in the first chapter of that letter, he has much to say about their wonderful bishop. And what is the bishop's name? It is *Onesimus;* and Ignatius makes exactly the same pun as Paul made—he is Onesimus by name and Onesimus by nature, the profitable one to Christ. It may well be that the runaway slave had become with the passing years the great bishop of Ephesus.

WHAT CHRIST DID FOR ME

If all this is so, we have still another explanation. Why did this little slip of a letter, this single papyrus sheet, survive; and how did it ever get itself into the collection of Pauline letters? It deals with no great doctrine; it attacks no great heresy; it is the only one of Paul's undoubted letters written to an individual person. It is practically certain that the first collection of Paul's letters was made at *Ephesus*, about the turn of the century. It was just then that Onesimus was bishop of Ephesus; and it may well be that it was he who insisted that this letter be included in the collection, short and personal as it was, in order that all might know what the grace of God had done for him. Through it the great bishop tells the world that once he was a runaway slave and that he owed his life to Paul and to Jesus Christ.

Did Onesimus come back to Paul with Philemon's blessing?

Did he become the great bishop of Ephesus, he who had been the runaway slave? Did he insist that this little letter be included in the Pauline collection to tell what Christ, through Paul, had done for him? We can never tell for certain, but it is a lovely story of God's grace in Christ—and we hope that it is true!

PHILEMON

A MAN TO WHOM IT WAS EASY TO APPEAL

Philemon 1–7

This is a letter from Paul, the prisoner of Jesus Christ, and from Timothy, the brother, to Philemon our well-beloved and our fellow-worker; and to Apphia, the sister, and to Archippus, our fellow-soldier, and to the Church in your house. Grace be to you and peace from God, our Father, and from the Lord Jesus Christ.

I always thank my God when I make mention of you in my prayers, for I hear of your love and your faith, which you have to the Lord Jesus, and to all God's dedicated people. I pray that the kindly deeds of charity to which your faith moves you may be powerfully effective to increase your knowledge of every good thing that is in us and that brings us ever closer to Christ. You have brought me much joy and encouragement, because, my brother, the hearts of God's people have been refreshed by you.

THE letter to Philemon is extraordinary, for in it we see the extraordinary sight of Paul asking a favour. No man ever asked fewer favours than he did, but in this letter he is asking a favour, not so much for himself, as for Onesimus, who had taken the wrong turning and whom Paul was helping to find the way back.

The beginning of the letter is unusual. Paul usually identifies himself as Paul *an apostle;* but on this occasion he is writing as a friend to a friend and the official title is dropped. He is not writing as Paul *the apostle* but as Paul *the prisoner of Christ.* Here at the very beginning Paul lays aside all appeal to authority and makes his appeal to sympathy and to love alone.

We do not know who Apphia and Archippus were, but it has been suggested that Apphia was the wife and Archippus the son of Philemon, for they, too, would be very much interested in the return of Onesimus, the runaway slave. Certainly Archippus had seen Christian service with Paul, for Paul speaks of him as his fellow-campaigner.

Philemon was clearly a man from whom it was easy to ask a favour. He was a man whose faith in Christ and love to the brethren all men knew, and the story of them had reached even Rome, where Paul was in prison. His house must have been like an oasis in a desert, for, as Paul puts it, he had refreshed the hearts of God's people. It is a lovely thing to go down to history as a man in whose house God's people were rested and refreshed.

In this passage there is one verse which is very difficult to translate and about which much has been written. It is verse 6 which the Revised Standard Version translates: "I pray that the sharing of your faith may promote the knowledge of all the good that is ours in Christ." The phrase translated *the sharing of your faith,* is very difficult. The Greek is *koinōnia pisteōs.* As far as we can see, there are three possible meanings. (*a*) *Koinōnia* can mean *a sharing in;* it can, for instance, mean partnership in a business. So this may mean *your share in the Christian faith;* and it might be a prayer that the faith which Philemon and Paul share in may lead Philemon deeper and deeper into Christian truth. (*b*) *Koinōnia* can mean *fellowship;* and this may be a prayer that *Christian fellowship* may lead Philemon ever more deeply into the truth. (*c*) *Koinōnia* can mean the *act of sharing;* in that case the verse will mean: "It is my prayer that your way of generously sharing all that you have will lead you more and more deeply into the knowledge of the good things which lead to Christ."

We think that the third meaning is correct. Obviously Christian generosity was a characteristic of Philemon; he had love to God's people and in his home they were rested and refreshed. And now Paul is going to ask the generous man to be more generous yet. There is a great thought here, if this interpretation is correct. It means that we learn about Christ by giving to others. It means that by emptying ourselves we are filled with Christ. It means that to be open-

handed and generous-hearted is the surest way to learn more
and more of the wealth of Christ. The man who knows most
of Christ is not the intellectual scholar, not even the saint
who spends his days in prayer, but the man who moves in
loving generosity amongst his fellow-men.

THE REQUEST OF LOVE

Philemon 8–17

I could well be bold in Christ to give you orders as to where your
duty lies, but for love's sake I would rather put it in the form of a
request, I, Paul, such as I am, an old man now, a prisoner of Christ.
My request to you is for my child, whom I begat in my bonds—I
mean Onesimus, who was once useless to you, but who is now
useful to you and to me. I am sending him back to you, and that
is the same as to send you a bit of my own heart. I could have
wished to keep him beside myself, that he might serve me for you in
the bonds which the gospel has brought to me; but I did not
wish to do anything without your approval; so that the boon which
I ask might not be forcibly extracted but willingly given. It may be
that he was parted from you for a time that you might get him
back for ever; and that you might get him back, no longer as a
slave, but as more than a slave—a well-beloved brother, most of
all to me, and how much more to you, both as a man and a
Christian. If you consider me as a partner, receive him as you
would receive me.

PAUL, being Paul, could have demanded what he wished from
Philemon, but he will only humbly request. A gift must be
given freely and with good-will; if it is coerced it is no gift at
all.

In verse 9 Paul describes himself. The Authorized Version
translates—and we have retained the translation—Paul *the
aged*, and a prisoner of Christ. A good number of scholars
wish to substitute another translation for *aged*. It is argued that
Paul could not really be described as an old man. He
certainly was not sixty years old; he was somewhere between

that and fifty-five. But on this ground those who object to the translation *aged* are wrong. The word which Paul uses of himself is *presbutēs*, and Hippocrates, the great Greek medical writer, says that a man is *presbutēs* from the age of forty-nine to the age of fifty-six. Between these years he is what we might call *senior;* only after that does he become a *gerōn,* the Greek for an old man.

But what is the other translation suggested? There are two words which are very like each other; their spelling is only one letter different and their pronunciation exactly the same. They are *presbutēs*, *old*, and *presbeutēs*, *ambassador*. It is the verb of this word which Paul uses in *Ephesians* 6: 20, when he says, "I am an *ambassador* in bonds." If we think that the word ought to be *presbeutēs*, Paul is saying, "I am an ambassador, although I am an ambassador in chains." But it is far more likely that we should retain the translation *old*, for in this letter Paul is appealing all the time, not to any office he holds or to any authority he enjoys, but only to love. It is not the ambassador who is speaking, but the man who has lived hard and is now lonely and tired.

Paul makes his request in verse 10 and it is for Onesimus. We notice how he delays pronouncing the name of Onesimus, almost as if he hesitated to do so. He does not make any excuses for him; he freely admits he was a useless character; but he makes one claim—he is useful now. Christianity, as James Denney used to say, is the power which can make bad men good.

It is significant to note that Paul claims that in Christ the useless person has been made useful. The last thing Christianity is designed to produce is vague, inefficient people; it produces people who are of use and can do a job better than they ever could if they did not know Christ. It was said of someone that "he was so heavenly-minded that he was no earthly use." True Christianity makes a man heavenly-minded and useful upon earth at one and the same time.

Paul calls Onesimus the child whom he has begotten in his bonds. A Rabbinic saying runs, "If one teaches the son of his neighbour the law, the Scripture reckons this the same as though he had begotten him." To lead a man to Jesus Christ is as great a thing as to bring him into the world. Happy is the parent who brings his child into life and who then leads him into life eternal; for then he will be his child twice over.

As we have noted in the introduction to this letter, there is a double meaning in verse 12. "I am sending him back to you," writes Paul. But the verb *anapempeim* does not mean only *to send back*, it also means *to refer a case to;* and Paul is saying to Philemon: "I am referring this case of Onesimus to you, that you may give a verdict on it that will match the love you ought to have." Onesimus must have become very dear to Paul in these months in prison, for he pays him the great tribute of saying that to send him to Philemon is like sending a bit of his own heart.

Then comes the appeal. Paul would have liked to keep Onesimus but he sends him back to Philemon, for he will do nothing without his consent. Here again is a significant thing. Christianity is not out to help a man escape his past and run away from it; it is out to enable him face his past and rise above it. Onesimus had run away. Well, then, he must go back, face up to the consequences of what he did, accept them and rise above them. Christianity is never escape; it is always conquest.

But Onesimus comes back with a difference. He went away as a heathen slave; he comes back as a brother in Christ. It is going to be hard for Philemon to regard a runaway slave as a brother; but that is exactly what Paul demands. "If you agree," says Paul, "that I am your partner in the work of Christ and that Onesimus is my son in the faith, you must receive him as you would receive myself."

Here again is something very significant. The Christian must always welcome back the man who has made a mistake. Too often we regard the man who has taken the wrong turning with suspicion and show that we are never prepared to trust him again. We believe that God can forgive him but we, ourselves, find it too difficult. It has been said that the most uplifting thing about Jesus Christ is that he trusts us on the very field of our defeat. When a man has made a mistake, the way back can be very hard, and God cannot readily forgive the man who, in his self-righteousness or lack of sympathy, makes it harder.

THE CLOSING APPEAL AND THE CLOSING BLESSING

Philemon 18–25

If he has done you any damage or owes you anything, put it down to my account. I, Paul, write with my own hand—I will repay it, not to mention to you that you owe your very self to me. Yes, my brother, let me make some Christian profit out of you! Refresh my heart in Christ. It is with complete confidence in your willingness to listen that I write to you, for I know well that you will do more than I ask.

At the same time get ready a lodging place for me; for I hope that through your prayers it will be granted to you that I should come to you.

Epaphras, my fellow-prisoner in Christ, sends his greetings to you, as do Mark, Aristarchus, Demas and Luke, my fellow-workers.

The grace of the Lord Jesus Christ be with your spirit. Amen.

IT is one of the laws of life that someone has to pay the price of sin. God can and does forgive, but not even he can free a man from the consequences of what he has done. It is the glory of the Christian faith that, just as Jesus Christ shouldered the sins of all men, so there are those who in love are prepared to help pay for the consequences of the sins of those who are dear to them. Christianity never entitled a man to default on his debts. Onesimus must have stolen from Philemon, as well as run away from him. If he had not helped himself to Philemon's money, it is difficult to see how he could ever have covered the long road to Rome. Paul writes with his own hand that he will be responsible and will repay in full.

It is interesting to note that this is an exact instance of a *cheirographon,* the kind of acknowledgment met in *Colossians* 2: 14. This is *a handwriting against Paul,* an obligation voluntarily accepted and signed.

It is of interest to note that Paul was able to pay Onesimus's debts. Every now and again we get glimpses which show that he was not without financial resources. Felix kept him prisoner for he had hopes of a bribe to let him go (*Acts* 24: 26); Paul was able to hire a house during his imprisonment in Rome (*Acts* 28: 30). It may well be that, if he had not chosen to live the life of a missionary of Christ, he might have lived a settled life of reasonable ease and comfort on his own resources. This may well have been another of the things which he gave up for Christ.

In verses 19–20 we hear Paul speaking with a flash of humour. "Philemon," he says, "you owe your soul to me, for it was I who brought you to Christ. Won't you let me make some profit out of you now?" With an affectionate smile Paul is saying, "Philemon, you got a lot out of me—let me get something out of you now!"

Verse 21 is typical of Paul's dealings with people. It was his rule always to expect the best from others; he never really doubted that Philemon would grant his request. It is a good rule. To expect the best from others is often to be more than half-way to getting it; if we make it clear that we expect little, we will probably get just that.

In verse 22 there speaks Paul's optimism. Even in prison he believes it possible that through the prayers of his friends freedom may come again. He has changed his plans now. Before he was imprisoned it had been his intention to go to far off Spain (*Romans* 15: 24, 28). Maybe after the years in prison, two at Caesarea and other two at Rome, Paul felt that he must leave the distant places to younger men and that for him, as he drew near the end, old friends were best.

In verse 23 there is a list of greetings from the same comrades as we meet in *Colossians,* and so there comes the blessing, and Philemon and Onesimus alike are commended to the grace of Christ.

FURTHER READING

Timothy and Titus

D. Guthrie, *The Pastoral Epistles* (TC; *E*)
W. Lock, *The Pastoral Epistles* (ICC; *G*)
E. F. Scott, *The Pastoral Epistles* (MC; *E*)
E. K. Simpson, *The Pastoral Epistles*

Philemon

J. B. Lightfoot, *St Paul's Epistles to the Colossians and Philemon* (MmC; *G*)
C. F. D. Moule, *The Epistles of Paul the Apostle to the Colossians and to Philemon* (CGT; *G*)
E. F. Scott, *The Epistles to Colossians, Philemon and Ephesians* (MC; *E*)

Abbreviations

CGT : Cambridge Greek Testament
ICC : International Critical Commentary
MC : Moffatt Commentary
MmC: Macmillan Commentary
TC : Tyndale Commentary

E : English Text
G : Greek Text

THE DAILY STUDY BIBLE

Published in 17 Volumes

Also by Gert Hofmann

THE SPECTACLE AT THE TOWER

OUR CONQUEST

The Parable of the Blind

The Parable

Gert Hofmann

of the Blind

Translated by *Christopher Middleton*

Fromm International
Publishing Corporation
NEW YORK

Designed by Constance Fogler
Printed in the United States of America
First U.S. Edition

Library of Congress in Publication Data

Hofmann, Gert.
The parable of the blind.
Translation of: Der Blindensturz.
1. Bruegel, Pieter, ca. 1525–1569—Fiction.
I. Title.

PT 2668.0376B5513   1986   833'.914   85–24600

ISBN 0–88064–051–0

The Parable of the Blind

1

On the day when we're to be painted—yet another new day!—a knocking on the barn door drags us out of our sleep. No, the knocking isn't inside us, it's outside, where the other people are.
What's going on? we call. And it's hard to find the way back. We're in a dream. Lying in a fresh furrow, in a boundless field, half on the surface, half below ground, clouds probably overhead. One leg is stuck in the earth already, the other still outside it. Around us thick soft flakes of snow, clearly remembered, are falling into the gentle folds of the countryside and burying everything: the plow, the weeds, the trees, as well as all the other things we gave up long ago, but which probably still exist. Eventually the snow buries our second leg too, which had been lifted against the

sky, like a black stone, until the last moment.
Good, it's over now, we say, and we've been buried.
First as far as others are concerned, then as far
as we ourselves are. We're beginning to be for-
gotten. Back again to themselves they drag us,
with their knocking. Yes, we call as we crouch
there. Now what do you want of us?
Easy now, easy, the knocker says, and he's standing
close to the door. And he asks if we've forgotten
about being painted today.
Painted? we ask.
Yes, painted.
And why are we going to be painted?
But the knocker doesn't know.
Not forgotten, we call nevertheless, and we kick
our way out of the straw we've shared all night
with the mice.
Good, so we must get up now and go to the village
green, it's time, the knocker says. We must refresh
ourselves before being painted. Also we have to
walk around in the village a bit, to practice.
This village? we ask and tap on the barn floor.
Yes, this one.
What's it called?
Pède-Sainte-Anne.
Is the sun up yet?
No.
And why not? Won't it be coming up today?

The Parable of the Blind

But the knocker doesn't know that, either.
And why walk around?
Because we've got to practice the walking that will
be painted, the knocker says. Especially the stum-
bling and falling, the different kinds of fall.
But aren't we going to be painted sitting?
No, not sitting, the painter says.
So we're going to be painted walking?
Stumbling and falling and screaming.
Do we have to practice screaming?
He doesn't know. Probably we'll have to.
Wait, we call, we're coming.
Slowly, clawing at one another, we get out of the
straw, struggle to our feet. Then we grope at
ourselves and at one another. For there are several
of us, even if only one speaks, the others listen.
(Even if one speaks for all, each thinks for himself.)
Then we pass our hands over our bodies. Yes,
we're still the same people as yesterday. And
probably to the end we'll be yesterday's people
and gradually now we remember ourselves better,
down to the smallest details. Everything comes
back again, even what was buried, and we're very
startled. We remember our names again too, the
names we call one another. And this morning, as
we feel our heads, arms, and sticks, we're probably
the same for others. We wear thick hairy doublets
festooned with grass, straw, and feathers, with

long cords trailing down to our calves (recently
one of us hanged himself with just such a cord),
round bonnets pulled well down, and long sticks
we've cut for ourselves, to pass over the ground
when we walk, so that we can feel what's ahead
or coming our way. What we haven't got is a
nozzle or sucker, not necessarily a long one.
Something with which to pull close to us, without
our having to stoop, whatever might be lying
before us, draw it up to our faces, so as to snuffle
it, smell it. Also people could recognize us by such
nozzles, even from a distance, and see what was
coming. Yes, we should all have nozzles, but we
haven't. Instead, we have our sticks and a begging
sack thrown around our shoulders. And the horse
blanket which we wrap around ourselves at night
and which in the morning hangs down fore and
aft, like a second skin. So we stoop and slide about
on our knees and hit on a shoe, finding then the
second shoe too we slip into them. And around
our legs and calves we wind wrappings. Then we
pull on our smocks, that's to say each of us pulls
another's on for him. Bellejambe pulls Ripolus'
on for him, Ripolus helps Slit Man, we pull
Malente's on for him, and Malente helps us. The
smocks are buttoned up at the throat, they reach
to our calves. Some are badly stitched, the hems
are frayed. This is how we'll be painted, it will be

quite a big picture, because there are several of us, six perhaps. And we pick from one another the twigs, earth, and straw left on us from the night. We grope at one another's faces, we want to clean our faces too. Doing this we feel the nose, the forehead, the eyelids, how long, how high, how broad and angled this way or that, in this or that way smashed. On top, our hoods and our bonnets. (No hat, the wind would take it away.) But we don't want to think about that now— everything in its own good time—instead we trot, sticks in hand, to the barn door. Which, with our first combined effort of the day, we push open, to break out into the village, if only with our heads at first, gasping. The morning breeze is waiting out there, it blows toward us. We stand and look in the direction where we suppose the sun should be. Yes, that's where it must be! And we rub ourselves against the doorposts right and left and stamp our feet a bit, so that our clothes will hang from us properly in folds.

Is it them? a child asks, standing just in front of us.

Yes, it's them, the knocker says.

And they really don't see me? the child asks.

That's right.

And you, the child asks, do they see you?

No, the knocker says, not me, either. And he

7

pauses, so that the child will have time to look at us closely. But they don't need to, he says then, they've got eyes in the back of their heads, like some animals. With those they feel what's going on around them, they don't need any in front. Isn't that so? he asks, you don't need any eyes?

That's so, we say, we don't need any eyes.

And we hesitate, want to say something more, but our thoughts slip away from us.

Even then, the child says, I don't believe they're blind, and he comes closer still, breathing hard up at us. Then he asks if he can touch us.

Where? the knocker says and rustles in the leaves.

Their face.

All right, touch if you want, he says.

Then through the morning breeze the child's warm hand comes and strokes our cheeks, right and left, and creeps into our ears.

Can you feel that? the child asks.

Yes, we say, we can feel it.

And this? he asks, passing his fingertips softly over our eyelids.

Yes, that too, we say.

And how is it, the child asks, does it hurt?

No, we say, it doesn't hurt.

And if I press a bit?

No, we say, you mustn't press.

But you don't see anything anyway.

8

The Parable of the Blind

All the same, we say, you mustn't press.
Oh well, the child says, if I'm not allowed to press
I won't touch, and he steps back again. No, I don't
think they're blind, he says a moment later, probably after wiping his hand on his trousers. Last
year there were some here too, they said they
were blind as well. And then they stole three
chickens and vanished again.
Yes, we've heard about that, we say, but it wasn't
us, and we arrange ourselves in a low row facing
the child. Those are the people who always arrive
before we do and say we're them.
Since when?
Ah, we say, it started several years ago.
And why do they arrive before you and say they're
you?
We don't know that, we say.
And who are they, really?
We don't know that either, we say. Anyway people
tell us, wherever we go: You've been here before.
But we haven't, at least we don't remember. We
don't steal chickens either. We can't even see
chickens.
But if you're really blind, the child asks, how can
you always be looking at me when I talk?
Are we looking at you?
Well, the child says, sometimes you do look past
me or over my head.

GERT HOFMANN

You see? we say. That's because we don't see you,
little angel, we don't even look at you, we only
look in the direction your voice is coming from,
silly.
All the same, the child says to the knocker, they
aren't all blind.
They are, every one of them, the knocker says, or
else they wouldn't be going to be painted today.
One evening in the summertime when it was very
hot they were sitting underneath a cherry tree
and birds came. The birds sat on their shoulders
and pecked their eyes out.
What sort of birds?
Crows, or ravens.
And they let them do it?
Ah, the knocker says, it all happened so fast.
Is that true? the child says and turns to face us
again.
Yes, we say and nod, it's true.
And why then did they peck your eyes out?
Because we killed their young.
And why did you kill their young?
We'd had enough of their noise, we say, at least
we thought we had.
Except that some people say, the knocker says,
that it wasn't ravens or crows, but jackdaws.
Jackdaws, the child says, ah yes, I've heard about
the thing with the jackdaws.

The Parable of the Blind

Yes, we say, perhaps it was jackdaws.
Well, the child says, if it was jackdaws, then I
know about it. And hearing, the child asks the
knocker, can they still hear?
Hear, yes, the knocker says and walks around us.
So they hear everything we're saying now?
Yes, the knocker says, that much they do hear.
And what the people in the houses say?
They hear that too, but not everything.
So they hear as much as we do?
Yes, just about.
Well, at least they're strong, the child says and
takes hold of our arms.
They have to be.
Why?
Because they have to walk a lot.
And where are they going to walk to now?
Now, the knocker says, they're going to be fed,
the painter has paid for it. Then they'll go to the
pond, to practice falling.
Falling? the child asks, why?
Because it'll be painted, the knocker says.
And why will it be painted?
I don't know.
May I guide them to the pond? the child asks.
If you like, the knocker says. Then he claps his
hands and calls: Right, now let them pass.
Cautiously, heads down, sticks right or left, bon-

nets pulled still farther down, we shove our way out through the barn door and enter into nature. Where at once a wind is blowing from above, from the trees, around our heads. The houses we'll be walking between are gathered already around us, quietly we ramble in among them. Windows and doors are being unbolted, people walk out and yawn, acknowledge us, utter little cries, and think: How strange that they have heads with brains inside, like other people. And they wonder if we're wise or foolish, and probably they gaze after us too as we pass.

Hey, you, we say as we walk on, are there any people here?

Yes, the child says.

How many?

Shall I count them?

No, just roughly.

Ten, perhaps.

Where? we ask.

In front of their houses.

And what do they want?

To see you.

So they're looking at us? we ask.

Yes.

Now?

Yes, now.

Well then, we say. And we huddle closer together,

as we always do when we're being watched, we
look more steeply upward. And feel how we're
being *seen*, partly from close, partly from afar.
When we lurch along their streets, we're a deep-
sea monster, a general, noiseless, dark, laboriously
shifted thing. Which, when displayed, is met with
fear, pity, and disgust. This knot of gray bodies
rolling along our street and unfolding at the
windows, they think, it's them. How closely they
cling to one another, how they wobble in the slight
wind! And they ask themselves how such beings
are possible, but that's something even we don't
know. Then a church bell rings, necessarily, but
it startles us.

Pity for the blind! we call and wave our sticks, so
that people will get out of our way. (When they
stop being afraid of our sticks, we show them our
eyes.) Then we ask about the crows. Also we ask
about the season, because we're never sure of it.
Certainly it's a cool day, but what does that mean
in a country with so much winter? We ask: Springtime? Yes, they say, springtime. We ask: Soon?
Yes, soon. Well then, we think, so it's springtime,
and we try to sniff a little warmth out of the wind,
and we tap our way onward, a little heartened.
Perhaps it's the village green we're creeping over,
perhaps we aren't there yet.

Should I guide you? the child asks, but we don't

answer. We call: Pity for the blind! Yes, take them by the hand, guide them to the table with the food, the knocker says, they'll be hungry.

Are you hungry? the child asks and rustles through the leaves.

Yes, hungry, we say.

You're always hungry, the knocker says, aren't you?

Always hungry, we say. Then we say: Spare a thought for the blind, and we wave our sticks.

Then the child says we'll soon reach the table, just a few more steps. Then you can eat whatever you want, just take it. But you mustn't drop anything, because you'll never find it again.

And where's the table, we ask, and already we can smell the food. And from sheer greed we stamp our feet a bit.

There, the child says, there's the table.

And the food, we ask, where's the food?

Here, the child says and takes us by the arm.

2

After the child has led us to the table and we've placed our hands on it and have drawn our fingers around its edge and over its surface, we do then find the food, its smell floats toward us. On the table heavy bowls have been placed and fat jugs set up.

There's the food, the child says, it's all for you.

And he takes our hands and lays them on the bread and the vessels and pushes us around the table. We grope for the food, we want to know what's been provided. And our hands even go into the milk, which stands by the food, it trickles down us, lukewarm. But that's usual. We're always lunging into things we can't count on. Or else we reach out for something that doesn't exist.

Don't you sit down when you eat? the child asks.

Certainly we do, we say, is there anything to sit on?

There, the knocker says, push them onto the bench.

And why, the child asks, don't they go indoors?

No, the knocker says. They'll eat here by the door.

Sit, you may sit down, the child says and pushes us onto the bench we're to sit on. Then they put spoons into our hands for the liquids, the soft things. And so, early this morning, after they've pulled us out of our furrow and questioned us thoroughly and guided us to our table and un-buttoned our smocks and pushed our bonnets back from our faces and tied something too, a rag, across our chests, so that we won't spill anything on our doublets, we sit with our legs spread, in the cool of the season, probably around a long table by a house door on the street, and we begin to eat. We tear the bread, which is moist and still warm from the oven, we gobble into the mash.

Hey, bring us the pepper, we call and lick our fingers.

There isn't any pepper, the child says.

Then bring us salt, we say. And we scatter the salt he gives us over the bread and our hands and we feel how they're watching us.

Hey, we call, why are you staring like that?

16

The Parable of the Blind

They're not staring, the knocker says.
But we feel they're staring.
They're not staring, he says.
Ah, we say, why should we care? And we eat, first
from one, then from another bowl, first cold, then
hot, then lukewarm. Then a little wind comes and
we're glad of our smocks. And we spoon up the
mash, which is sweet, not salty, smear it into our
mouths.
Look what a mess they make, they say.
Yes, we're making a mess, we say.
Then they laugh and say: Get on with it then. Get
on with your sweating and stuffing yourselves.
Thanks, we say.
And so, reaching out in wider and wider circles
over the table we slowly eat up every scrap and
drink up every drop, first the shallower bowls,
then the deep ones. The jugs, when we knock
against them, sound hollower and hollower. Then
we place our hands before us and they ask: Are
you full now?
Yes, we say, full now.
Then they come and untie our rags and give us
back our sticks. We bang on the ground with
them.
You've eaten a lot, the child says.
Eaten a lot, we say.
And did you enjoy it? the child asks.

17

Enjoyed it, we say. Except that one of us, it's Slit Man, says the meat was hard.

Hard? the knocker asks, and he leans over us.

He means the meat was tough, we say, he's forgotten the word.

Is that true, the knocker asks him, did you mean to say tough?

Yes, Slit Man says, I meant to say tough.

He's Slit Man, we say and hold his head up. He didn't mean to complain about anything. It's just that he hasn't got any teeth left, he finds everything tough.

That's right, Slit Man says, I find everything tough. I didn't mean to complain.

Well, the knocker says, if it was tough we'll cook it longer next time, if there's a next time. Then he calls out: They've spilled things on themselves, Lise. So she comes and stoops over us and rubs at our smocks.

Yes, we say, clean us up, Lise, we're going to be painted today. Hey, we say, come closer. And we take the woman by the wrist and shoulders and pull her down to us. And now, we whisper, listen, Lise. Can you see any tobacco on the table?

No, she says, I don't see any tobacco.

Have you had a good look?

Yes, she says, I don't see any tobacco.

The Parable of the Blind

And are there any other tables here, where there
might be some tobacco?
No, there aren't any others.
Just listen, the child exclaims, they've only just
eaten all that food and now they want to smoke.
Don't shout so, we say, what we want is between
you and us, not everyone need hear of it.
If it's tobacco you want, the knocker says, there
isn't any, at least not for you. Perhaps the painter
will give you some, if he's satisfied with you. And
to the child he says: Take them away now.
To the pond?
No, behind the barn.
We wipe our hands on our trousers and bless
those who fed us. In the name of the most
important saints, we say and grip our sticks more
tightly and are even meaning to kneel down when
the child takes us by the arms and leads us away
from the table.
Hey, we call, and where are you taking us?
Behind the barn, the child says, or don't you need
to?
Yes, we might, we say and trot along. And we ask
if the sun has risen *now*.
No, the child says, not yet.
So we still haven't got any shadows?
No, not yet.

And crows, we ask, are there crows?

Yes, there are crows.

Where?

Above us.

Can you count them? Are there five?

Yes, the child says, how do you know?

There are always five, we say. What are they doing?

They're flying.

Did you hear that, Slit Man? we ask.

Yes, Slit Man says, I heard.

And then, when we've gone a little way: Hey, we call, is it here, your barn? Here, where we're standing, or a bit farther?

A bit farther, the child says.

And we walk a bit farther and ask: So it's here? and we push our sticks into the earth, which is soft and loose hereabouts.

Yes, the child says, here.

Are there bushes?

Yes, bushes, the child says.

And are we alone now?

Yes, alone.

And then, after we've quickly kicked away a dog that had been circling us at the table and had followed us when we'd left it and is still trying to snuffle at us, and when we've unbuttoned our smocks and trousers, we call out: Hey, where are you?

Here, the child says, I'm here.

Then come closer, we say, you needn't be frightened. We want to put our hands on your head.

Why?

So we can feel you.

And why do you want to feel me?

So we'll know you're there.

As close as this? the child asks, and he comes very close.

Yes, we say, as close as that. And now tell us, little angel, we say after putting our hands on his head and pressing it a bit and imagining him for such a long time that we can almost see him, do you live here?

No, the child says and places his hand on our shoulder and tries to push us down into the damp grass.

Don't do that, we say, we have to wait a bit. First tell us where you come from.

From the forest.

Do you know your way around here?

A little.

Then listen carefully, we say. Is Pède-Sainte-Anne a big village?

No.

So it's small?
Not small either.
So it's neither big nor small?
Yes.
And what are the people like?
Same as everywhere else.
So not rich?
No.
Poor then?
Yes, more like poor.
Do they take pity on the blind?
Same as everywhere else.
Then listen, we say and let our hands rest on his hair a bit longer, who paid for our food this morning?
The painter.
He had us brought here?
I think so.
So he lives in the village?
No. In the town. But he has a house here. The one by the pond. Sometimes he comes here.
And what does he do when he comes?
He walks around and stands in front of the trees.
Which ones?
One after another.
So all of them?
Yes.
And then?

22

The Parable of the Blind

He looks at them.
Are the trees here different from other trees?
No, they're the same as everywhere else.
And then? What does the painter do then?
Then he paints.
Aha, he paints, we exclaim and pinch his cheeks.
And what does he paint, little angel?
Everything. The bridge, the church, the river, but especially the trees.
And people?
People too.
And blind people, listen, does he paint blind people? we ask and shake the child a bit, so he'll remember better. Because indeed we know that the painter wants to paint us, but we don't yet believe it. (We've never been painted before!) Isn't there anybody else for him to paint?
Yes, there is, trees.
Ah, trees, that's not much, we exclaim. We mean: people like us.
I don't know about that.
You don't know about that?
No.
Strange that he wants to paint us, we're thinking. For we know that people don't like to see us, even when we're unpainted, that's to say as we *are*. Still far off, when they see us coming, they keep out of our way, squeeze past us. We're the opposite

of our friends the cripples, we don't bring good luck, they think. And if they had their way they'd gladly throw us into a deep hole they'd dug in the earth and bury us safely, so we'd be out of their way. Certainly they wouldn't paint us. Least of all want to hold on to us by painting, make us double by painting us. No, we say, a hole's better.

What?

Nothing, we say, the hole slipped out because we were just thinking about it, don't let it bother you. Instead, answer our question: Has he ever painted people like us?

No, the child says, mostly trees.

And why does he paint trees?

I don't know, the child says, so they can be seen.

Little angel, we exclaim, you're a big fool, can't they be seen in any case? Trees, we exclaim, trees, there, and there, can't you see them, and we point straight ahead and behind us, where there are probably trees that the child probably sees. Or aren't there any trees?

Yes, there are, the child says, but only little ones.

That makes no difference, we say, they can still be seen.

Yes, the child says, they can be seen.

You see? we say.

But not always, the child says and finally pulls his head away from beneath our hands. In the winter,

The Parable of the Blind

for instance, they can't be seen, they're covered
with snow.
Yes, we say, the trees perhaps, but not people.
Are people covered with snow too, perhaps?
No, but they can't always be seen, either.
Why not?
Because one day they die, the child says, then
they can't be seen anymore, and that's why he
paints them. And that's why he also paints himself,
so that he'll always be seen.
Did he tell you so?
No, but that's what I thought.
At least you know him?
Yes.
And what does he look like? we ask.
He's tall and thin, with wild hair and paintbrushes
in his hand. Sometimes I grind colors for him.
Does he talk to you?
Hardly ever.
So he's not friendly?
Yes, he is, but he doesn't talk.
And how should we know that he's friendly?
Now and then he smiles.
Stupid, we say, we can't see that. Doesn't he at
least laugh sometimes?
I've never seen him laugh.
What if something's funny?
Perhaps he thinks nothing is funny.

25

Well, perhaps he's friendly, we say, but silly too, we say, or else he'd never have hit on the idea of painting us. A picture of us—you might as well throw it away.

Why?

Because nobody wants to see it, we say. Do you think we could ask him why he wants to paint us?

You can always ask.

Then tell us when we should ask.

Yes, I'll tell you.

And the sun, we ask, after we've stood around for a bit longer and digested our food and thought about things, is it there now?

No.

Then show us at least where it rises, just in case it does, we say.

And the child takes hold of our smocks and turns us around and says: That's where it'll rise, there, and he pushes us to face in the direction of the sun. And we hearken in that direction for a while and say: Good, we'll remember it. And now, angel, look the other way a bit, so we'll be alone a bit, when we're relieving ourselves, we say and push the child aside and let our trousers down. But when we're crouching in the cold and tickly grass we sense that we're not alone at all, there's a breathing and gasping and giggling in front of us and behind us. They're all still there! Probably they followed us from the table and are standing around us now.

Hey! we call, who's there and what do you want? But they only giggle. Go away, whoever's there, we call and, still crouching, strike out around us with our sticks but only hit one another. Animals! we call.

Then somebody says: Animals yourselves.

Who said that?

I did.

We aren't asking who it was, we say, you should be ashamed of saying that, whoever you are.

You should be ashamed too.

Beast, we exclaim.

Ah, the knocker says, don't shout so loud. And you there, leave them in peace.

Peace, we exclaim, what's that? We're punished, we say, till the end of our days, but soon we'll have passed on. Yet we're still alive and we still have our dignity, while other people are human only in form but in all other ways they're beasts. For we are the Lord's elect, because He punishes those whom He loves, amen. (Even if His Love goes a bit too far, sometimes, we're thinking.) Then a girl or a young woman, perhaps in a cow shed or a yard, suddenly starts to sing. Her song comes to us across a few roofs, or so we imagine. We sob a bit and hum along with her a bit, then the girl stops and everything goes quiet again. And then, shoulder to shoulder and with our thighs apart, probably behind the barn, hands clenched on our knees, after we've relieved ourselves side by side before them and the men and women of the village of Pède-Sainte-Anne have seen their fill of us and giggled their fill, well, then we're ready and we want to leave this place just as quickly as we can.

Hey, we call, we want to leave this place, we want to forget about all this right away. We've still got to practice falling, so we have to cross the village green. Hey, we call, where's the village green? Can somebody guide us?

You're on the village green, somebody says.

Oh, we say and cover our nakedness and pull up our trousers, aren't we behind the barn?

Yes, he says, you're behind the barn.

Are we? we ask, so is the barn on the village green?

Yes, on the village green, he says and laughs. Then somebody kicks us in the calf, but it doesn't hurt much.

Hey, we exclaim, why are you kicking us?

And the knocker says: Yes, why did you kick them?

28

The Parable of the Blind

I didn't kick them, the child says—the one who'd
wanted to guide us to the pond.
But somebody did, we say, we felt it.
He did kick them, another child says, I saw.
And why did he kick them? the knocker asks.
Ah, says the child who wanted to guide us to the
pond, just because.
Well, we say, just so long as he doesn't kick us
again, this time it didn't hurt. Will you promise
not to kick us again?
I don't know yet, the child says.
Won't you take them to the pond now? the knocker
asks.
No, the child says, I don't like them.
No matter, we'll find the pond, even without you,
we say and step back, because it's our duty to step
back so we won't get in anybody's way. And so
we've emptied ourselves on the village green, not
behind the barn, but this doesn't surprise us. We're
always too quick to believe people when they say
we're somewhere. When they say: You're in a
church, we feel: A church, yes indeed, even if
it's only a mill, or, let's say, a tavern. And when
they say: You're on a hill, we feel: Ah, a
hill. Even when, surrounded by a lot of flat
country, we're in a hollow. This isn't important,
though. The fact is that anywhere we are is

where we are. All right, we say, we're leaving
now.
Fine, the knocker says, off you go then.
And which way should we go? we ask.
Just go straight ahead, he says.
All right, we say, straight ahead.
And we go with God, to the pond.

3

We're always hearing it said that anyone who walks in front ought to be able to tell light from dark. Even if he doesn't see every little detail, for instance his shadow, he must be able to recognize blatant things, for instance the sunlight. Not, like us, from warmth on the skin, but as light in the eyes. Even if he can't really see, he must *almost* be able to see. This is what Ripolus is for us, Ripolus with the longest stick.

Hey, we call, Ripolus.

Yes, Ripolus says, who's that calling me?

We're calling you, we say, it's us.

And where are you, Ripolus asks and gropes for us with his stick.

We're here, we call, here.

And what do you want? Ripolus asks.

Nothing, we say, we don't want anything.

Then why are you calling me?

Because we want to hear you.

Why?

So we'll know you're still there.

And where else might I be? Ripolus asks.

Well, we call, you might . . .

No, Ripolus calls, and he stamps his feet on the ground, I'm still here.

Yes, we say, we can hear you. And we line up against a fence or lattice, for we'll be walking in single file so we won't take up so much room on the way, in nature. Right, and we take hold of one another, probably by the shoulder or by the stick of whoever's walking in front of us. Or we take him by the hand, so as not to lose him. And then, after we've turned our backs on the morning sounds of the village, we walk on behind Ripolus, who probably has the same name as his father. If he does have a second name we don't know it. Perhaps he doesn't know it anymore himself, or won't reveal it. Isn't that so? we ask.

Yes? Ripolus says, what's that?

We're wondering, we say, what your name is.

Ripolus.

Ripolus or Ripolust? we ask.

Yes, Ripolus says.

And what else, we ask, what else are you called?

The Parable of the Blind

Nothing else, Ripolus says.

Well, we say, that'll have to be enough. Well, we ask, have you got your stick?

Yes, Ripolus says, my stick's here. And he taps his stick over the ground, for us to be able to hear it.

Good, we say, and now stretch it out, so you'll know where you're going. So we'll know where we're treading when we walk behind you. Stretch it out, Ripolus, stretch it out, we call.

Yes, Ripolus says, I'm stretching it out now. And where are we going? he asks after we've walked a little way. For God's earth, which is infinite for everyone, is even bigger than that for us. All the same, we're making some headway, it's just a question of where to. Because we certainly don't always walk straight ahead, sometimes it's back and forth and not only forward, but back too, or in a circle. This soon prolongs, more than infinitely, the tiniest village, we'll be clinging to one another for support, one of us will be leaning on his stick and having to take deep breaths before he can go on. When that happens, a crutch mightn't be a bad thing. Helped by it we'd fly over the earth, horizontal, with our heads drawn in. But that would mean we were cripples, not just a bit blind, the way we are. So let's be satisfied with what we have, let's creep onward supported by sticks! Or we'll wave the sticks at whatever stands in our way, people, their cattle, their dogs. True, we haven't yet collided with any, the way to the pond seems to be clear, yet if we walk a bit farther they'll certainly come. (People, who speak to us, touch us, are sorry for us, give us food and drink, and, since we can take a joke, shove us into ditches or spit into our eyes.) Yet there are birds, not only crows, close to us and they draw us onward, and they're flying, probably in smallish flocks, probably to the right, above our heads. To the left, in any case, a cow shed, whence a stamping comes. Also we can smell the cow shed smells, they come out through the cracks. One of us, we forget who, can even *feel* the cow shed, he comes from the country.

There's a cow shed, he says, and there's another cow shed. And here comes another.

And how do you know that? we ask.

Because I can feel cow sheds.

And what do you feel them with? we ask.

But he doesn't know that either. Also he can't feel all cow sheds, even if he can feel some.

And ponds, we ask, can you feel ponds?

No, he doesn't feel ponds.

And why don't you feel ponds?

I simply don't, he says, and on we trot.

Hey, Ripolus, we call, did you hear that, he can't feel the pond. Hey, Ripolus, when will the pond be coming?

The Parable of the Blind

Any moment, Ripolus says, the pond will be there
any moment.
And what's stopping us, we ask.
It's the distance, Ripolus says.
We walk and walk, we say, and aren't and aren't
there yet.
Any moment, Ripolus says, any moment.
And when's that, when's any moment? we ask
because we're in a hurry to get to be painted at
last. And Ripolus doesn't know *when* that will be,
either. And what's it *like*, we ask, to be painted?
What'll it be like? Ripolus says, it'll be fine.
Fine like pissing? we ask.
No, Ripolus says, much finer.
You see, that's why we're in a hurry, we say. And
we're trotting through a region which is probably
one of the more beautiful, or anyway less ugly,
on earth, so they say. A region where brown and
green melt quietly into one another and the
ground is soft and fat and moist and level. And
the flatness of the fields is relieved by trees,
crooked or straight, which look as if they'd been
dabbed into it. So beautiful it looks almost artificial,
they exclaim. And they tug excitedly at our smocks
and pant into our faces. And what's so beautiful
about it? we ask. Everything, they say and stamp
their feet for joy, as if they were going to dance
at any moment. Yes, we say, we can smell all that,

35

GERT HOFMANN

but we'd rather talk about something else. And so
the subject is quickly changed. And Ripolus now,
with the sky of the region, which we seldom
mention, probably high above his head, suddenly
stops, because instead of leading us to the pond,
he doesn't himself know where he's leading us.
Hey, Ripolus, we call, what's the meaning of this?
I'm stopping again, he says.
And why, we ask, are you stopping again? Do we
have a shadow? Is there light overhead at last?
Can we be painted now?
Perhaps.
How light, Ripolus, how light? Quick, we call,
don't just stand there, describe our shadows for
us. But Ripolus can't describe them for us, because
instead of long and big and broad shadows, if
any, we've only got short and thin ones, which he
can't see.
And why did you stop then, if you haven't seen
anything? we ask, are you tired again already?
But Ripolus doesn't tell us, he only trudges around
us in silence. For, while he's still able to speak, he
only speaks a little, perhaps even less than we do.
Since he has only a dim picture of what exists in
front of us, around us, and behind us—it was
always much and apparently there's more and
more of it—he forgets the words for it, just like
we do. (Also for what's inside him, or was, or

36

could be inside him, those words too he forgets, as we do, exactly as we do.) Many of the words he once knew, the *words from before*, as he calls them, he's already forgotten, at least half of them, no wonder his sentences (and ours) are getting shorter and shorter. Compared with the sentences from before they aren't even sentences. But none of this disturbs him, because he believes that when all the words have been forgotten, then there'll be nothing above, beneath, before, or inside us. And if he does (or we do) still remember an old sort of word, or if somebody speaks such a word, he doesn't know if the thing is still behind the word and how he's to think about it. A larch tree clearing? Good, but how? A twilight? Fine, but what's that? And he wonders where it belongs, what are the connections? Then there always has to be somebody who'll explain it for him (or us). Other words that he hears don't remind him (us) of anything anymore, all he can do is shrug. Possibly there used to be some such thing a long time ago. Or a word means to remind us of something, but of what, of what? We stop in our tracks, or, if we happen to be lying down, we sit up, and we pull close to us with clammy hands the expression from before, hold it, in a manner of speaking—everything is in a manner of speaking—close to our eyes or nose or mouth. And we snuffle at it, smell it, and lick it, gently, gently, gently. Is it possible that we once really understood this expression or this word, carried it around inside us? Unthinkable! We don't even know anymore how many words we've forgotten, we've forgotten even that. Even if the world slipped away from us entirely, we wouldn't miss it. Instead of pressing forward into it with words, we curl up without words inside what's still there. And, to punish ourselves for doing so, we often hit ourselves in the face, often bite our fingers. Even Ripolus does, walking in front and still feeling the light. Possibly he's not only duller and tireder than us, but older too. Yes, he's older, we think, he *must* be older. And then again: No, he's not. Perhaps he only walks and breathes as if he were older, perhaps he wants to deceive us. Admittedly, he's got no more teeth in his head, we felt that when we shoved a carrot into his mouth once and went too far with it. Yes, those were his gums, but there wasn't anything else in Ripolus' mouth. Yet even if he hasn't got any teeth left, that still doesn't prove much. Lots of people have no teeth and still aren't older than we are. Anyway, walking uphill Ripolus starts to gasp, sweats when he's arrived at the top, has to stop for long spells to catch his breath, and likes to lean against trees, particularly birches and lime trees. And he ex-

The Parable of the Blind

claims that he's forty already, but can he prove it? Hardly, because he then says he doesn't think of his age and has forgotten it, just as we've forgotten ours. Now he's leading us in the direction of the sun, that's to say, in the direction he thinks is the brightest.

Hey, Ripolus, we call.

Yes, he says, I'm here.

All right, Ripolus, what can you see? Simply describe for us what you see.

Oh, Ripolus says, not much.

Why, we ask, because not much is there or because you can't see it?

I can't see it, he says, I can't see anything, but probably there's not much to be seen, either. This region, just as I thought, he says and taps his foot on it, is not heavily populated.

But there's a village, isn't there? we ask.

Yes, he says, a small one.

And people, we ask, can you see people?

People, he asks, and probably he's looking around. No, he says.

Can't you see any, we ask, or is that only what you think?

It's what I think, he says.

Right, we say, but *what can you see*, really?

What I can really see?

Yes.

I see, Ripolus says, and probably he makes a sweep, probably with his right hand. Also in describing what he sees he makes something of a wide sweep. He sees a plain, something flat, at least that's what it all comes down to. Yes, it'll be a plain I'm seeing, he says, a plain that we're facing, no, beneath us. Then he pauses again.

So it's a plain? we ask.

Yes.

But, we bellow, it isn't a plain we're looking for, you fool, you shouldn't be seeing a plain!

Shouldn't I?

No.

All right, he says. Then perhaps I'm not seeing one. I'm probably seeing . . .

Yes?

What should I be seeing? he asks.

A pond, we exclaim.

A pond?

Yes, a pond.

No, Ripolus says, after probably gazing for a while over the plain before us, which he perhaps sees, but also perhaps only imagines. I don't see any pond. But of course it might be covered up.

What by?

By trees, for instance.

And the trees, we ask, can you see them?

40

The Parable of the Blind

No, Ripolus says, I can't see them. I'm not seeing much at all today. I can't even see the sky.
What, we exclaim, can't you even see the sky?
No, Ripolus says, probably I can't.
So you're not sure?
Not altogether.
Then don't just stand there, we exclaim, move about, move about, at least inside your head. It could just be that something's there and you'll end up seeing it. Ripolus, we exclaim, you've got to find the pond, take a really good look around. It must be very close, we can almost smell it. And we give him a little time too, so that he can look around, and we turn as he turns and ask him if there's anything there.
No.
And over there?
No, nothing there either.
And this way, we ask, do you see anything this way?
But Ripolus, because he's having a bad day, simply doesn't see the pond even that way. Either there isn't one, he says, or we've lost our way.
Curse it, we say.
Yes, he says, we've lost our way. So what do we do now? he asks.
You'll have to turn back.

And where, Ripolus asks, will you be going?
We'll follow you, we say, we'll follow you.
And where, Ripolus asks, will I be going?
To the house with the painter.
Right, Ripolus says, so we'll turn back.

4

Then, as we carry on walking, in another direction, there's Slit Man coming up behind Ripolus. Unfortunately he's a thief. We forget his name while we're walking, it comes back to us at night. So that we'll be able to imagine Slit Man to ourselves, Ripolus has often described him to us. He tells us that he's small and nimble, with thick wrists and thick knees on which he rests his hands while he sits down. And we believe him. In fact, we believe everything Ripolus tells us about the look of things, their *exterior*, whenever we want to have a picture of what's in front of us and behind us. Anyway Slit Man lost his eyesight not in the natural way like us, but in the other way, the human way.
I had amazing eyes, he often says, and I'd still have them today, if . . .

Then he likes to weep. The eyes were supposedly blue, at least that's what he says. And, as people kept assuring him in those days, they always took on a green tint near the sea, but also near fairly large lakes and rivers. At night, like cat's eyes, they shone. With eyes like those, Slit Man says, one can see everything.

Well, we say, a lot perhaps, but—everything?

Yes, he exclaims, everything.

Well, we say, a lot perhaps, but surely not . . .

Anyway everything one wants to see, Slit Man says, everything that interests one, even if one didn't remember the details. Even on darkish nights he could discern every star, and in the grass every butterfly.

And the worms, we ask, did you see the worms too?

Yes, he says, the worms too.

Well, we listen to this, but should we believe him? Perhaps he did have eyes like that, perhaps he didn't. Perhaps he only imagined them, when it was all over, when he no longer had any. It's said that in the village of Peer, just as he was stealing the foot bone of Saint William from the church, he was caught with the relic in his hand and only by a hair's breadth escaped being hanged. Now to enter eternity with a rope around your neck is terrible, of course. So, on account of a plea made by the canon of the church, who has guests sitting around his oak table with him at the time, to the regret of everyone in the neighborhood Slit Man isn't to be hanged but only slit. How Slit Man screams for mercy, as soon as he hears this! All right then, the slitting is postponed. How he breathes again! Just so that for one more day he can consider and absorb the edifice of the world, which in its incomprehensible beauty the Lord established, after all, for him too. Good, and now comes the day set aside for him and his eyes. Over his face he has smeared dirt and ashes, to let everybody know he's penitent. He stands at the window of his small prison, where, despite the dull weather, huge masses of light assault him. His hands rest on the window bars, his gaze rests on the square outside, where he sees the people going past, but only up to their calves. Every so often somebody stoops and looks in on him. Eyes and mouth agape, he considers the world now as he never did before, and he discerns it and absorbs it. Even if not as a whole—nobody can do that— still some parts of it: by day the clouds, by night the stars, and at all times the random but inexhaustible patterns on the wall of his small prison and the small animals creeping on him, which he crushes to death with his thumb. He's so greedy that he even starts to *count* the little hairs on his right hand. All this he absorbs, but he feels it won't be enough (for the rest of his life, what's left of it). On the day before he got slit, the door had opened, creaking, and he'd been shown the instruments, so that he'd be able to include them in his picture of the world. These are, in a flat leather case, two knives, which the executioner has hastily brought from Brussels and now places ceremoniously in front of him. For they are part of the world which had not been apparent before and which must now be quickly *absorbed*, along with everything else: two butcher's knives, with handles of bone, blades thin but long and broad. The longer of the two is already a bit rusted near the handle, that's just part of its peculiarity. Both, when he holds them in the light, look notched and old-fashioned, and they seem to have been put to various uses, as well as frequently sharpened. After the future Slit Man has wrestled for a long time with Satan, shoulder against shoulder, staring at the knives, the executioner takes them away from him, having now tied a long leather apron around his own waist. It is Sunday, the people of the neighborhood must be given time to arrive. But birds too, mostly ravens and crows, come and sit around hungrily in the trees and on the rim of the well in the marketplace. And here, after evening Mass, when everyone is gathered in fine weather and with a good view right up into the sloping streets, he becomes famous, if only for a little while, at least people are talking about him a lot. After this, as if a signal had been given, the hush of the crowd, he alone screams. Up till the last moment he'd believed that what's now happening can't happen, because he can't imagine it, that it's only a threat, the lords and masters having only wanted to give him a fright. Now he discovers he was wrong. Ever since that evening the crows, which in his hour of trouble sat before him on the rim of the well, with him, have been his traveling companions, so he believes. He can clearly remember four, but more arrive. Mornings they flutter around him, travel above him from tree to tree. Toward nightfall they descend around him, sit at his feet and try to perch on his shoulders, but he chases them away.

Get away, what more do you want of me, he calls, and he's convinced that on that day in May they ate up his eyes.

It's you they're after, we say, you.

Can anyone here see them? he asks.

Not us, we say, not us. And you, Ripolus, can you see them?

No, Ripolus says, not quite.

Curse it, Slit Man says, and how many are there?

Probably five, Ripolus says.

Curse it, Slit Man calls, more and more of them.

They want you, we say, and we laugh.

Whether or not their number increases we don't know, perhaps yes, perhaps also no. We don't know where they are at night, either, in the trees, we believe. Or on a barn roof, it occurs to us, if one's nearby. And we hearken, but can't hear any roof or trees. Or they fly into the nearest forest, to break out of it again in the morning and wait for us, when we push our way out of our barn. Even now, quite a while after being slit, Slit Man can't understand them. He'll finally see the true light, you'd think, but he doesn't. Instead, he deludes himself into thinking it's all only a dream. And that he only has to raise his eyelids and the world will be there again. (Yet he has no eyelids to raise now.) And he sleeps, if at all, briefly, burrowed deep into the straw, when he thinks it's nighttime, and moans and wails when he lies down, but also when he gets up again. Yes, even in his sleep he moans. There's never a morning comes but he looks up and wants to see the sun.

The sun, he exclaims, I don't see the sun, when we commonly suppose it's somewhere in the sky.

That doesn't matter, we say, we don't see it either.

I don't care if you see it, he exclaims, *I* should be the one who's seeing it.

48

The Parable of the Blind

Quiet now, we say, it's all over and done with, but he can't keep quiet.

I sat there, he says, they'd tied me up . . .

Don't think about it anymore, we say.

They'd tied me up and . . .

Come on now, we say, let's take a walk.

And we take him among us and hold him by the arms and haul him along with us a little way, perhaps underneath some trees. So that he'll have different thoughts and be moving around a bit. An ugly person, who, when we pass our fingers over his forehead, has no eyebrows left, probably not even ears. They slit everything off him. We're also surprised when we feel his bonnet, which is made for a much bigger head, it hangs down over him. With the head he's got, how can he wear a bonnet like that? Well, it's the only bonnet he's got. He's even plucked his hair out. All the same, he'll be painted together with us.

But he's not one of us.

Yes he is, they tell us, now he is.

But he hasn't got any ears.

That makes no difference.

And if he's a thief?

That doesn't matter.

All right then, we say. And we're thinking: Yes, it'd be foolish not to say good-bye to him soon. And at the right moment not to push him into a

ditch, or, while he's having a drink, into a stream.
Except that moment hasn't arrived yet, but it will,
it will. Hey, Slit Man, we call and spit between our
feet, you know something?
No, he says, what?
You're going to be painted.
I know.
And why are you going to be painted?
I don't know.
Nor do we, we say. Do you steal things still?
Why, he asks, are you missing something?
Not yet, we say, not yet.
Yes, we know a lot about him, more than he
thinks, and God knows even more. Sometimes
from the floor of a barn he'll take a piece of wood
or a smooth stone and hide it on his person, in
the most unbelievable places. A habit, we think.
Under other circumstances, if the light were bet-
ter, of course he'd have taken something else from
the barn floor, or from the kitchen, but he can't
find things anymore now. Isn't that so, we ask,
you don't steal anymore?
It's difficult, Slit Man says.
Why, we ask, isn't there anything left to steal?
Certainly there is, Slit Man says, only I can't see
it.
And he's restless, takes wheat kernels from the
pockets of his smock and munches them and hangs

his mouth in every stream we hear murmuring. And walks only if we push him forward, always stooping low over the ground. And if he goes on creeping like that he'll surely be a hunchback soon. And he croaks and drools and froths at the mouth and if we're not careful he'll pass his restlessness on to us, then we'll froth and croak too, but we don't let things go that far.

Quiet now, quiet now, we say when he's all set to start frothing, and we leap on him and grab him and throw him to the ground and sit on him. Or we take him by the arms and legs and drag him to the nearest tree. And even if he struggles, we tie him to the tree trunk with our cords, until his throat and shoulders slacken and slowly he quiets down. This is on our way to the pond, so we hope, still in the village, or on the edge of it, and everything is probably bare and empty, the path, the sky, the countryside. Later we walk, probably, out of the village called Pède-Sainte-Anne—or so they told us. Unless it's already behind us and we're in the next village already. In any case, a village with its church, around the tower of which birds are flying, birds we can hear squawking.

Are they mine? Slit Man asks.

Yes.

How can you know?

We recognize them.

What by?

The way they screech.

Get away, if you're mine, Slit Man shouts, and he's thinking of his eyes and he starts to froth at the mouth again. And we pull him to the nearest tree and tie him up and let him froth and then ask him: Right, are you quiet again now?

Quiet, Slit Man says.

So quiet you can be painted? we ask.

Yes, quiet as that.

But we don't believe him. His throat full of screams, his mouth full of curses! Well, he can go along with us a little, but not much longer. We'll wait until we've been painted and then we'll leave him behind. Or else we'll sit on him and try to suffocate him, then we'll be rid of him. One thing's for sure: We won't be sorry for him, he's not one of us. If he's walking with us at all, he's walking in the place that doesn't belong to him at all but to one of us who doesn't walk anymore and now lies at rest. His name was Lamme and recently he was farting along with us. Before a meal he felt sick, he lay down, turned over, and after the meal, he died. Yes, our friend Lamme is dead, we won't be seeing him again, because he had to be buried. At all events, his smock, doublet, and boots were suddenly available and belonged to us. We tossed them into a heap and crouched around them, and touched them and listened to them and sniffed at them and shared them out among us. Slit Man got most of them, because he didn't have anything and shouted loudest. Because in despair at being slit he'd torn his clothes from his body and in doing so had quite forgotten he'd need his clothes. So it turns out that he's now wearing the doublet that doesn't belong to him. Or trousers that don't belong to him. And if he's got tobacco he stuffs it into a pipe that doesn't belong to him, but which Lamme used to puff not long ago. Also his bonnet doesn't belong to him and it looks ridiculous on him. How often people who can still see laugh at this bonnet! All the same, he'll be painted with us, we don't know if it'll be in front of us or behind us. Even the stick he waves around him, which will probably be painted too, he stole even that. Well, we say and chuckle a bit, he won't be going along with us much longer. All the same, it's said he looks very like the person whose place he's walking in now. Does he think like him too?

No, he exclaims, I think differently.

And feel, we ask, do you feel as he did?

No, he feels differently too.

Fine, we say, but how, but how?

But he doesn't know that, either.

You see, we say, you're not different at all, you only think you are.

No, he says, I'm different. And then, after thinking a bit, he says that, for example, he doesn't hear well anymore, the sounds are getting fainter.
Then can't you even hear us? we ask.
Yes, I can still hear you, he says. What are you getting at?
Nothing, we say, we aren't getting at anything.
So let's be moving along now, Ripolus says.

5

So we turn back again meaning to find the house by the pond and the painter who wants to paint us. Ripolus supposes he's turning back again, he's not certain. Walking behind Ripolus, we aren't certain either. Sometimes we think we're turning back, sometimes we think we're walking onward. Who'd have thought it was such a long way? All the same, we did dress up warm. In doing so (dressing up) we thought as much of ourselves as of our painting. For if somebody wants to paint us, then he must paint us with everything we have: the smocks with the frayed hems, the bonnets, the sticks, the legs wrapped up and lifted, the faces turning up to the sky, as we're always being told, with a slightly transfigured look. Perhaps too it'll start to rain, then the day will be particularly long.

True, they say springtime is coming, but there's rain and snow in the air. So we keep our feet warm too, that's why they're wrapped. Also in wrappings one falls more softly, if one must needs fall. Besides this, there's not much to paint, if we're to be painted. Of course, there are pockets in our smocks, with various things in them, but since the things can't be seen they can't be painted. (Also what's in our heads, for the same reason that can't be painted either.) Only our sticks and our bodies in our smocks are left, and today they weigh (the bodies) particularly heavily on the crust, the earth crust. And are walking, one behind the other, probably down a sunken lane or a narrow alley, at the end of which, as we find out with our sticks, there's a fence blocking our path. So weren't we going straight ahead after all? No, it seems we weren't. Seemingly we've gone in the wrong direction, unless from the very start we were sent in the wrong direction. The only thing left for us to do is lean against the fence and, with eyes closed, regret we're here. Better still we could have lain down and fallen asleep. But we must press on, on, for we're going to be painted. And so we creep along the fence and call: Hey, here's a fence! Hey, we call, isn't there anybody here to tell us what this fence is doing here? And we pull our way, lath by lath, along the fence, until it stops

56

The Parable of the Blind

and we're standing in a corner. Hey, we call and cling to the laths, hey, Ripolus, where are you?
I'm here, Ripolus calls, and he's standing right in our midst.
And where have you taken us?
To a fence, he says.
Yes, to a fence, we've noticed that, we call and shake the fence, but where do we go from here? Can you see where we go from here?
No.
And the fence, we ask, can you see the fence?
No, Ripolus says, I can't see it.
And anything else, we ask, can you see anything else?
As a matter of fact, Ripolus says, I can't see anything at all.
Why not? we exclaim. And isn't there anybody else who can see the fence? And who could tell us perhaps how we get to the pond? Hey, we call, is anybody there?
Yes, a voice says, me.
Aha, we say, so there is somebody. And we'd been thinking . . .
No, the voice says, I'm here.
Good, then come closer, if you're here, we say.
Like this?
No, closer still, much closer, so we can put a hand on your head, we say.

Why?

So we'll know who you are.

Like this then?

Yes, like that, we say once he's come closer, and we put a hand on his head. True, we don't yet know who he is, but at least his head helps us to *imagine* something, even if each of us imagines something different. And now, we say, after each of us has imagined him in his own way, tell us: Where have you been all the time?

Here, he says, I was here.

Didn't you hear us calling?

Yes, I did.

Then why didn't you come and help us?

Because I don't meddle with other people's concerns.

But we'd lost our way, we've been walking in a circle.

Anyone can do what he wants.

But we hadn't wanted to walk in a circle.

How do you expect me to know that?

You could have thought it, we say. But it's all right, if you didn't know. And who are you?

Ah, the voice says, I'm just Balthasar.

No matter, Balthasar, we say. Just stay as you are and tell us: Are we still in the village?

Yes, Balthasar says, this is where it ends.

Where the church is?

58

The Parable of the Blind

No, Balthasar says, the other end.
And crows, we ask, are there crows here?
Yes, he says, there are crows here.
How many?
Six or seven.
Yes, we're thinking, that's them. They're flying
around the tower here, aren't they? we ask.
No, Balthasar says, those are other ones.
Which?
Starlings.
Aha, we say, starlings fly around the tower?
No.
Where then?
Around the lime tree.
And where's that?
On the village green.
So are we still on the village green?
Yes.
And where's the pond?
Which one? There are many of them.
Not only the one where the painter lives?
Oh no.
Did you hear that, Ripolus, we say and turn
probably to Ripolus, there are many ponds here
and you couldn't find a single one.
Ah, Ripolus says, I'd find it if only I could see
better today.
Yes, Ripolus isn't seeing anything today, we say

and laugh and turn probably back to Balthasar. And ask: And where's the pond where the painter lives?

That's one of them, Balthasar says.

So we're close to it? we ask.

Yes, close, says Balthasar. And explains to us in his quiet voice that we've gone the wrong way. We should have gone to the right, to the right! But can we, stricken as we are, talk of right and left at all? That would presuppose we know what's straight ahead, but do we really know that? But Balthasar should be telling this not to us but to Ripolus, who of course doesn't listen. No, Ripolus, like an old ram, walks to the left, and us behind him. To the right, Ripolus, you must walk to the right. Hey, we call, are you still there?

Yes, Ripolus says, I'm still here.

And you, Balthasar, are you still here?

I'm here, Balthasar says.

And where, we ask, is the fence?

That's here too, Balthasar says.

And can you see it?

Yes.

And where does it end?

There, Balthasar says, I'll show you. And he takes us by the hands and pulls us along with him and takes us to another place where there's probably no fence, we can feel there isn't. There, he says, that's where it ends.

Aha, we say, so that's it. And now the pond where the painter lives, now we want to go to the pond. Do you know the painter?

The one who paints the trees?

Yes, we say, but he'll paint us too.

Has he said so?

No, we say, he can't, because he doesn't know us.

Then he won't paint you.

Won't he? we ask, how do you know? Are you the person who grinds his colors?

No, Balthasar says, I'm somebody else.

But you could have been?

No, he says, it's quite impossible. And he thinks for a while and then says: Yes, it might be possible.

You see? we say. Anyway, you do know the painter, do you?

Yes.

Did he ask about us?

Not me.

So you haven't seen him yet today?

No.

And have you met anybody who asked about us?

No.

And anybody who hasn't asked about us?

Not that either.

Then we walk on a bit.

And you, Balthasar asks later, who are you?

Ah, we're the people with the crows, we say. Not the people who go ahead of us, so don't get us mixed up. We can't be the people who go ahead of us, because we can't see chickens. And since he doesn't understand and hasn't yet heard of us, we tell him how, one summer night, we were sitting and talking beneath a tree and crows suddenly came and pecked out our eyes.

What sort of a tree?

A cherry tree.

And what were you talking about?

We've forgotten, we say. But it was a great misfortune and there was a lot of talk about it at the time. Haven't you ever heard of it?

No.

So perhaps you don't believe it?

No, I don't believe it.

Well, we say, whether or not you believe it is your concern, at least we've told you, so you won't be able to say you've never even heard of it.

All right, he says, I've heard it. And he thinks, when he sees that we really are all stricken in the same way and form a group, one walking so close behind the other, all keeping step, even if we aren't sure where we're going, that we're related.

The Parable of the Blind

A numerous but united and like-minded family, hurrying on our way to the pond.

Well, we say, that's so. We may look like a family, but we aren't. One day we came out of a forest, one after the other, and since none of us had any definite plans, we walked on together, that's all. Since then, people think we belong together.

So you're not fathers and sons?

No.

And brothers, he asks, aren't you even brothers?

No, we say, we aren't brothers either. And then we stop walking and say: Hey, Slit Man, and we seek him out quickly and feel him and know him by the ears that are missing and push him toward Balthasar and say that *he*, for example, isn't one of us, he's only going along with us, taking somebody else's place.

And since when have you been going along together?

Since recently.

And how long will you stay together?

Not much longer.

And how many of you are there? Balthasar asks— he wants to test us.

We don't know exactly, we say.

And how many were you before, he asks, or don't you know that either?

Seven, we say, we were seven before, but we lost one in the noontime.

And what happened to him?

We don't know.

And the sticks, he asks, why do you have the sticks?

Because we haven't got nozzles.

So you can't even see the earth?

No, we smell it.

And the sky? Balthasar asks after walking for a while with us across a stubble field, do you smell it too?

No, we say, we hear it. And then we call: Hey, are you taking us the right way?

Yes, Balthasar says, straight ahead.

And where's that, straight ahead? Don't forget we're going to be painted any moment.

Ah, Balthasar says, but not right now.

And why not? we ask because we want to have it over and done with as soon as possible.

Because it's still too dark.

And when will it be light?

Later, Balthasar says. And now, he says after we've walked a bit farther and fallen down and gotten up again and walked on, I'll tell you something. Over yonder, where the path leaves the village, a pig is going to be slaughtered anytime now. I've seen the butcher with his knife already sharpened. So you mustn't be startled when you hear it squeal. If you like, we can go and look.

Ah, we say, we wouldn't see it anyhow.

But I could describe it for you.

No, we say, it's not the same. Besides, we've got to hurry, we're going to be painted very soon.

Well, Balthasar says, then we won't go. We can hear it squeal just as well, I needn't describe that for you.

No, we say, we'll hear it.

And then we walk a bit farther and imagine the pig so precisely that we can even hear how, not far from us, it's still alive and grunting and snuffling the earth. We can even smell the fire with the caldron on it, into which the pig will be chopped up. (But it could be another fire we're perhaps smelling.) And we hearken and wonder at every step why it doesn't finally squeal.

Was that it? we ask.

No, that wasn't it.

And that? we ask later.

No, not that either.

So nothing has squealed yet?

No, he says, not yet.

Yes, we say, just as we thought, we didn't hear anything. We only thought we should have heard something, time's getting on. And on we walk again. And ask: Hey, Balthasar, why doesn't anything squeal? But he doesn't know.

Yet it will, he says. And you, he asks later, do you see one another?

No, we say, we don't see one another either. And we think about it and then say that we feel one another.

What with, Balthasar asks, with your hands?

No, we say, we don't know what with: We feel it must be us when we say *us*. Even if we can't prove it.

And who are you?

The people in the middle.

Very well then, Balthasar says, you walk straight ahead now. I've got to be getting along to my work now.

And us, where are we going?

Straight ahead.

But we've been going straight ahead all the time.

No matter.

Are we still in the village?

Yes, he says, but not much longer.

And what comes then?

The end of the village.

The one by the church?

No, he says, the other. And then comes the pond.

Listen, we say, you must tell all that to Ripolus.

The Parable of the Blind

But he'll have none of it. No, he says, I'm having my bad day, I can't see anything at all. Then he stops, nevertheless, and asks: So where must I go?
Then naturally we have to stop. Balthasar probably stops too. Unless he simply walks on and leaves us.
Hey, Ripolus, we call, why are you stopping? Why aren't you walking on? Hey, Balthasar, we call, where are you? The pond, Balthasar says—already he's some way off—comes later, just walk straight ahead. Or can't you anymore?
Yes, we say, we can, but Ripolus can't. He's got warts on his feet. Quick, Ripolus, show him.
And then, while Ripolus is probably taking off his shoes to look for his warts, we ask Balthasar if he's got a toad on him, by any chance, with which to rub the warts, so Ripolus will be able to walk better, but Balthasar, who's far away already, hasn't got a toad, it's still too cold for toads.
Well, he'll just have to wait, until it gets warmer and we can find one, we say. Isn't that so, we say, you'll wait?
Yes, Ripolus says, I'll wait.
Hey, we call later after we've waited a while and Ripolus has put his shoes back on, is anybody here besides us? Hey, Ripolus, can you see anybody?
But Ripolus can't see anybody either. No, he says, unfortunately I can't.

And then, since we're not certain whether Balthasar is still with us, we call: Hey, Balthasar, are you still here? But Balthasar doesn't answer, so we must be alone. Even then—always this feeling that somebody is seeing us, from above, at an angle, somebody who doesn't say anything. So we take one another's hands again and call: Hey, who's looking at us? But apart from the sounds of the air and the earth and the ones we ourselves make (with our hearts, our lungs, our throats, our mouths) everything around us is hushed. Then Malente, who's walking last, suddenly starts to sing, something we've never heard before, and which perhaps doesn't really exist. How His Kingdom is mighty, ahead and behind, above and below. Something he thinks up on his own, simply inventing it as he walks along.

Hey, what's that? we call.

A song, Malente says, I'm singing a song.

Yes, we say, but why?

But Malente doesn't know that. Whenever he can't go on walking, when it's very hot, or very cold, he starts to sing, isn't it disgusting? We think we're lost and Malente sings! Us, anyway, his song disturbs, at least it's no help to us. What we want is to be getting along, who knows who'll be painted, otherwise? And we wonder what to do, so as not to be late. Should we let go of one another, should each of us go it alone? Or should we stay together here in this damp-seeming hollow? No, we won't let one another go, we think, and we stay where we are, even if, so as to keep moving, we walk in a circle. And you, Malente, don't you be singing now!

Why not? Malente asks.

So nobody will hear us.

And who's likely to hear us? Malente asks.

The people who could be here. Here in the hollow, we say. And then, a bit louder, we call: Hey, who's that creeping around us, we can hear you tapping about. But he doesn't announce himself. Till we suddenly hear something else, quite unexpected. Till the pig, which we'd forgotten about again, but which, even if it was on the far side of a field or meadow or some plow land, was always together with us in the world and breathing along with us, though close to the ground, gives a piercing squeal, probably behind his pig house. Well, so that's over and done with! And then, as if an expectation had been lifted from all around, we at once hear voices from the hills or the vales, distant and blending, people flocking to look at the dead pig, and to turn it over on its other side and walk around it, people who, if only they'd look in our direction, would surely see us too. (For even if we can't see anything, we can still be seen, very much so!) Probably we're manifest as dark points in the wavy but generally flat countryside, which (the points) aren't rooted in the earth like trees or rocks or other natural things, but move back and forth, so that, once one has sighted them, one can follow them with one's eyes moving through the region. So that's us, being seen and becoming smaller or bigger. Anyway, nobody comes to us in the hollow, also nobody calls to us, but probably people can see us walking with soft uncertain footsteps out of the hollow and vanishing over the horizon. Then people will soon have seen enough and told themselves: O, it's only *them*! And they turn their backs on us again, to contemplate the dead pig.

Hey, we call, isn't there anybody around to take us away from here? Some helpful person who'll lead us to the pond we're expected at? May God lead him into heaven by the hand, just as he leads us away from here. Hey, is there any such person here?

But probably there's nobody here, it's the same as ever. We hear only the earth and the air and ourselves, even the pig is hushed now. And we won't hear it, even if we listen for it. So in this empty place, probably the edge of a hollow, we position ourselves in a semicircle, for, as far as we can remember with our foot-memory, we were last going downhill, therefore it *must* be a hollow. Or it's a snake pit and we just don't know it yet. Then one of us—it might be ourself—says: This wind brings rain! And immediately we draw our heads in. And we stand, unless we're quite mistaken, with our backs to the village green, for we don't want to go back there. And we join hands and softly curse and we prop one another up, because, whether from sadness or walking, our legs tremble. So that if somebody saw us from a distance standing with these legs he'd naturally think we were going to dance at any moment, but he'd be wrong. We *can't* dance at all, at least not properly. We wouldn't know which direction to step in, we'd dance past one another and farther and farther off into the remote distance, and we'd finally get lost. True, we run and crawl and chase a lot, but that doesn't mean we dance too. And even if we were able to dance, in the dark, when nobody's looking, alone on a level spot especially meant for us and kept vacant for us, why should we? Certainly, to loosen our legs we sometimes hop and kick them up, and straightaway we're misunderstood. Straightaway people call: Quick, look, now they're dancing! But that's a delusion, no, we never dance.

6

Later this wet springtime—they say whole countries are underwater—when we've been standing and stamping the earth flat for a long time in this snake hole or hollow He's led us into—we notice, yes, it's raining. At first we think it's even snowing. Naturally we'd like to find shelter, but where? There we stand, under a sky which hangs down black probably around our ears, and we feel it's a steady rain now. Our rage at the rain, that He should make it fall on us! And the smell of wet earth! What heaps of last year's leaves we hear around us now, not rustling, but rotting! The situation we're in, how clearly it shows us, at least, His Will! How we beg Him to lead us out of the hollow, if it's a hollow we're in! Instead, He leads us into a part of the hollow where the water comes up to our calves. If we go any farther this way we'll end up drowning! Turn back, turn back! But there's water behind us already too, we'll drown there as well. In any case we'll catch cold and not be fit to be painted anymore. How heartily we implore Him to save us, and He can't hear us because He's too far away! Instead, just as we get clear of the water, He sends us a dog, which isn't wanting just to sniff at us, not at all, he immediately attacks us.

Hey, Ripolus, we call—our feet in muck—there's a dog here, it seems.

Yes, there is, Ripolus says, I can hear him.

Good, we call, then hold him.

But Ripolus says he can't. He can't even see the dog, how can he hold him? Certainly he gives a shout, he grabs at him, but grabs nothing. We kick and lunge at him too, but our kicks miss.

Hey, dog, we shout, why are you attacking us?

Hey, we shout, call him off!

Instead, the dog snaps at us and hangs on to our legs. A new pain, never felt before, piercing, but quickly we get used to it. We hold one leg up in the air and thrust it back and forth, we swivel around. But the dog has sunk his teeth into us and he doesn't let go.

You dog! we scream and kick our legs about and probably swing the dog around in the air, but he doesn't give up. O Lord, we call, why don't You hear us, why don't You call for Your dogs?

All the same, He does then send us a man, we can hear his voice. Perhaps a shepherd, who speaks to the dog and calms him down and probably scratches his throat and takes his teeth out of us. And then perhaps puts him on a chain, or a leash. And says we'd irritated him and made him lose his temper and that ordinarily he's a good dog and we'd spoiled him.

Hey, is somebody there? we call and put our hands on our wounds.

Yes, the man says, I'm here.

And where exactly are you? we call, come closer, we can't see you.

Like this? the man asks, and then he's very close and we stand around him and, in spite of our pains, put our hands on his head. And feel over his face and make for ourselves a picture of him and tell ourselves he's this way or that and probably not this or that other way. Then we ask who sent him. Nobody. But somebody surely sent him? No, he saw us walking over the field and came of his own accord.

And why didn't you come sooner? we ask, we could have been drowned.

Yes, that's true, in the pond.

So there's really a pond here?

The Parable of the Blind

Yes, over there.

Where?

Then the man takes us by the shoulders and turns us toward the pond and he says: There. You're lucky devils and you don't know it. Then he wants to see our wounds.

Ouch, we say when he bares them and his finger hits them, why are you doing that? Ouch!

Then he says the pain is a good sign, it shows we're still alive. And soon we'll forget about it.

But why didn't you come sooner? we ask.

Because, he says, I thought you were someone else.

Who?

Soldiers.

Soldiers! we exclaim, why?

Because you're so colorful.

Us?

Yes, from a distance.

But we aren't soldiers, we exclaim, even if we're colorful from a distance. We couldn't ever be soldiers, we'd never see the enemy. Only this one here has been a soldier, we say and take Bellejambe by the shoulders and pull him out from among us and push him toward the man.

Yessir, Bellejambe says, gunner, bangbang.

But then the gun went off backward, didn't it? we say and laugh.

Yessir, Bellejambe says, bangbang.

In short, even Bellejambe isn't a soldier now, he just used to be one. None of us is a soldier anymore, nor could he be. But we live in darkness, so to speak, forever. Look, we say, and pull Bellejambe back again, put him in his place, and pull up our eyelids and show the man our eyes. And tell him who we really are, and that we're going to be painted, we don't know why. But he doesn't know anything about the ravens.

In the summer, we say, while we were sitting under the cherry tree, don't you remember?

No.

Then you'll have forgotten about it.

Yes, he says, probably.

And what's your name? we ask after waiting a while to see if he might remember after all, but he doesn't, and he's meaning to tell us his name but we say: No, don't tell us.

Why not? he asks.

Because your name, we say, is only a word like any other, which, like the many other words we once knew, we'll only forget, and that only upsets us. Or it would make us feel sad.

All right, he says, so I won't tell you.

Much more important than your name, we say, is your finding us and not thinking anymore we're soldiers and taking us out of this hollow.

76

The Parable of the Blind

It's not a hollow, he says.
Not a hollow, we exclaim, then what is it?
Part of a field that belongs to me.
Well, we say, we think it's part of a hollow that belongs to you, but let's say no more of it. The main thing is for you to take us away from here to the house where the painter lives.
Why?
Because we're going to be painted.
But his house, the farmer says, is just over there.
To the right or to the left? we ask.
To the left.
Strange, we say, just now we were told to go to the right. Do you remember, Ripolus?
No.
No matter, we say. And to the farmer we say: So lead us over there, to the left.
If you want, the farmer says, but it isn't really necessary, it's only a little walk from here. And then, after taking us a little way in that direction, the direction we'd always wanted to go but then hadn't, because Ripolus was against it, he says that in any case the painter can't paint us as we are.
And why can't he paint us as we are? we ask as we trot behind him through the hollow.
Well, the farmer says, you can't see yourselves, but if you could . . .
Yes?

Then you'd see that he can't paint you as you are.

It doesn't matter that we can't see ourselves, we say. He'll paint us as we are.

Maybe, he says, if it's all right with him. And we carry on walking. Then he says that the painter's house by the pond can be seen ahead now, it's already looking out from among the trees. A pity you can't see it, he says.

That doesn't matter, we say, we're used to it.

A big house, he says, and if we could just turn our heads the right way we'd certainly feel its presence.

And which way should we turn our heads if we want to feel it? we ask.

There, he says, this way.

And actually, when he takes our heads in his hands and turns them the right way, we can feel the painter's house, at least we think we can. Or not, Ripolus? we ask.

Yes, Ripolus says, something's there.

Of course, we say, that's the house. And we tap our way with our sticks, full of expectation, probably toward the painter's house. Hey, we call, can't anybody see us, can't anybody hear us? Hey, we're expected here, isn't anybody here? And then, when everything stays quiet, we call: Hey, you, whom the hollow belongs to, or, as you think, the field, where have you gone? But he doesn't answer.

The Parable of the Blind

Hey, we call and cup our hands to our ears to hear him better, but everything's quiet. So the man who owns the hollow has left us standing! But no matter, we've found the house.

Hey, Ripolus, we call.

Yes.

Where are you?

I'm here.

Then come here quickly, we say. And ask him, once he's standing beside us, if there's anybody in the house or looking out from it because he's perhaps expecting us, but Ripolus doesn't know any of these things.

You can't see if anybody's looking out? we ask.

No.

Why not?

I'm not seeing well today.

And tomorrow?

I can't tell yet.

Oh well, we say, oh well. And we ask him to take us by the hand and lead us to the house, so that we can touch it and make a picture of it for ourselves. So Ripolus takes us by the hand and leads us to the house.

Is it it? we ask, are we at the house now? And we can feel something. And we even knock on it, first with our sticks, then with our fists.

Yes, Ripolus says, I think so.

What does that mean, we ask, aren't you certain?

No, Ripolus says, not entirely.

So you can't see the house either?

No, Ripolus says, actually I can't.

Nor can we, we say. In any case that must be the house wall, there, we say and pass our sticks over what we think is the house wall. At least, we say, it sounds like a house wall.

Yes, Ripolus says, that's true.

And this, we say, is this a cross beam?

At least it sounds like one, he says. A pity that you can't see it.

The cross beam?

No, the house.

Why?

Because it's a beautiful house, Ripolus says, oh yes.

It doesn't matter that we can't see it, we say, you can describe it for us.

The whole house? Ripolus asks.

Why not, we say. And we stand there with our legs apart, sticks between our feet, and feel a bit sad. Because all the things and objects that are scattered around the world now, so random and confused, the things we sometimes run into, once had their familiar and necessary places, in the old days we knew our way around, but now . . . Well, we'd better not think about that. Meanwhile Ripolus starts to describe what he might be seeing, the walls, the roof ridge, a door, but slowly, bit by bit, so we can absorb it and put it together anew for ourselves. In general, his description is probably correct, though of course not always, especially as regards details Ripolus is probably often wrong. In any case he walks alongside the house through the leaves we can hear being squashed, and he scratches the walls with his stick and describes what he can feel and scratch and perhaps see.

One thing's for sure, he says, it's a beautiful house.

Is it, we ask, high?

Yes, it's high.

And what else can you see? we ask. Can't you describe anything else?

I think, Ripolus says, that it has got windows.

So it has windows! we exclaim. And we'd like to pull the house closer, so that, even if we can't see it, at least we could smell at it.

Can one see through the windows? we ask.

Yes, Ripolus says, I think so.

And what's to be seen through the windows? we ask.

Us, Ripolus says, we're to be seen.

And what, we ask, are we doing?

We're waiting.

What for?

For somebody to notice us at last, and come out to us.

And through how many windows can we be seen?

But again Ripolus doesn't know, perhaps *two*, or three.

And can't you describe anything else for us? we ask after standing there in silence for a while.

Ah, probably it has two floors, Ripolus adds. He won't tell us anything more.

Well, we say, if it has two floors we'll all fit into it.

Do you think he'll let us all in? Slit Man asks.

Why shouldn't he let us in, if he wants to paint us? we say, and we stump up and down in front of the house.

But he doesn't want to paint us inside the house, Ripolus says, he wants to paint us in front of it.

Perhaps, Malente says, he'll paint us twice, once outside and once inside.

Nonsense, Ripolus says, he wants to paint us when we're falling.

And what if he paints us once when we're sitting and once when we're falling? Malente says.

Anyway, Bellejambe says, the house as I know it is big enough for us.

There they are, a woman's voice calls, and we hear footsteps in the gravel and somebody, probably a maid, comes to a stop in front of us and probably stands there with her arms resting on her hips, probably she's looking at us. We can catch a whiff of her breath as it passes over our foreheads and goes into our noses and eyes or eye sockets. Then she comes with her hands and takes our face and turns it toward her, so that she can see us from the front and take a good look at us.

My God, she says after looking us over for a long time.

Yes, we say, it's us, and we cross ourselves and say: The blind people, who are supposed to be painted, we've come, probably through the hollow.

My God, she says once more. And then she calls high over our heads: Yes, it's the ones with the ravens.

Yes, we say and breathe toward her and then tap our way toward her too, so as to reach out for her and make for ourselves a picture of her, helped by her neck, shoulders, breasts. But she shrinks from us. She doesn't want us to touch her, she's afraid our infirmity is infectious. All the same, we can feel her in front of us, in curves, in contours, and at this moment—the birds arrive. In short low arcs they're fluttering above us and whipping the air into our faces and they caw and plunge down at us and try to settle on us, mostly, of course, on our heads.

Hey, what's this? we call.

Suddenly crows, the maid says.

Are they always here?
No, not always. We'd brought them with us.
Nonsense, we say, and we feel them flying up and down and we stand there waving our arms and we call: Go away, crows! Then everything's hushed again.
Hey, we call, are they still in the air?
No, the maid says, in a tree.
Which one?
The ash tree.
All in the same ash tree?
Yes.
Take us to it, we say. And when she's taken us to the ash tree and probably we're standing beneath it, we wave our sticks over our heads and shout: Go away, go away! And we knock on the trunk of the ash tree and chase the crows away. Then we ask her: Well, how was that?
Yes, they've gone now.
So we'd have thought. And where are they?
They're fluttering again.
Where?
Up there, above us.
In the clouds?
No, lower.
Then Slit Man suddenly asks her if she knows that these crows ate his eyes.
His eyes, the maid asks with a start.

The Parable of the Blind

Stop it, idiot, we say, why can't you keep quiet?
Why? he exclaims, it's all right for her to know.
No, we say, she needn't. And we tell the maid not
to take him seriously. It wasn't long since he was
slit and he still didn't know what he was saying.
Yet it was true: The crows had sat on the well and
had been the last thing he saw, so he couldn't
forget them and was certain they'd eaten his eyes.
And then, a bit louder, with a gesture: Now, good
woman, tell us—who is waiting for us in this
splendid place? And loudly, so that we'll be heard
inside the house too—Blessèd be the hands and
fingers and eyes of him who has invited us into
his house, so that he may paint us, as we were
told yesterday or the day before. And may God
bless the patience, we say, with which he has
waited for us, but his house was hard for us to
find.
They couldn't find the house, the maid shouts
probably across a garden full of flowers or weeds
or across a field with stubble or fruits in it. Then
she says we're wet and asks if we aren't cold.
Yes.
Your hands?
Yes, our hands.
And where else?
All over.
Then put your hands in your pockets, she says.

And she takes us by the arms and leads us up a path, we notice that it's sloping upward.

Careful, she exclaims, there's a cart here, you see, I'm leading you past it now.

Well now, we say, we just thought there was something there.

So you guessed about the cart?

Not the cart, we say, but that something's there.

The higher place we're led to—the hush of the dust and stones, and over them our puffed groans, silent dogs all around us, perhaps enormous ones.

Then we ask if the sun's shining.

Yes, the sun's shining.

Thought so, we say, we can feel it, mostly on our faces. And we hold our faces up to the sun, which shines into them. It's shining on our faces, isn't it? we ask.

No.

But on our hands?

Not on them either.

And why not?

It's shining on the other side.

Of the hill?

No, of the pond.

And here?

Nothing's shining here.

Then we start to groan, to curse and stamp our feet. Why doesn't the sun shine here? Why does it shine on the other side? Why does it always shine where we are not and cannot be? And altogether everything. The blows of fate we endure, the trials and tribulations we pass through! We make too much of it, of course, for our misery isn't the worst in the world. Certainly there's much greater misery elsewhere. Then there's the misery that was and the misery still to come. All the same, we gasp and groan, so as not to be overlooked. And ask if we can be painted as we are, with our curses distorting our faces, with our wounds and our sopping clothes. And we prod our sticks into the ground and twirl around, so that the maid can see us from all sides, but she doesn't say anything. Either she doesn't want to tell us, or she's not there any more.

Hey, aren't you there anymore? we call because we can feel the gap she's left. Hey, we call, where have you gone?

Then a man who's arrived in the meantime—perhaps a gardener or a coachman—takes us by our hands that are torn by thistles and bushes and leads us back down the path again. First sand crackling under our feet, then earth, fat and moist. Yes, we've only just been taken uphill and now we're taken downhill again. Naturally we're wondering about several things. For instance: Is it still us that all this is about? If it's somebody else, who could it be?

7

And why are you so late? the gardener or coachman asks when we're down below again.
We doff our bonnets and say that unless we're
mistaken we got lost, twice. And that somebody
had meant to guide us, but then nobody had. So
we'd walked on our own and lost our way. Ripolus
had always led us to the left, instead of to the
right. First to a fence, where there was no way
onward, then into a hollow that was flooded and
where it rained on us, we even thought it was
snow. Also that we'd been attacked by at least one
dog. Back there, we say and point in some direction or other. Are you the painter? we ask him.
They lost their way and got bitten and think you're
the painter, the maid exclaims, she's back with us

again now. And to us she says: Let's have a look
at you now!

Ah, we've been looked at already, we say.

Never mind.

So we stand close together, pull our shoulders
back, and keep still, and now she's in front of us,
then behind us and probably looking at us.

Well, sit down now, she then says.

Where?

On the ground.

But isn't it damp?

No, here on the stones.

Good, so we sit on the stones and stretch our feet
out, as best we can.

And now take your shoes off, she says.

All right, so we take our shoes off—one should
take them off once a day in any case—and unwind
the wrappings from our feet and stretch our legs
again, so she'll see our wounds. The maid leans
over us and looks at everything.

Yes, they've been bitten in the legs, she exclaims,
by dogs. And us she asks: And how could you
have lost the way? Because the barn we'd slept in
was only a stone's throw away.

Because nobody guided us, we say.

Nobody guided them, so they lost their way, the
maid exclaims. Now they're wet and bitten, he
won't want to paint them like this. Bring some

wood for a little fire, so they can get dry and look like something again.

But he doesn't have to paint them wet and bitten just because they're wet and bitten, the gardener exclaims—perhaps he's the knocker from this morning, even if he won't admit it. Can't he paint them unharmed and dry, even if that's what they aren't?

No, the maid says, he has to paint them as they are.

Why?

Because he has to paint what he sees.

But can't he paint *roughly* what he sees and change it a bit, improve it?

No, the maid says, that would be a lie. He has to paint *exactly* what he sees, otherwise he wouldn't have needed to send for them.

Yes, we exclaim, that's why he sent for us, to paint us as we are.

Then we hear her taking our shoes and tipping the shoes so that the water still in them will finally run out of them. (Yet he wouldn't in any case have painted the water in the shoes.) Then she wrings out our leg wrappings, they drip onto the ground. We can't tell if the wrappings are bloody from the biting. Then she rolls up our trouser legs, because our trousers are wet too, but we

90

don't need to take them off, they'll dry in time by themselves.

Yes, they've been bitten, the maid exclaims, and she probably looks at our wounds, not touching them, though, at least we don't feel anything. Does it hurt? Yes. How much? Unbearably. Then she goes away again.

Hey, we call, where are you going? We're going to be painted today! And for a while we sit on the stones and slide around and think of our various pains, the ones in our legs and the ones in our heads. Then she comes back and stoops over us and rubs fat or grease on our wounds and rolls our trousers down again and says the pain will go away now, we just shouldn't think about it.

But if it hurts how can we help thinking about it? we ask, and we take one another's hands. Hey, we call, isn't there somebody who'll help us a bit to stand up? We can't do it, otherwise. If we'd known that nobody would help us up, we wouldn't ever have sat down. Then we wouldn't need to stand up, we'd be standing up already. Hey, we call, if somebody doesn't help us soon, we'll go away again.

But they take no notice of us, or else they're inside the house taking the fat back or bringing wood. So we stand up on our own and walk around feeling the pain, and we ask, if anybody's there to be asked, whether we'll be painted with our wounds, if that's possible. Hey, we call, is that even possible, a picture of us with wounds? But probably there's nobody there who could tell us. Later, the gardener comes back with dry branches and throws them down before us. And he starts to make a fire for us, because if we don't get dry soon we can't be painted, but will get ill, as the maid tells us when she comes back again.

First you'll cough, then lie down, and then you'll be dead, she says.

Yes, we say, God has punished us.

And then the devil will take them, the gardener says and laughs into his fire. For it's alight now, and, with hands outstretched, we go toward it, but not too close, so that we won't walk into the fire and perish in it. Instead, we have to crouch around the fire, then we feel it too, and something rises up out of us, but not smoke or fumes, which stink, it's steam, which is just damp, and slowly we get dry. And we smell the fire and hear it and hold our hands out to it, and the steam rises into our noses, and we mayn't put our feet into the flames, because then we'd be set on fire, and what then? How should he paint us if we're dry, to be sure, but, on the other hand, charred?

92

The Parable of the Blind

Have you understood that? the maid asks.

We understand, we say.

All right, the maid says. And to the gardener, who is probably standing beside her, she says: Put a few more branches on, so they'll get dry soon and won't get frozen, but only little ones. And then take them behind the trees, if they want to relieve themselves before being painted. Hey, she asks, do you want to relieve yourselves?

Probably we shall want to, we say, but not just yet.

When's that?

A bit later.

Then she goes away again. And the gardener goes away and we hear the crows and feel the wind blowing a bit, but then the wind goes away too and we're alone with the fire.

Hey, fire, we exclaim, we're alone with you. And the fire crackles. Hey, fire, we exclaim, and we're thinking: We're alone with it. And then we fart and belch a bit, so people will notice we're still here. And then, when we've been alone with the fire long enough, we call to Slit Man, just to be calling to him.

Hey, Slit Man, we call, are you still there or have we lost you?

I'm still here, he says.

Then tell us something, we say.

What about? he asks.
Old times, we say. Where did you last steal something?
In the village of Peer, he says.
And what did you steal in that village?
A foot, he says, a sacred foot.
Why?
Because at the time nobody was looking.
And then?
Then they caught me and almost strung me up, but then they reprieved me. Then they just . . .
No, he says, I'm not going to talk about it.
Just as you wish, we say. And now? we ask.
Now I'm going to be painted.
Yes, we say, we know that. Are your feet smoking or are they only steaming?
I think they're only steaming.
Then you should shift aside a bit, we say, and let us come close to the fire too, so we can get dry at last. And then, after we've pushed him aside and stretched our legs a bit, we call: And you, Ripolus, where are you?
Here, Ripolus calls, I'm here.
And Malente, we call, are you here too?
Yes, Malente calls, I'm here.
And Bellejambe, we call, where's Bellejambe?
I'm here, Bellejambe calls.

94

The Parable of the Blind

Fine, we say, so we're all together. Or is someone missing?

No, Ripolus says, probably not.

And is anyone else here, besides ourselves?

No, Ripolus says, I don't see anyone.

And the stream, we ask, do you see the stream we're supposed to fall into?

No, Ripolus says, I don't think so.

And hear it, we ask, can you hear it?

No, Ripolus says, I can't hear it either. And you, he asks, can you hear it?

No, we say, we can't either. And then we're warm from talking and from the fire and are steaming a lot out of our smocks, and again we call: Hey, Ripolus!

Yes, he says, what now?

Ah, we say, we were going to ask if we're steaming, but we won't ask.

And we stretch our legs to get dry even more quickly, but then our feet are suddenly too warm and the steam begins to smell. Quickly we draw our feet back, so as not to get dry too fast, and call: Hey, our steam smells. Hey, Ripolus, we call, does your steam smell too?

Yes, Ripolus calls, my steam smells too.

Then we call: Watch out! The fire! but we're already in flames. At least we're smoldering and will be in flames at any moment. Help, we're smoldering! we call and lie on the ground and roll over the ground, so that our wrappings and shoes and trousers, which are probably burning or smoldering, will go out again. Help! we call, can't anyone hear us? And then we really do feel the heat. There's a burning especially around our ankles, perhaps a bit higher up too. And we roll and burn and smolder and are speechless with fright, but then we take a hold on ourselves again and go on bellowing. The maid, when she's there again, calls: Quick, pull them away! And the gardener jumps among us and pulls us to the side and probably tramples the fire out or pulls it to pieces. And they haul and drag us over the earth and knock and beat around on us, up, down, and in the middle.

Hush now, they say.

Are we really burned, we ask, or just singed?

You got a little hot.

And our trousers, we say, are they burned up or just scorched?

Your trousers, they say, are dry now.

So then he'll be able to paint us? we ask and cough because of the smoke.

Why not? they say. And they finger us and handle us to see if we're dry now, but not *too* dry, and if our shoes and doublets and smocks can still be painted as they *are*. Then they tell us, we're not hurt but are warm and dry now, and the fire is out.

Yes, we say, but now we're tired, because we've walked so far.

They're telling lies, the gardener or coachman says who's perhaps the knocker too, on account of his voice, and probably he's standing before us, they've been resting all the time. They've even been dancing, he says.

Saving your presence, we say and look in his direction, that wasn't us, it was the people before us.

And who are they supposed to be: the people before you?

The people who say they're us.

No, he says, it was you.

Well, we say, perhaps we lifted up our legs, but we didn't dance. We can't dance.

Quiet, the gardener exclaims, don't tell lies. And that of course we could dance. Proof: He'd seen it himself. You dance when you think people aren't looking, and later you won't admit it. I know you, he says.

Well, we say, if you know us, then probably you're the knocker.

Who? the man asks.

The knocker, we say, or aren't you?

No, the man says, I'm not.

Yes, we say, we'd been thinking that probably, in fact, you weren't.

Then why did you ask?

Because your voices are alike, we say. But whether or not you're alike in other ways . . .

I'm not, I'm not.

Yes, we say, we were wrong. But even so, you could have been the knocker, couldn't you?

Never, the man exclaims, me, never!

Yes, we say, probably.

And then the man who isn't the knocker suddenly flies into a rage and jumps around on the ground in front of us. Perhaps because we mistook him for the knocker, perhaps for another reason. And he shouts that it's wrong to talk with us and to be concerned with us and to let us run around, because we bring disorder into everything, thoughts, people, the air. And that we trample down everything that's in our way. Look at them, he exclaims, and probably he's pointing at us.

At once we think we might be standing among flowers and we step back, but aren't certain if we're stepping out of one lot of flowers into another. Then the gardener again: Had she— probably the maid, if that's what she is—had she seen the vegetable patch behind the house, she'd get the shock of her life. We'd stamped through it like pigs through a maize field. It was an outrage

98

The Parable of the Blind

to let wretches like us go running around on the loose and tripping over their own beards. As for wanting to paint us, he just couldn't get that at all.

And where would you put them, the maid asks, if you didn't let them run around?

I'd put them . . . , the gardener exclaims, and probably he makes a gesture, only we don't know which one.

Yes? we ask, what is it you'd do?

Well, the gardener says, well. And he doesn't say where he'd put us. In any case we'd better be more obedient and do what we were told, we were old enough.

And if they can't find the house straightaway? the maid asks.

Then they should ask, he says, asking never hurt anybody. Really they ought to be . . .

But we're going to be painted! we exclaim, and we stand up tall with heads thrown back.

Ah, his wanting to paint you was just one of his whims, the gardener says, he doesn't even paint me.

He'll have a pretty good idea why he doesn't paint you, the maid says.

But us he'll paint, he even had us brought here, didn't he? we ask, and we stretch up even higher, in our partly still damp, partly singed clothes.

Don't worry, the maid says, he'll be painting you all right.

Yes, we say, he'll paint us falling over. Would he have paid for the meal otherwise?

So when did you eat? the maid asks.

This morning, we say.

Then you're hungry again?

Yes.

Then she asks if we'd like something more to eat. Well, a knob of cheese would be good, a loaf of bread, an apple, some milk. And she: Can we eat by ourselves? We can, we can do everything. Good, then we should stay sitting there as we are now, and she'd bring something straightaway. And she really does bring bread and milk and cheese and places them on the ground, probably in the midst of us.

And the pot with the milk? she asks. Shall I put the pot into their hands, or better not?

Better not, the gardener says, they'll spill it all over themselves. Pour the milk into their mouths.

But no, she needn't, we say, she can easily put the pot into our hands. Everybody puts the pot into our hands.

We don't, the gardener says. Open your mouths, one by one, then she'll come with the milk.

All right then, we stretch out our legs, probably into the ashes, and lay our heads back and open our mouths, and then comes the pot, probably a heavy one, smelling strongly of cow shed, with the milk. And then comes the milk itself and falls through the air into our mouths. Some of the milk runs into our throats, some over our chins. Look now, the maid exclaims when she sees how we're treating her good milk and how we're spilling it on ourselves, but we simply can't drink as quickly as we're supposed to. So finally she does give us the pot and we drink the milk by ourselves and pour it into ourselves and feel it roll in big leaps down our throats into our stomachs. So the pot goes from one of us to another and we drink it empty. Then the cheese and the apples and the bread, quickly we shove them down after the milk. Then we're pulled to our feet and are led among the trees, not behind the barn, because, before we can be painted, we quickly have to empty ourselves. (We don't ask if anybody's watching.) Then we're brought out again and arranged for the picture. For this we're made to line up side by side and they walk past us. Each one of us has something wrong about him, they don't like anybody the way he is. Not one of us is good enough as he is for the painting. A bonnet is straightened, a smock is tugged around, something left hanging from our sleep is picked off, because it doesn't belong in the picture.

And the painter, has he arrived? we ask.

Soon he will, the maid says.

Will he come out to us for the painting?

No, he stays in the house.

And how will he see us, if he stays in the house?

He'll look through the window.

Is it open?

He opens it. Perhaps he'll come out to see you as well, to take a close look at you.

Will he pick at us too?

If it makes it easier for him to put you on the canvas.

Describe the canvas for us. Is it big?

Yes. Big.

Fine, we say, then he won't need to squeeze out any part of us, we'll fit into it.

Are there seven of them? the gardener asks from far off.

No, there are six.

But he wanted to paint seven.

No, the maid says, there are only six.

Well, the gardener says, that'll have to be enough. Take them to the stream now, they'll have to line up there and walk up and down a bit.

On the bridge?

Yes.

Did you hear? the maid says, and she claps her hands, we'll make a line and walk onto the bridge. Take hold of the arm of the person in front of you or put your hand on his shoulder.

The Parable of the Blind

Like this? we ask and line up and stamp our feet
a bit, so we'll be able to walk better.
Yes, that's right.
And fall, we ask when we're on the bridge, should
we fall now?
No, the maid says, we'll wait a bit for the falling.
The painter isn't there yet. Just keep on walking
up and down, but be nice and natural.
But how can we be natural if we're not allowed to
fall? At least pretend, she says.
Listen, we say, before we were stricken by our
misfortune, while we were still trading in sheep
and pigs and honey . . .
Ah, she says, so you don't come from the poorhouse, after all?
The poorhouse came too, we say, but much later.
Before that, we traded in sheep and honey and
we . . .
Hush, she says, there he is.
Benedictus! we call, raising our arms, and we hear
a window being opened, but where? And we look
in some direction or other, but probably too high
up. Hey, you, we call, describe him for us. Is he
smiling, or is he serious? Is he looking our way?
Had he imagined us like this, or is he disappointed
with us? And since one of us got lost: Will only
six be enough for him?

8

The painter, who probably noticed us at once and is probably striding up and down by the probably wide-open window of his house, says—we can't hear it all—that he's always been surrounded by whole spaces full of pictures, *afflicted* by them. These spaces, he says, come to me, they come into my house. These are the spaces in which he lives, though of course there are also the other ones. How many times he's sat, especially on the long winter evenings, in the middle of those spaces and the pictures have shown him the world. More and more often now, since the slaughter at Liège, the pictures are of people dying and dead. The pictures in these spaces, now without a sky, with a high horizon, are all filled, to the limit of the frame, *gold, my good friend*, with images of people

104

and things dying, perishing, or dead already. All *in extremis*, he says. Like these here, he adds and probably points out through the window, thus probably at us.

God's mercy upon this house! we call at once in the direction of the window, and we make a bow.

What was that? the painter asks.

They were greeting you, the good friend says.

They needn't, the painter says—he's completely absorbed in describing his interior spaces and he pays no attention to us. The sea boiling and very far off, the sky covered by a pall of smoke, glare of a fire behind soaring mountains—a memory of the far Alps—are signs that even the remoter parts of the world have been *devastated*. In the foreground, among their foothills, the last people have been gathered together to die. Even himself the painter can easily identify in the pictures of these spaces—we can hear him come to a halt in his room and draw breath—himself dying, dead already. At night he is *walled in* by these spaces with their pictures, thus also by himself. In the daytime too he only has to close his eyes and look away from other things. Then he's tempted to pick up his brush and copy the inside pictures. Yet he wonders whom he can show them to, who could endure them. Then he comes to a halt and asks: Well?

Yes, the good friend says.
And why so late?
They'd lost their way.
Have they lined up?
Yes, the good friend says, the way you wanted it.
And have they been told they have to fall, that I'll
be painting them as they fall?
Yes, the good friend says, they know.
And where did you find them? the painter asks.
Not far from here, they came out of a forest, the
whole place is seething with them, the good friend
says. Would you have preferred to look for them
yourself?
No, no, the painter says, it's fine the way it is. And
probably he puts his hand on the good friend's
shoulder or takes his elbow. I know it's a terrible
thought, he says, but the main thing is that they
really are blind.
Completely, the good friend says.
You promise me?
They're exactly as you wanted.
You looked at them?
I had them led up and down outside the house
here. They really are blind.
So they move like blind people too? the painter
asks, that's important, you see.
Yes, they do.
And hold their heads accordingly?

The Parable of the Blind

It's all as you wished, the friend says. They walk, talk, and carry themselves like blind people, yes, probably they even dream that way. (If one only knew their dreams, and if only one could paint those.) He only had to look, then he'd see for himself.

No, I don't want to look at them, the painter says after hesitating a bit, *not yet*. The mere sight of people like that had a devastating effect on him in his present state, because at once he put himself in their place. He couldn't see people who've been broken without thinking of being broken himself. So before he sees us he'd like to imagine us for a while, without actually seeing us, picture to himself how we'd be and how it'd be when he did see us. Only then, after he'd pictured and imagined us for long enough, would he look at us, that's to say, while painting us, and then he'd do it professionally and precisely. Then he'd enter into us, true, going as deeply into us as might be humanly possible. Yet, although he'd be entering into us then, he wouldn't feel close to us, so he'd be able to endure his meeting with us, this *collision*. For he was in such a state—alas, it was the case—that he couldn't allow anything to come close or excite him, except in his art. Us close—out of the question.

I know, the friend says, your health . . .

My health, the painter exclaims near the window, is just the same as last year. That's to say, I still eat and drink and digest and breathe—*still*. That he didn't sleep was no secret. But why should he talk of it? Talking of it only made him twice as sleepless.

And your eyesight, the good friend asks hesitantly, how has it been these last weeks?

My eyesight, the painter says . . . Let's forget about it, he says. And them, the painter asks—he's no longer concerned with his friend—how did they go blind?

One after the other, sometimes in surprising ways, nobody knows in what order, the good friend says. Yet they say that they all went blind at the same time, in the same summer night . . . It was our legend: that we'd been victims of a hot night, victims of ravens.

Ravens? the painter asks in astonishment.

Yes, the good friend says, one night. The ravens—but it could have been crows or other black birds—had suddenly settled on our shoulders and pecked our eyes out.

And people believe that?

Some do.

Well, what can one say about that? the painter says. Then comes a pause.

Good sirs, we call into the pause, we're completely

blind, even if we can hear well, and we take probably one step toward them, with sticks slightly raised. We walk and move too like blind people and dream that way too, we say. And we arrange ourselves, as if we'd come to the age at which one makes oneself smaller, with outspread arms and straight backs, thus almost as if we were about to sing, probably at the window.

Is that them? the painter asks.

It's them, the friend says.

And who are they talking to? the painter asks, are they talking to one another?

No, the good friend says, they're talking to you.

Then they must be very close.

Yes, they're very close.

But I don't want them to come so close and talk to me, the painter exclaims, I'm not ready for them. Just a moment ago I didn't even know if they'd be coming, and now they're so close. They must stand farther back, please, back among those trees there.

Did you hear? You must go into the trees, so you won't be seen, the good friend calls, and he claps his hands a few times, probably out through the window.

Are there trees here then? we ask.

Yes, behind you.

We didn't know that. Are they single trees or is it

a forest? we ask and tap around with our sticks.
It's a little forest.
So it's a clearing? we ask because we haven't used
that word for a long time and don't want to forget
it.
Yes, the good friend says, there's a clearing too.
Good, so we'll go into the clearing now, we say.
And we go back among the trees, into the little
forest. But we don't ask which forest we're going
into, or how deep we're going into it.
Have they gone? the painter asks.
Yes, the friend says.
And what are they doing?
They're looking out from among the trees.
Can you still see them?
Yes.
Then talk to them.
What should I say?
Ask them if they can scream.
Scream? the friend asks.
Yes.
All right, I'll ask them, the friend says. And then,
to us: Listen, he says, he wants to know if you can
scream.
Scream? we say and trot up and down a bit on
the edge of our forest, we don't scream much
anymore.
Why not?

The Parable of the Blind

We haven't thought about that, we say, probably it's just the way it is. And after a few wrong steps we're suddenly standing in a sort of thicket that the friend hasn't told us about, but which is there, all the same, even if it's withered and faded, perhaps. And out of this thicket, which comes up to our knees, we speak, after trampling it down a bit, in the direction from which the painter's voice comes. While we were still trading in pigs and honey, we say, we were always honest.

Well, but don't they come from the poorhouse? the painter asks.

We've been asked that, we call from our thicket, but the poorhouse came later. Now we don't scream much anymore.

Then there's another pause.

So you want to paint them screaming? the good friend says—not to us but in the other direction.

Yes, screaming, the painter says.

And at the window he explains to his good friend that, ever since he was a child, he's been hoping to portray convincingly one day the human scream, and with a picture like that to make all the other pictures he'd painted forgettable. (Also all the pictures painted by other people.) Into this concluding and ultimate picture he'd like to put everything he had to say about the world, but so far he hadn't been able to paint a picture like that.

III

Perhaps he'd never be able to, perhaps a picture like that is impossible. All the same, he wasn't giving up and was trying again and again to do it, in the same picture, which, as it turned out, was different each time, with the firmest intentions, naturally. But what actually resulted came from the work itself and couldn't be foreseen. Not only that the picture he'd wanted didn't result, but also that the result was often the reverse. Yet he worked hard day after day and in his head there was always the same question: if it was really worthwhile to look more precisely at this beehive or this cypress tree, this horse or this landscape.

Look at them?

So as to portray them.

And why portray them?

I don't know, the painter says, probably to capture something. Something that moves and falls and gets up again and moves onward and falls again. He didn't know why he had to capture it, or why the *scream* had to be portrayed. In any case, if he ever gets down to painting at all, he'll show the *poor people* (us!) screaming, so that they (we!) can be seen better. So that they (we), who are always being ignored, will finally be seen for once, and people will know what a human being is, what being human is about. He had marvelous views, though frightful ones, of course, into the interior of our mouths, and these views he'd take up into his portrayal. Although at the end of last winter, when, after the flooding, during which the water had risen two meters outside his house and it hadn't been heated, so that the walls had sweated whole pounds of saltpeter out . . . In short: When, at the end of last winter, he'd first stumped his way out here through the last snow, he'd decided, considering his failures of last year, never to paint again. And now he was going to paint again, not just soon, but now, this very moment! Although it was so long since he'd painted from life, because the people he'd painted from life earlier had all died or been killed, and because to him it made a difference whether he painted someone who was still alive or a dead person. And, either way, of course he knew it was hopeless. Hopeless to paint the picture as it appeared in his mind, as he saw it before him, at the same time so real and so general and in its details revealing the whole, thus their (our) bodies, unmistakable, as well as what lay behind them (us), out of which they (we) briefly stepped forth to enter his picture. In short: Without hope he walks up to his easel, or up and down before it, or he sits down before it, as now, if walking has tired him. True, he always resolved to paint in a casual way, but the moment he took a brush in his hand he became as if possessed.

And without much hope, as he said. Because it's quite impossible to paint the picture the way it has to be painted, terrible *and* beautiful enough. With this conviction he walks up and down before his canvas—which also worries him. For he has the impression that it will not endure what is put upon it and will soon, under the charge of the colors applied to it, simply fall to pieces, perish. Yes, it was something strange, the brush stroke, *la touche*. Thus his life was passing away as he became more and more deeply trapped in his brush strokes and felt more and more keenly that he wouldn't be able to apply them much longer.

If the signs he spoke of just now are . . . ? the good friend asks.

I won't be painting much longer, the painter exclaims, probably standing close to the window. And always he paints, so as not to waste a moment, after his long doubtings, with speed and frenzy, not thinking of much else. For when he looks around him . . . So then he doesn't look around him. His excuse: that, in his case, painting, even just the thought of it, kills all thought of anything else in the world. (Although he knows that it's probably more important to live, to *survive*, than to capture life.) But he can't at the same time paint or want to paint and think of other things as well. Meanwhile, he's even doubting, of course, whether painting has any use. First comes life, which mustn't be sick or dead, then comes painting.

And the scream, what's the scream?

Well, the scream is naturally the terror, the cause of which, I willingly confess, the painter says, I haven't till now looked for patiently enough—and he starts to walk again. But he wants to look for it. And when he wants to paint the *scream*, he also wants to paint the terror, what can be seen of the terror. The way, for instance, the mouth changes when it screams, yes, that interests him. He's fascinated by the arch of the mouth cavity, the position of the teeth, the condition of the gums, the shaping of the lips, the colorings, the *discol-orings* of the palate. On the other hand, admittedly, he'd like to have painted a smile sometime, but hadn't been able to do that, either. And if he says the smile might come later, he thinks it won't come anymore now.

And why does he stress the terror so much, at the expense of everything else?

Terror? Ah, does he really do that? He doesn't feel it that way at all. What people call *terror* is the element he lives in. Certainly he doesn't want to give people a fright, far from it, and he doesn't make too much of it, either, he simply brings together what people, not wanting to think about what's terrible, fail to see. On the other hand the friend is right. He too sometimes wonders, while painting: In what house, in what room, among what people, for heaven's sake, would your picture be in the right place, be at least *endurable*? Because at that moment he can't imagine such a place, such a wall, for the pictures he paints, *must paint*. Then he asks how things are in Ghent, in the southern provinces.

Slaughter, the good friend says.

And the slaughter in Liège?

Still going on.

You see? the painter says, and probably he puts his hands over his ears, wanting not to hear the details of the slaughter. And is probably led by the hand, by his good friend, out of the corner from which he was speaking, to the canvas, which we imagine to be empty. And he is placed before this great emptiness. Then the good friend probably places a brush in his hand, but the painter probably pushes it away and says: I can't, dear friend. But the friend won't give up, he comes again with the brush and probably even ties the brush to his hand with string, so that he won't drop it, because his fingers are gouty, or set it aside again immediately. And tells him everyone is hoping that this time he'll achieve *the scream*. Then the good friend probably puts his head out

of the window and probably looks in our direction.
(Looks to the edge of the forest, we're still standing
on the edge of the forest.) In any case he calls to
the maid, who's standing among us, and he tells
her that she can lead us around now.
So he'll paint us now? we ask and rub our hands.
Yes, he will, she says.
So you'll lead us around?
Yes, she says, and she pulls us one by one out of
our bushes and out from among the trees and
pushes us close together, so that we'll all go onto
the canvas, even if it'll quickly fall to pieces.
Hey, we call, can you see the painter now?
Yes.
Then describe him to us, we say. Is he tall and
thin, with a pointed beard?
No, he hasn't got a beard.
Then he's not the one who wants to paint us.
But he's certainly tall and thin.
Then it'll be him. Then we ask: Is it light enough
for painting now?
Yes, she says, light enough.
And the sun, we ask, is it shining on our faces
now?
No.
On our hands then?
Not on them either.
And him, we ask, if it's him, is he looking now?

No, she says, but he'll look any moment now.
And when he looks, we ask, will we be allowed to
ask him something?
Walk now, she says, walk.
But, we say, isn't there a stream, a ditch?
Yes, she says, and you'll be falling into it.
And she takes Ripolus probably by the hand and
leads him probably onto the bridge, which probably crosses a stream, which we can hear murmuring. And now, she says—as we stand on the
bridge and feel the wood of the bridge—do exactly
as I tell you. You, she says probably to Ripolus,
stretch out your stick and step onto the bridge.
You go this way.
Which? Ripolus asks.
This way, she says and sets him straight. After a
few steps there'll be something you won't find
with your stick, and then you'll fall over it. You'll
fall into the stream, it isn't deep, we'll pull you
out again straightaway. But it's important that you
fall.
Good, Ripolus says, I'll fall.
And you, the maid says and turns probably to Slit
Man, take hold of his stick with your right hand,
he'll pull you along with him. So you'll fall after
him, simply fall over him. And you, she says and
positions us close together, hold his stick with your
left hand. You fall too.

The Parable of the Blind

Yes, we say, we'll fall too.

So she goes all the way down our line, walks from one to another of us and tells each of us how he's to walk and behave and stumble and fall. All the way to the last, to Malente, who has to fall too, though he won't be painted falling, but upright, just beforehand, expecting to fall.

Has he seen us now, your painter? we ask.

Perhaps he has, perhaps he hasn't, she says.

But he's looking? we ask.

He'll be looking any moment now.

Is this how he imagined us?

Yes, she says, he'll be looking any moment now.

9

No, the painter exclaims at his window, I don't want to look, I can't. He still needs some time to get used to the idea of seeing us. Poor people, he keeps on saying.

Yes, the good friend says, they are rather clumsy.

Clumsy? the painter asks, what are they doing then?

They're practicing walking.

Have they been painted before?

Not that I know.

Yes, people do fight shy of being painted, at least the simple ones do, the little people, the painter says, and he's speaking half inside his room, half out of his room. Perhaps they're obscurely afraid of the genuine thing, at least they're more honest than the others. They're afraid of being captured

The Parable of the Blind

in a particular moment, one that's unrepeatable, of course, and then of decaying, themselves, bit by bit. Or they're afraid that later they'll find the part of them that was painted is missing. What they've got left, they think, is only the covering, the painter paints the essential thing out of them. That's why they often can't endure the sight of the picture when it's shown to them.

Yes, the good friend says, there are lots of prejudices about that.

Well, the painter says, and probably he imagines, still turned away from us, at his window, how awkward and clumsy we are as we practice walking. Cautiously, keeping close to the ground, which is very creased, we place one foot before the other on the grassy bridge and know that we'll fall at any moment. Often in the past we've fallen, to be sure, singly or together, on our hands, knees, faces. We're continuously hurting ourselves, we knock deep bloody holes in ourselves. Ripolus has a hole in his knee, Slit Man one in his elbow, there's a hole in Malente's chin, and we won't even mention ourself. Yet we never knew till now when a fall lay ahead of us and when we'd be hurt, and now that's precisely what we do know. Now we'll be falling, now, we think, and while doing so, what's more, we'll be painted. This thought, how it hampers our steps, we even creep instead of walking! Meanwhile, the painter has probably gone to his painting table and is preparing his colors: the white lead for our weathered smocks, cool gray for our bonnets, pine soot, which must be very black, for the shoes, the crows, and the branches. Sheer toil, he exclaims, getting this hard black—and probably he shows his friend the black he's obtained so laboriously. And, of course, the rose for the inside of our mouths, which has to be seen when we scream.

So should we scream now? we ask, and we're probably on the bridge.

Yes, the maid says, scream now.

Very well—and to get going we take two or three steps back and stretch our sticks out and walk forward again. While doing so we begin to scream, but, at first, with caution, softly.

Aah, we scream, *ooh* and *eeh* and *no*, and *no, don't*, and slowly we get into the swing of it, becoming more independent and noisy. And we hear how the screams escape from us and float around us, and, after they've settled over us (our shoulders, our heads) and have enveloped us for long enough, spread out across the country and settle over the neighborhood. Of course, this doesn't stop the world, but it does seem to be listening. And we open our mouths wide and close our eyes and listen to our screams, each of us to his own. And we imagine to ourselves the fields, the space around us we've been separated from since our affliction began and which we sense as a dark corridor we have to pass through, enveloped in our screams. Yet probably it isn't a dark corridor at all, but a bright expanse, a damp region lying all around us, through which we tap our way and which we fill with screams, each in his own way. With a mud hole here and there, a stream ahead of us, behind and beneath us.

Is it still frozen? we ask after we've caught our breath.

Yes, the maid says, but only at the edge. Wait, she says, I'll show you.

And she goes away, climbs down probably to the stream, and breaks off a piece of it. Then she comes up the slope again and holds it out to us.

There, she says, can you feel it?

We can feel it, we say, throw it away.

Or in another direction a probably boundless and still unplowed field beneath a sky which is always the same black for us, without sun, moon, and stars. Somewhere, probably, a farmyard from which the sound of a hammer blow comes. Also the crows in the air or in trees with probably vast leafy crests which for us exist only as a rustling. And we have the feeling that here, where we're screaming and where there's also a pond somewhere, one region of the world ends and goes over into another. And on this limit we stand, facing toward the other region, and into that region, which is put together and taken apart quite differently in the thoughts of each one of us, we scream now with gaping mouths which anyone with eyes to see can study. Malente, glass-eyed, as Ripolus thinks—we haven't felt his face yet, and he's supposed not to have a neck either—screams especially loud, but the scream refuses to escape from him, he'll be suffocated by it if he's not careful. They say his throat is slowly closing, his rattling sounds at night give this away. When he speaks we hush and listen, for how much longer will he speak? Sometimes too we feel the air which comes out of him when he speaks, or the air he sets in motion when he draws his rattling breath. Unless we're quite mistaken, it's likely he'll become religious soon.

Then, altogether surprisingly, although we'd been waiting for it, like the sudden squeal of the pig, we fall and this is probably how it happens.
Probably Ripolus, who's leading us, strikes one of his feet against what the maid had spoken of, probably it's a stone which the gardener has rolled onto the bridge. (The maid says it won't be in the picture.) In any case, Ripolus loses his balance,

The Parable of the Blind

starts probably to topple, probably jerks his arms upward, and falls probably backward into the stream, which, up till now, he'd only heard murmuring. Meanwhile, Slit Man probably trips over Ripolus' legs and, as he falls, pulls us along with him, for we fall too. And scream and, as we fall, reach all around us in midair for a moment and drag Bellejambe with us onto the stones, down into the stream.

Yes, that's how I'll paint them, exactly like that, the painter says to his good friend—surely he's watching us now, he's probably been looking, has seen us fall, while, in the stream we've fallen into, we're collecting ourselves and feeling for the limbs we've knocked and scrambling to our feet again in the shallow water.

Hey, you, the maid calls from high above us, have you hurt yourselves?

Yes, we call up to her.

Where?

Everywhere.

Is it bad?

We can't say yet.

Then she comes and we're led up the slope cursing and grumbling, of course (us!). What must they be up to, treating us like this, do they think we're not people?! Pushing us into a stream like that, or rather, telling us to fall into it! Once we've climbed to the top again, Ripolus is even trying to talk about our dignity, and he blurts the word out several times, but can't put it into sentences, he's too shaken. And while our voices go in and out among one another and we've hardly got our breath back, the painter, whom our fall has evidently excited and who has probably captured us in outline already, says that now he knows how he must paint us: on a bridge, over a slope, as a dark procession making a descent. And, while the maid lines us up on the path again, the painter is again at work drawing or painting, we can hear him brushing the strokes on. Whereas he'd talked a lot to begin with, he keeps silent a great deal now. And he asks the other people still in his room—we don't know how many there are—not to say anything, because he's painting now and, as he quickly explains to them, he has to scrutinize our appearance, which is only our appearance for an instant, then we'll have changed and we'd present a quite different appearance, which might cancel and contradict the previous one. And through his good friend—he doesn't speak to us himself—he directs us, please, not to fall so quickly next time, but to prolong the fall or drag it out, because it's not possible for him to capture us at such a speed. Even us, slow and clumsy as we are, we're always on the move, if not our limbs, then the looks on our faces. But at once he contradicts himself, since he admits that our *appearance*, which is easily painted, is quite superfluous, because it takes attention away from his subject, which is the constitution of the world and of human beings. And this constitution has to be caught in some other way than any direct rendering, so traps were needed. Like the length or brevity of the brush strokes, pigmentation, peculiarity of texture, the arrangement of the background, which for every picture has to be reinvented, to strengthen the figures. As to that, he'd often thought of a sort of framework which to some extent would stress what he wanted to show, even if it might look a bit artificial, yet everything in art was artifice. The trees, the clouds, plowed fields, the eye sockets, the nose, and the mouth were nothing but colors to which a form had been given, abbreviations invented each time anew, which had nothing to do with real clouds, trees, eyes, or noses, such as we see around us. Except that the colors and the forms, when they passed across from one realm to another, produced likenesses that seem deceptively real, and then we'd say: It's painted. Thank God one could paint *over* what had been painted, though one had to wait until the color was dry, or else one couldn't scratch it off.

Right, and now, my good friend, tell them to fall

again, the painter says then, because he wants to capture us not posing but picking up speed, as a downward motion.

And then he goes quiet and stands probably at his easel and outlines us or fills us in, while the maid brings us closer together, pulls our bonnets farther down over our faces, and, clapping her hands, chases us back onto the bridge.

But we're going, we're going, we exclaim.

And then we walk and stumble again and scream and fall, as slowly and distinctly as we can, into the stream and lie for a while on the stones, and then we're pulled upright again. Conversely, on the canvas, as the good friend says, the superfluous and hideous blind people are rapidly being transformed into their true and beautiful and terrible picture, which will grip every one of us.

Sir, we say—after we've gone over the bridge several times, stumbled and fallen, screaming (the inside of our mouths, the terror inside our mouths!), and have been pulled dripping wet from the cold stream and up the slope for another fall—we have a few questions to ask. All this time we've been walking and falling we'd had these questions. Yes, even on our way to the pond we'd had these questions. And although the painter calls from his room, Fall! Don't ask questions, fall!, we come to

a standstill on some grass, with bushes probably
behind us, and look toward where we suppose the
house to be, with the window and the painter.
Well then: some questions.
Now what's this? the painter exclaims, they're
talking, haven't I told them not to?
They're rather worn out, the good friend says.
I don't care, the painter says, they talk too much.
It's because they're worried about something.
They needn't be.
What if they have only one small question? the
friend says.
All right then. What do they want?
Hey, did you hear? Just for once you may ask a
question, the good friend calls—he has the advantage of being able to see our picture as well as
ourselves, and he can compare us with each other
in our different forms. So what do you want?
We take a few steps forward, doff our bonnets,
and say, in the direction of his voice, how surprising this has all been for us. Only a moment
ago we'd been walking through the countryside,
and now we were suddenly being painted. Could
we be told why he's painting us and what he,
ourselves, and the world had to gain from it? Just
see how we probably look, why would anyone
want to paint that? we say and point down at
ourselves, our smocks, trousers, leg wrappings,

which are now, we can feel it, even damper than they were in the hollow. Shouldn't one rather be grateful if we disappeared, unpainted, as quickly as possible, we exclaim, wouldn't it be better to paint, instead, something that's not like this? For us he could do something else, help us, or console us, surely, instead of just strolling around and painting a picture of us? And then, when there's no answer, because the good friend doesn't know one and the painter, who should know one, instead of answering just goes on painting us, we ask: Why then must he paint us, isn't it enough that we exist? Or is he trying to make fun of us? Or is it (sh!) a secret? At least if everything goes well, will we be like it?

Ah, like it, is all the painter says, and probably he waves us away.

Well, the good friend says, when he sees that the painter is unwilling to speak, only very few people could judge what was really a likeness, we certainly couldn't. As for all the other questions you've asked, he says, instead of the small one you were wanting to ask—yet we'd never said we had only *one* question and a small one at that—they certainly couldn't answer them so fast, there were far too many. Isn't that so? he asks the painter.

Yes, the painter says, far too many.

And they're far too big, the friend says.

The Parable of the Blind

Yes, the painter says, far too big.

Very well, we say, if that's too many and they're too big, then perhaps he can answer a small one, at least, so we can see his goodwill.

Just one? the good friend asks.

Yes.

What do you think, the good friend asks the painter, would you answer one small question for them?

Well, a small one perhaps, the painter says, and probably he's gone very close to our painting now, if not crawled right inside it.

Did you hear? the good friend says, you're allowed one question, but only one. Isn't that so? he asks the painter, But the sight of us, which he endures effortlessly now that he's painting, seems only to make him want to paint, not to speak, for instead of his voice—and we're listening attentively—we hear only the scratch of his various brushes as they fill his canvas, probably more and more distinctly, with our fall, the way he wants to see it.

Good, he finally says, one then.

Did you hear? the good friend exclaims, just one, no more, and then go back to your bridge, to get on with it. Well now, he asks, what do you want to know?

Well, if we're allowed to ask only one question,

then we'd like to know, we say and raise our right foot a little, then draw it over the earth . . . Then we'd like to know, we say, but we notice that during the short time we've not been at the bridge and falling we've forgotten all the questions we'd wanted to ask or have asked already, we can't think of a single one. We draw our foot a few more times over the earth and our fingers over our heads and search a bit longer for the questions we wanted to ask, but we simply can't remember.

Well, the good friend exclaims, where's your question now? What do you want us to explain?

Oh, perhaps he can explain to us, we say and hope that if we take a bit of a run at it and collect everything in one long leap of a sentence and stress the sentence right, then the questions will come back. For instance, we say, can he explain to us . . . But we can't think how to end the sentence. The fact is: We simply don't want to know anymore why the painter is painting us. All we want to know is whether he'll be finished soon. Sorry, we say, but no question occurs to us at the moment. And we put our bonnets back on. It seems, we say, that at the moment we have no question. So we'd rather not ask anything now, later perhaps, when something occurs to us again.

All right, the good friend says, then go back to your bridge, if you haven't got any questions.

The Parable of the Blind

Yes, we say, we'll go back again now.

And we're led by the maid, who has probably been standing among us all this time—so our breath was passing through her hair—but who also hasn't told us what we wanted to ask the painter, back to the bridge, where we . . .

Well, we just scream and fall again, more or less as they wish, and scramble to our feet again and crawl up the slope, and the painter says: That's right, and he goes on painting us. With new strength, as he says to his good friend, for he hadn't been able to paint all winter, but that was over now, as one could see, the dead were coming to life again. Or he says that if it goes on like this, then his blind people, even though he's showing them as horrors, must soon be worth five hundred talers to any shopkeeper with eyes in his head, God Almighty! When one thinks, he says, that in a few weeks we'll be able to see the trees blossoming, whereas they, he says pointing probably at us, all they see is blackness. And he's convinced that as a painter he'll never be or produce anything significant, distinctly he feels this to be so. Supposing everything had been different, the times, his character, circumstances, the world's and his own, yes, then perhaps something might have come of it, but the way things are, the way things are . . . In spite of all the paintings he'd done,

everything still remained to be done, but he had
it all in his head. As fate would have it, he hadn't
yet been able to paint the pictures that were in
his head, but perhaps that would come in time.
Yes, he then says, at about this time last year he'd
begun to work with just as much zest, but what
had become of that year? And then, after a few
summary brush strokes, perhaps over a painted
sky or a painted field: In a biggish composition
that was leaning unfinished against his bedroom
wall, he'd begun an avenue of red and white
blossoming chestnut trees flecked with sunlight.
As well as many pencil studies for other paintings,
of course: a burning bridge with collapsing towers
and smoking roofs in Ghent, and a pretty view of
Antwerp in ruins, both from memory, frontal
views. And now tell them to fall again, he exclaims,
and the maid lines us up again.

10

We'd been thinking our time with the painter by the pond would be short, but our visit lasts quite a long time. Again and again we have to scream and fall and walk over the bridge. (Because the painter wants to bring out the fine points, easily overlooked, of the looks on our faces and our movements, our faltering and gaping.) Since the sun is actually shining now, and since our comings and goings have been many, our day is becoming a hot one. We pull open our smocks, but then have to close them, because, as the good friend calls to us from the window, we have to be captured and passed down with buttoned and not open smocks. Also the wrappings around our legs—we don't know if he's painting them—we'd like to unwind them, but then two voices call from the window at the same time: No, don't unwind them, don't unwind them, leave everything as it is.

The bonnets, too? the maid asks.

Yes, the bonnets too.

And if they're sweating?

That doesn't matter.

Naturally we go on hoping for a long time that we'll remember *the question* we wanted to ask, but we hope in vain. For a while we go on looking for it, then we forget about it. So we'll probably never know why, on this day, we're being painted. We'll never know whether we're a likeness (or how much of one we are), but perhaps that's not important. At least the painter is content.

Just look, he keeps saying to his good friend.

Yes, the friend says, it's coming along.

The eyes, do you see their eyes?

Yes, I do, precisely.

Isn't that it? the painter says, and he's very excited now by the sight of us (the sight of us on the bridge and on the canvas). Which, as he exclaims again and again, does wondrously sum up the ways of the world and the fate of man, but the good friend, who may have a different idea of these ways and this fate, or who might be horrified, only says, each time: If you think so—and he doesn't argue. Nor do we know what the sight of us sums up for the painter, we just go on saying:

136

The Parable of the Blind

All right, now we'll fall, all right, time to fall. And let ourselves be led back to the bridge, stumble, scream, and fall. But after the falling, during which we've torn all our clothes bit by bit and have begun to bleed all over, it's not the maid who comes now, it's the gardener who picks us up from the stones. And he has to strain every muscle to pull us up the slope again, because, naturally, we're completely worn out, completely out of breath. Or else he (the gardener), who leaps around us in his nasty mood, may already be standing in the stream bed and waiting for us, head tilted back, anticipating our fall. (The maid, for whom we've called several times, has probably left the scene, perhaps she's in a cow shed, perhaps after a short sit she came from the cow shed again, to carry a pail past us, if that was her.) Of course, we're at the end of our tether too, so is the gardener, probably, but we can't leave the scene yet, we're still being painted. The painter is the only person who isn't worn out, in spite of his many infirmities (stomach, eyes, head), he never stops painting us, for now he's completely at home with the sight of us, while his good friend, probably looking over his shoulder, calls out to him over and over again how *excellent* he finds what's being painted, and that if the painter means to paint a masterpiece he only has to go on like this. Until we suddenly feel we're not needed anymore, until somebody even shouts this to us. Somebody who'd been silent till now shouts it from the window.

Stop now, he shouts, take them away.

So he doesn't need them anymore? the gardener asks.

No.

Did you hear that? the gardener says to us, you can go now, he doesn't need you anymore.

Us? we ask, and we stand there.

Yes, who do you think?

And where are we supposed to go? we ask.

Home.

We can't, we exclaim at once.

Why not?

Because we don't live hereabouts, we're only passing through, we say and point to the neighborhood we've passed through.

Then go where you do live.

We can't do that either, we say, we're always passing through, everywhere.

Quiet, the gardener exclaims, you're always contradicting. It upsets everything, all this contradiction.

All right, we say, so we'll be quiet, so we'll go away.

And nobody holds us back, either, as we walk, not pushed, a few steps in a direction we've probably never gone in before.

138

The Parable of the Blind

All right, we say as we pass the house probably for the last time, we'll go now. We won't be a burden to you anymore, we call quickly over our shoulder.

And how will you do that? the gardener asks—probably he followed us a little way—not be a burden to us anymore?

And with the house behind us, making a grand gesture to include the countryside we've been incessantly imagining ever since we arrived, but which, for the gardener, for the maid, for the painter and his good friend, is probably quite different, we call: We're going, but we don't say where we'll be going or for how long we'll be gone or if we'll come back one day or if we'll have disappeared forever. We detest the gardener at the house by the pond, we detest the whole neighborhood, because something here is coming to an end, or it should be.

And where are you going? the gardener asks—from the very start he's only made things difficult for us. And we think for a while and say: Over there, and we point high over the ground, far into the distance.

You can't go there, the gardener says, that's where everything stops.

No matter, we say, we already knew that, but it's where we'll go. And we point in another direction

and call: You hear, Ripolus? That way, let's go!
But I don't see much in that direction, Ripolus
says.
Then what do you see?
Nothing, actually.
No matter, we say once more because the words
are still warm. And we grope for Slit Man's hand,
who's walking in front of us, and for Malente's,
who's walking behind us. What's more, we find
the two hands and press or squash them and
follow Ripolus, first one way, then another, and
then to the side, first this side, then the other.
Then Ripolus stops and doesn't know where to
go. We stop too.
You can't go anywhere, the gardener says—perhaps he's moved a fair distance from us in the
meantime—you'll have to stay where you are. And
wait until somebody takes you away, but I'm not
going to.
We wouldn't even have wanted you to, we exclaim.
No, he exclaims, I'm not going to. And he turns
probably in some direction or other which we
haven't foreseen and probably goes away. We
follow him with our heads turning to listen for
his footsteps and tell ourselves: Good riddance.
And we imagine the interval between us increasing
and the mere distance making him steadily smaller

and smaller, and he no longer sees us and finally he's no more.

So we'll just wait until somebody else comes, we call to him quickly, but most likely he can't hear, at least he doesn't call back. So we'll just wait, we're thinking. And we crowd together and drag our feet a bit this way and that and stump around one another a bit, all keeping step. And finally we're all standing like a dense clump, all on the same spot, and we grumble and moan again, just as we'd moaned and grumbled on the path going uphill, except that now it's a slower and more feeble grumbling. Possibly too we take a nap, upright, propping one another up. Or we think about something, call something up from down inside us, perhaps a memory, or something we think is a memory. And then, after we've stood around and moaned long enough, it starts to rain again. When Slit Man hears the rain he starts to curse, but Malente is almost proud of the rain, as if he'd made it. A rain coming as if through a fine sieve, which, it occurs to us, we'd probably have called in earlier times a drizzle, and so distinguished it from all other kinds of rain, but does the word still exist?

Hey, Ripolus, we call.

Yes, Ripolus says, I'm still here.

And where are you? we ask.
Here.
Good, we say, then listen, we have a question.
Fine, Ripolus says, I'm listening.
Right: What's falling now? we ask and hold him by the elbow.
Falling? Ripolus asks, has somebody fallen down?
Idiot, we say, on us, on us, falling on us. Isn't that a drizzle?
A what?
Or isn't it?
But Ripolus can't remember, he doesn't know the word anymore, even the thought that he might have forgotten it doesn't occur to him. No, he says, the word doesn't exist, never has existed.
But to us, if we remember rightly, we say, it seems . . .
Doesn't exist, Ripolus exclaims, doesn't exist!
In short: At this point in time—soon to be our last—we doff our bonnets, to let the elements refresh us a bit up top. And we hold our faces up to the sky—the wild ducks overhead are probably flying back north again—hold them into the fine rain, the thin wind.
Then a voice says: Come on now.
Hey, we call, is somebody there?
Yes, the voice says, somebody's here.
How's that?

The Parable of the Blind

Always was.
And how long still?
Yes, over here, by the bush.
We tap our way across. Is there a bush here?
Yes, there's a bush.
If the . . .
Bush?
No.
The speaker?
Here then?
No.
Here?
That's right. And he takes us firmly by our hands and draws us across a meadow, which could also be a field or a pasture, so that we can't even try to imagine what's beneath us, but something's there. Also we don't know which clouds we're turning our backs on or which are ahead of us. Quickly along under these clouds, until we've gone far enough. Until we're pushed into a barn—at first we think it's a big cupboard—and the rain goes away again, and a door is slammed shut behind us, of course. Then the wind around us goes away too, the rattle of leaves in the trees.
Hey, we call, what have you pushed us into?
Sleep now, the voice says, it's raining.
Yes, we're thinking, and it'll snow. And we stand there and put our bonnets back on and cock our

143

heads up high, because that way we hear better, but we don't hear anything. We only feel the air, how quietly it stands around us, the roof, the darkness. Darkness that we only suppose to be there and of which we can't tell if it's the night's or the barn's. (We'd like it to be the night's, then we'd feel more protected, or certainly less exposed.) In the hush that now comes we imagine the snow descending on us from very high up and how we sink down into this snow, legs, shoulders, heads. Then we think: Yes, it's night, the real one, not just the other. And we hope that nobody will come and talk to us about the stars. For who knows, perhaps there are stars today, or a rotten tree is glowing and it's only a question of time before somebody will talk to us about it. Then it occurs to us: But how can it be night, we haven't had anything to eat! All we've done is walk and fall, won't anyone give us food and drink? And we put out fists to our forehead and stay like that for a while. This hush around us! (The hush of things that don't move and probably never will move, whatever happens.) Then we grip our sticks more tightly—what else should we do?—and since we've stood long enough we walk a few steps softly over the earth of the Lord and through the darkness of the Lord and through the barn, the *rubbish pit* of the Lord, into which we've been pushed. For we begin to shiver and shake if we haven't been moving for a long time. Move, we say at daybreak, and off we march. And in our ears we have the shuffling of our feet over His ground. And in a single day we walk through three villages, sometimes even four. Or at least we think we're walking through four villages, but actually we'll be walking around in the first village all the time. Or else they capture us and put us in the sun, where we have to weave baskets. In any case, we move a lot, also before and after the weaving, so the shaking won't come up, won't even grope around for us. In the evening we're much too tired even to shake. Anyway, after a few steps we come up against a lath wall. Which, no doubt about it, is an old acquaintance.

Hey, there's a lath wall here, we call at the end of this Lazarus day of ours or thereabouts, and we knock on the wall. Hey, what have you pushed us into, we know this already.

What do we know already? Bellejambe asks.

All this.

And how come we know it? Bellejambe asks.

Because we've been here before.

Me too? he asks.

Yes, you too.

And when do you think we were here? Bellejambe asks.

Probably this morning.

Me too?

Yes, we say, you too. But perhaps it was another morning, we aren't quite sure. Can't you remember?

No, Bellejambe says, you've been dreaming.

Yes, we say, we've been dreaming, but of something else. And we tell him how somebody woke us up, took us out of our dream. Do you remember somebody waking us up?

No, Bellejambe says, not me.

But he did. We were under the earth already, only one leg was still hanging outside. And that wouldn't have been there much longer, because snow was falling on it. But then he knocked on the door and took us out again.

Who?

The knocker, we say. And after we'd been stood back up on our feet somewhere in this neighborhood, we say and grope around with our stick, we were led outside and to the table, where the bowls were. Which were all for us to eat from and which we could empty.

Not me, Bellejambe says.

Not you?

No, not me.

So you mean you've forgotten it all? we ask and know exactly what he's thinking. Like us, we think, exactly like us! How often we tell ourselves: Let's just go to sleep!—and forget that we're already asleep. Or we think we're dreaming while we're really awake and—we'd forgotten it—eating or walking.

I didn't empty anything, Bellejambe says.

Yes, you did, we say, you've forgotten, that's all. Have you forgotten the child too, who wouldn't believe us?

What child?

The one who took us behind the barn.

And what didn't he believe about us?

That we're blind.

He wouldn't believe I was, either?

That's right.

He didn't believe I was blind! Bellejambe exclaims and strikes the ground with his stick.

No, he didn't.

And why not?

Because you kept on looking in his direction when he said things. Do you remember now? we ask.

No, Bellejambe says, you've dreamed it.

All right, we say, and we give up and step aside a bit and wonder if a person who remembers so little is still alive. If what was so in the morning ceases to be so in the evening. If that's the case, then it's unfortunately certain that many of us must be dead already.

Hey, Bellejambe, we call, why don't you say anything? Are you dead?

No, Bellejambe says, not yet.

So you can still hear us?

Yes, he says, you've dreamed it.

Yes, we say, but then somebody woke us up.

Not me he didn't, Bellejambe says, not me.

Well, we think, at least we're back again where we
probably started, probably this morning, after a
long and strenuous, but uneventful and boring
walk. At least that's how it feels here. Hey, we call,
is anybody else here, or are we alone?

And we stoop and hunch our back and are on the
verge of collapse, or sinking into the ground
almost, that's how far gone we are. But then we
only fall to our knees and ask for enlightenment.
Lord, we think or call, Thou knowest that for a
long time we haven't seen Thy earth, which Thou
hast established also for us, grant us that we too,
we too . . . But we don't know how to go on,
because it's always hard for us to complain and
suffer consecutively for a long time.

Ripolus, we call and stand up again and walk up
and down, because we don't want to get stuck in
one place.

Yes, Ripolus says, what do you want?

We want! we call.

The Parable of the Blind

What you want is nothing, Ripolus asks, isn't that it?

No, we say, we want to know something. We want to know if you think somebody's here, looking at us.

Yes, Ripolus says, if only one knew whether it's dark.

And whether, Malente says, dark or light, anybody at all is looking.

Do you think it's dark? we ask.

Who could be looking? Bellejambe exclaims.

I don't think anybody's looking, Slit Man says— we'll certainly push him into a ditch soon.

And why not? we ask.

Because there's nobody here who could see, Slit Man says, otherwise he'd announce himself.

Hey, is anybody here? we call. But it's true, nobody announces himself.

And then, when nobody has announced himself for long enough, we reach forward with our sticks and tap along the lath wall, first Ripolus, then the rest of us. Later, to make even more sure of it, we also touch it with our fingertips. The lath wall is rough and cold and we scratch at it and knock on it. And feel cracks in it, through which fingers can be put, or fingertips at least. Until we come to a corner, a barn corner. A corner, at least a corner! We stop, draw breath, fill the corner up. And stay in the corner for a while, establish ourselves in it.

Hey, we call, isn't there anybody here?

And then, after hesitating a bit, then leaving the corner and the lath wall as well, we go deeper into the interior of the barn and hit on straw. Straw, of course, there had to be straw, we'd smelled straw! Also there'll be animals here perhaps, only they're not announcing themselves. Perhaps if we go a bit farther like this we'll even hit on animals, run into them. Probably they'll have lain down already and settled into the positions in which they spend the night, thus close to the ground. Anyway we smell not only straw, but also animals. But we smell and feel ourselves too. On top we smell like damp, down below it's like fire and dust, and in the middle, we smell . . . Well, we're alive, all the same. Then suddenly we start to laugh, we astonish ourselves. For a long time we stand up to our knees in the straw and can feel ourselves laughing, the shoulders, the throat, the belly. Even our legs, which mostly are hushed, join in the laughter. At first we laugh softly and each by himself, each in his own direction, then loud, in chorus, all of us together. And we feel the tears running down our cheeks and throats, into our shirts.

150

The Parable of the Blind

All right, we call, is anybody here? For the last time: yes or no?
No, a voice says outside the barn.
Aha, we say, so we weren't mistaken?
Yes, you were, the voice says, because he's going now.
And us, we ask, have you shut us in?
Yes.
Why?
So you won't hurt yourselves in the darkness.
In which darkness, we ask, the barn's or the night's?
The night's.
So it's night again, we exclaim. And by our voices we can tell: Yes, it's night, it must be night. Because it has a different sound from day when one calls into it, even inside a barn.
We are in a barn, aren't we, or . . . ? we ask.
Yes, in a barn.
The same one as last night? we ask.
Yes, the same one.
Ah, we say, we thought so. Then you'll be the knocker who came this morning?
Yes, the knocker says, this morning.
We ask: Why did you wake us up?
And the knocker says: Because you were going to be painted.

Curse it, we say, couldn't you have waited? We'd almost disappeared.

Yes, the knocker says, woken up.

And we, the people in the middle of the picture, we say: So are we painted?

And the knocker, going quickly on his way: Yes, you're painted.